# Oxford KS3 Science

M000303955

# Activate

## Question • Progress • Succeed

# 2

Philippa Gardom Hulme
Jo Locke
Helen Reynolds

**Assessment Editor**
Dr Andrew Chandler-Grevatt

**OXFORD**
UNIVERSITY PRESS

# Contents

# Physics P2
## Physics P2 Unit Opener

## Chapter 1: Electricity and magnetism

## Chapter 2: Energy

## Chapter 3: Motion and pressure

# Introduction

## Learning objectives

Each spread has a set of learning objectives. These tell you what you will be able to do by the end of the lesson.

## Key Words

The key words in each spread are highlighted in bold and summarised in the key-word box. They can also be found in the Glossary.

## Link

Links show you where you can learn more about something mentioned in the topic.

## Summary Questions

1 ⚗ Questions with one conical-flask symbol are the easiest.

2 ⚗⚗ The questions get harder as you move down the list.

3 ⚗⚗⚗ The question with three conical-flask symbols is the hardest. In these questions you need to think about how to present your answer.

Welcome to your *Activate* Student Book. This introduction shows you all the different features *Activate* has to support you on your journey through Key Stage 3 Science.

Being a scientist is great fun. As you work through this Student Book, you'll learn how to work like a scientist, and get answers to questions that science can answer.

This book is packed full of fantastic (and foul!) facts, as well as plenty of activities to help build your confidence and skills in science.

**Q** These boxes contain short questions. They will help you check that you have understood the text.

### Maths skills

Scientists use maths to help them solve problems and carry out their investigations. These boxes contain activities to help you practise the maths you need for science. They also contain useful hints and tips.

### Literacy skills

Scientists need to be able to communicate their ideas clearly. These boxes contain activities and hints to help you build your reading, writing, listening, and speaking skills.

### Working scientifically

Scientists work in a particular way to carry out fair and scientific investigations. These boxes contain activities and hints to help you build these skills and understand the process so that you can work scientifically.

## Fantastic Fact!

These interesting facts relate to something in the topic.

**Opener**

Each unit begins with an opener spread. This introduces you to some of the key topics that you will cover in the unit.

**Picture Puzzlers**

These puzzles relate to something in the unit – can you work out the answers?

**You already know**

This lists things you've already learnt that will come up again in the unit. Check through them to see if there is anything you need to recap on.

**Big questions**

These are some of the important questions in science that the unit will help you to answer.

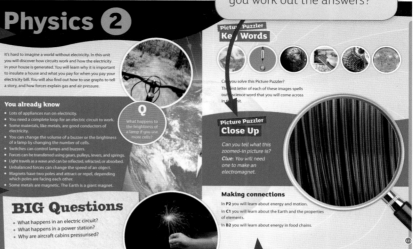

**Making connections**

This shows how what you will learn in the unit links up with the science that you will learn in other parts of the course..

**Topic spreads**

Each topic in the chapter has a double-page spread containing learning objectives, practice questions, key words, and task boxes to help you work through the chapter.

**Summary**

This is a summary of the chapter. You can use it to check that you have understood the main ideas in the chapter and as a starting point for revision.

**End-of-chapter questions**

You can use these exam-style questions to test how well you know the topics in the chapter.

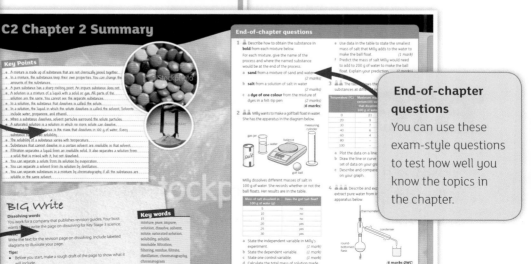

**Big write/Maths challenge/Case study**

This is an activity that you can do at the end of the chapter. It will help you to practise using your scientific skills and knowledge.

# Biology 2

In this unit you will compare the effects of healthy and unhealthy lifestyles on your body. You will look at why organisms need energy to function effectively. Finally, you will investigate the differences that exist between organisms, and why this is important for their survival.

## You already know

- The digestive system in humans is made up of different parts, each with its own special function.
- Diet, exercise, drugs, and lifestyle have an impact on the way the human body functions.
- Living things are classified into broad groups according to common characteristics.
- Fossils provide information about organisms that lived on Earth millions of years ago.
- Living things produce offspring of the same kind but normally offspring vary and are not identical to their parents.
- Animals and plants are adapted to suit their environment and adaptation may lead to evolution.
- Food chains include producers, predators, and prey.

**Q**

What are the five main groups that vertebrates (animals with a backbone) are classified into?

# BIG Questions

- What is a healthy diet?
- Why do organisms need food to survive?
- Why don't we all look the same?

  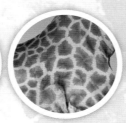 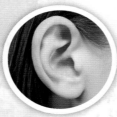  

Can you solve this Picture Puzzler?

The first letter of each of these images spells out a science word that you will come across in this unit.

Picture Puzzler
# Close Up

*Can you tell what this zoomed-in picture is?*
**Clue:** *It's made from flour.*

## Making connections

In **B2** you will learn about how life evolved on Earth.

In **C2** you will about the origins of the Earth.

In **P2** you will learn about how we use energy in our daily lives.

# 1.1 Nutrients

## Learning objectives

After this topic you will be able to:

- describe the components of a healthy diet
- explain the role of each food group in the body.

## Foul Fact

If you eat a lot of beetroots your urine turns pink. Eating a lot of asparagus turns your urine bright yellow!

▲ Carbohydrate-rich foods.

▲ Fat-rich foods.

We all know that sweets should only be eaten as a treat and you have probably heard many times that you should eat a balanced diet. But what does this mean, and why is it important?

**Nutrients** are important substances that your body needs to survive and stay healthy. There are different types of nutrients. We get most of them from food. The types of nutrient are:

1 **carbohydrates** provide energy

2 **lipids** (fats and oils) provide energy

3 **proteins** are used for growth and repair

4 **vitamins** keep you healthy

5 **minerals** keep you healthy

6 water is needed in all cells and body fluids

7 **fibre** provides bulk to food to keep it moving through the gut. Fibre is not a nutrient but it is important for a healthy diet.

To remain healthy you must eat a **balanced diet**. This means eating food containing the right nutrients in the correct amounts.

**A** State what is meant by a nutrient.

## Carbohydrates

Carbohydrates are your main source of energy. They are found in sugary foods such as sugar and fruit, where they provide a quick source of energy. They are also found in starchy foods such as pasta and bread. These foods have to be broken down by the body, so the energy is released more slowly.

**B** State the function of carbohydrates.

## Lipids

Lipids include fats and oils. They have three important jobs. They:

- provide you with a store of energy
- keep you warm, by providing a layer of insulation under your skin
- protect organs like your kidneys and heart from damage.

## Proteins

Proteins are needed to repair body tissues and to make new cells for growth. Your muscles, organs, and immune system are mostly made of proteins.

**C** State two functions of proteins.

## Vitamins and minerals

Vitamins and minerals are essential substances for keeping you healthy but you only need tiny amounts. Vitamins are needed for you to grow, develop, and function normally. For example, vitamin A is needed for good eyesight. Vitamin D is needed with the mineral calcium to maintain healthy teeth and bones.

Fruits and vegetables are a good source of vitamins and minerals.

## Water

Your cells are made up of about 70% water. To keep them healthy you need to constantly replace the water your body loses in sweat, tears, urine, feces, and exhaling. You should drink over a litre of water every day. This can come from drinking water but tea, fruit juice, and squash all count.

**D** List four ways in which you lose water from the body.

## Fibre

Fibre is a type of carbohydrate but it is not classed as a nutrient. However, it is an important part of your diet as it adds bulk to your food. This means it keeps food moving through the gut, and waste is pushed out of the body more easily, helping to prevent constipation.

◀ Fibre-rich foods.

### Healthy eating

Design and film a healthy-eating TV advert on behalf of the government. The advert should aim to encourage young people to eat a balanced diet.

▲ Protein-rich foods.

### Link

You can learn more about balanced diets in B2 1.3 Unhealthy diet

### Key Words

nutrient, carbohydrate, lipids, protein, vitamin, mineral, fibre, balanced diet

## Summary Questions

**1** Match the nutrient to its role in the body.

| | |
|---|---|
| **carbohydrates** | growth and repair |
| **lipids** | remain healthy |
| **protein** | provide energy |
| **vitamins and minerals** | provide bulk to food |
| **water** | energy store and insulation |
| **fibre** | needed in cells and bodily fluids |

*(6 marks)*

**2** Describe the role of lipids in the body.

*(3 marks)*

**3** Explain in detail what is meant by a balanced diet. Provide examples of what a balanced diet should contain.

*(6 marks)*

# 1.2 Food tests

## Learning objectives

After this topic you will be able to:

- describe how to test foods for starch, lipids, sugar, and protein
- describe the positive result for each food test.

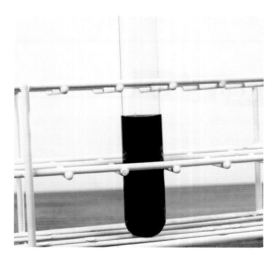

▲ This food solution contains starch.

## Key Words

food test, hypothesis

### Hypothesis

Scientists observe the world and come up with a **hypothesis** to explain what they observe. A hypothesis is an idea about things that always happen. A hypothesis can be tested in an investigation. You can use hypotheses to make a prediction.

You may be able to guess by looking at some foods which nutrients they contain. For example, you may know that oily foods contain lipids. Scientists use food tests to find out which nutrients are in a food product.

## How can you test foods?

A different chemical test exists for each type of nutrient. For most **food tests**, you will need a solution of the food. To prepare a food solution:

1 crush the food using a pestle and mortar

2 add a few drops of water, and mix well.

You should use a special type of water called distilled water – this is pure water that contains no other chemical substances.

## How do you test for starch?

To test for starch you use iodine solution. Iodine solution is an orange-yellow liquid.

1 Add a few drops of iodine solution to the food solution.

2 If the solution turns a dark blue-black colour, the food contains starch.

**A** State the colour change in iodine if a food contains starch.

## How do you test for lipids?

To test for lipids in a solid piece of food you use a piece of filter paper.

1 Rub some of the food onto a piece of filter paper.

2 Hold the paper up to the light.
If the paper has gone translucent, the food contains lipids.

**B** State how you would test a solid piece of food for lipids.

To test for lipids in a food solution you use ethanol. Ethanol is a colourless liquid.

1   Add a few drops of ethanol to the food solution.

2   Shake the test tube and leave for one minute.

3   Pour the ethanol into a test tube of water.

4   If the solution turns cloudy, the food contains lipids.

## How do you test for sugar?

To test for simple sugars such as glucose you use Benedict's solution. Benedict's solution is a blue liquid.

1   Add a few drops of Benedict's solution to the food solution.

2   Heat the test tube in a water bath.

3   If the solution turns orange-red, the food contains sugar.

**C** State the colour change in Benedict's solution if a food contains sugar.

▲ This food solution contains lipids.

▲ This food solution contains sugar.

## How do you test for protein?

To test for protein you use copper sulfate solution and sodium hydroxide solution. Copper sulfate solution is a pale-blue liquid. Sodium hydroxide solution is a colourless liquid.

1   Add a few drops of copper sulfate solution to your food solution.

2   Add a few drops of sodium hydroxide solution.

3   If the solution turns purple, the food contains protein.

**D** State the colour change in a solution of copper sulfate and sodium hydroxide if a food contains protein.

◀ This food solution contains protein.

## Summary Questions

1   🔺 Complete the table using the words below.

**turns blue-black**

**turns orange-red**

**makes paper translucent**

**turns purple**

| Nutrient | Colour change if nutrient present |
|----------|-----------------------------------|
| starch   |                                   |
| lipids   |                                   |
| sugar    |                                   |
| protein  |                                   |

*(4 marks)*

2   🔺🔺 Describe how to prepare a food solution of a breakfast cereal.

*(3 marks)*

3   🔺🔺🔺 Explain in detail how you would test a gingerbread-biscuit solution for the presence of starch, sugar, and protein.

*(6 marks)*

# 1.3 Unhealthy diet

## Learning objectives

After this topic you will be able to:

- describe some health issues caused by an unhealthy diet
- calculate the energy requirements of different people.

▲ This food pyramid shows a healthy balanced diet. The largest part of your diet should be carbohydrate based. Lipids, oils, and sweets should only be eaten in very small quantities.

## Link

You can learn more about energy in food in P2 2.1 Food and fuels

## Key Words

malnourishment, starvation, obese, deficiency

You may have seen pictures of people who are either extremely overweight or underweight. Both of these conditions are caused by **malnourishment**. This means the people have eaten the wrong amount or the wrong types of food.

## Where does your energy come from?

You need energy for everything you do, even to sleep. This energy comes from your food. The energy in food is measured in joules (J) or kilojoules (kJ). 1 kilojoule is the same as 1000 joules.

If you look on a food label it will tell you how much energy is stored in that food.

**A** State the unit that energy in food is measured in.

## Why is it unhealthy to be underweight?

Some people do not eat enough food. In extreme cases this is known as **starvation**. If the energy in the food you eat is less than the energy you use, you will lose body mass. This leads to you being underweight. Underweight people:

- often suffer from health problems, such as a poor immune system
- lack energy to do things, and are often tired
- are likely to suffer from a lack of vitamins or minerals.

**B** State three problems caused by being underweight.

## Why is it unhealthy to be overweight?

Some people eat too much, or eat too many fatty foods. If the energy content in the food you eat is more than the energy you use, you gain body mass. This is stored as fat under the skin. If a person becomes extremely overweight, they are said to be **obese.**

Overweight people have an increased risk of:

- heart disease
- stroke
- diabetes
- some cancers.

**C** State three diseases that obese people are more likely to suffer from.

## What are vitamin and mineral deficiencies?

If a person does not have enough of a certain vitamin or mineral they are said to have a **deficiency**. This can damage a person's health. For example, a vitamin A deficiency can lead to 'night blindness'. This makes it difficult for you to see clearly in dim light. A vitamin D deficiency can lead to a condition called rickets, where your bones become weak.

**D** Name the condition caused by a vitamin A deficiency.

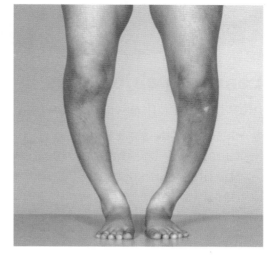
▲ This person is suffering from rickets.

## How much energy do you need?

Your body needs energy to function properly. The amount of energy you need depends on your age (as this affects your growth rate), your body size, and how active you are. The more exercise you do, the more energy your body requires.

### Energy requirements
Use the graph below to estimate the energy that a female computer programmer needs each day. How did you arrive at your answer?

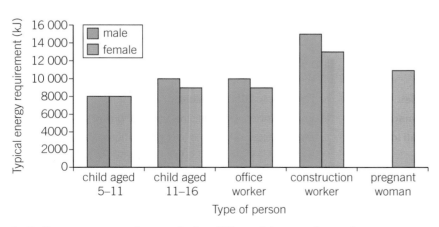
▲ Daily energy requirements for different types of people.

## Summary Questions

1 Copy and complete the sentences below.

You gain the _____ you need to survive from food. Energy is measured in _____ .

If you take in more energy than you use you _____ body mass. If you become _____ your risk of _____ disease increases. An underweight person is often _____ .

*(6 marks)*

2 Use the graph on this page to answer the following questions.

a Calculate the extra energy a female office worker would need each day if she became pregnant. *(2 marks)*

b A male office worker starts a new job as a construction worker. Calculate the percentage increase in his daily energy needs. *(4 marks)*

3 Compare the health problems of being underweight and the health problems of being overweight.

*(6 marks)*

# 1.4 Digestive system

## Learning objectives

After this topic you will be able to:

- describe the structure and function of the main parts of the digestive system
- describe the process of digestion.

### Link

You can learn more about molecules in C1 2.3 Compounds

### Fantastic fact

If you unravelled your small intestine it would be roughly four times taller than you – it is not very small!

You may sometimes notice your stomach rumbling. This is a hint that you need to eat. You know that the food contains nutrients. But how does your body get nutrients out of food?

## What is the digestive system?

The **digestive system** is a group of organs that work together to break down food. The nutrients in most of the food you eat are large molecules, like lipids and proteins. During **digestion** these large molecules are broken down into small molecules of nutrients. These nutrients can then pass into the blood where they are used by the body.

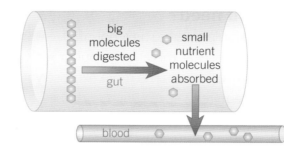

◀ During digestion large molecules are broken down into small molecules and pass into the bloodstream.

**A** State what happens during digestion.

## Structures in the digestive system

The diagram opposite shows the main structures in your digestive system. It is often referred to as your gut.

| | |
|---|---|
| Mouth | Food is chewed and mixed with saliva. Teeth help to break the food into smaller chunks. |
| **Gullet** | Food passes down this tube. |
| **Stomach** | Food is mixed with digestive juices and acids. |
| **Small intestine** | Digestive juices from the liver and pancreas are added and digestion is completed. Small molecules of nutrients pass through the intestine wall into the bloodstream. |
| **Large intestine** | Only food that cannot be digested gets this far. Water passes back into the body, leaving a solid waste of undigested food called feces. |
| **Rectum** | Feces are stored here until they leave the body. |
| **Anus** | This is a muscular ring through which feces pass out of the body. |

**B** Name the structure that food passes along to reach the stomach.

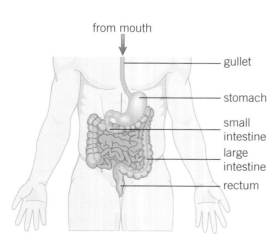

▲ Movement of food out of the digestive system.

## Moving through the digestive system

Fibre in your food isn't digested but adds bulk to the food. Muscles push against this, forcing food along the gut. Eating lots of fibre-rich foods such as vegetables and wholemeal bread helps prevent constipation.

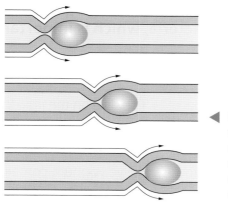

◀ Muscles in the wall of the gut squeeze food along – a bit like squeezing a tube of toothpaste.

**c** Describe how food moves along the gut.

## Passing into the blood

The small molecules of nutrients produced during digestion pass into the bloodstream through the wall of the small intestine. They are then transported around the body.

The small intestine needs to absorb the nutrients quickly, before the undigested food passes out of the body. The small intestine is specially adapted to this function. The wall of the small intestine is thin. It is also covered with tiny structures called **villi**. These stick out of the wall and give it a big surface area. They also contain blood capillaries to carry away the absorbed food molecules.

▲ Villi in the small intestine increase the surface area so more nutrients can be absorbed.

**Key Words**

digestive system, digestion, gullet, stomach, small intestine, large intestine, rectum, anus, villi

### Wordbank

Make a wordbank by listing all the scientific terms about digestion. You can refer to your wordbank as you progress through this topic.

## Summary Questions

**1** 🧪 Match each organ below to its role in digestion.

| | |
|---|---|
| **stomach** | food is chewed and mixed with saliva |
| **small intestine** | water is absorbed back into the body |
| **large intestine** | food is mixed with acid and digestive juices |
| **rectum** | feces are stored here until they pass out of the body |
| **mouth** | small molecules of nutrients are absorbed into the blood stream |

*(5 marks)*

**2** 🧪🧪 Describe the adaptations of the small intestine to its function.

*(3 marks)*

**3** 🧪🧪 Explain why it is important to eat a fibre-rich diet.

*(3 marks)*

**4** 🧪🧪🧪 Describe in detail the passage of food through the digestive system.

*(6 marks)*

## Learning objectives

After this topic you will be able to:

- describe the role of enzymes in digestion
- describe the role of bacteria in digestion.

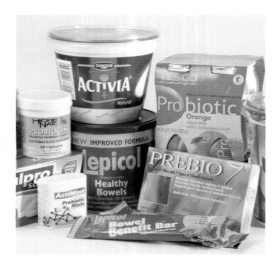

▲ Probiotic foods.

**Have you seen the TV adverts that say that yoghurts and yoghurt drinks are good for your digestive system? They contain bacteria, which is important for digestion.**

## Bacteria in digestion

Your large intestine contains bacteria. They live on the fibre in your diet. They make important vitamins such as vitamin K. These vitamins are then absorbed into your body and help to keep you healthy.

Some foods, called probiotic foods, like live yoghurt, contain these useful bacteria.

**A** State why bacteria are important in your digestive system.

## What's in digestive juices?

Your teeth begin digestion by breaking down food into smaller pieces. The digestive juices in your gut contain **enzymes**. These are special proteins that can break large molecules of nutrients into small molecules.

Large molecules in your food like starch, a type of carbohydrate, are made of lots of smaller molecules joined together. Enzymes chop these large molecules into the smaller molecules they are made from.

enzymes cut molecule here

digestion

◄ Enzymes chop large molecules into smaller molecules.

Enzymes are known as biological **catalysts** – they speed up digestion without being used up.

**B** State the role of enzymes in digestion.

## What's in a name?

The enzymes carbohydrase, protease, and lipase are named after the type of nutrient they break down.

## Different types of enzyme

Different types of enzyme break down different nutrients. There are three main types of enzymes involved in digestion – **carbohydrase**, **protease**, and **lipase**.

## Carbohydrase

Carbohydrase is an enzyme that breaks down carbohydrates into sugar molecules.

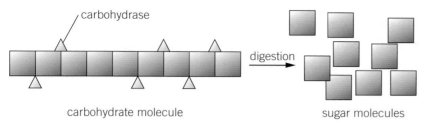

▲ Starch is broken down into sugar molecules.

Carbohydrates are digested in the mouth, stomach, and small intestine. Carbohydrase present in your saliva breaks down the starch in bread into sugar.

## Protease

Protease is an enzyme that breaks down proteins into amino acids.

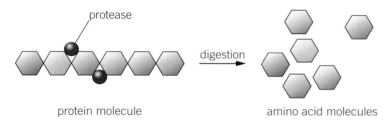

▲ Protein is broken down into amino acids.

Proteins are digested in the stomach and small intestine. Acid in the stomach helps digestion and kills harmful microorganisms in food.

## Lipase

Lipase is an enzyme that breaks down lipids into fatty acids and glycerol.

Digestion of lipids takes place in the small intestine. It is helped by **bile**, a substance made in the liver. Bile breaks the lipids into small droplets that are easier for the lipase enzymes to work on.

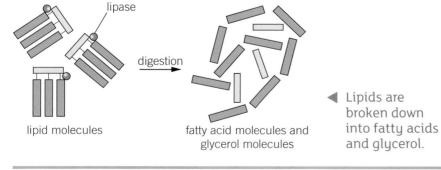

◀ Lipids are broken down into fatty acids and glycerol.

**C** State the function of bile.

---

### What happens to the bread you eat?

Describe the journey bread takes through your body and how it is digested. Present its journey as a flow diagram. Hint – bread contains a lot of starch.

---

## Key Words

enzyme, catalyst, carbohydrase, protease, lipase, bile

---

## Summary Questions

**1** ⚗ Copy the sentences below, choosing the correct bold word.

**Carbohydrates/proteins** are broken down into sugar by the enzyme **lipase/carbohydrase**. Proteins are broken down into **amino acids/lipase** by the enzyme **carbohydrase/protease**. Lipids are broken down into **lipase/fatty acids and glycerol** by the enzyme **lipase/carbohydrase**.

*(6 marks)*

**2** ⚗⚗ Explain why live yoghurt should be part of your diet.

*(3 marks)*

**3** ⚗⚗⚗ Make a visual summary of the ideas on this page to compare the roles of enzymes and bacteria in digestion.

*(6 marks)*

# 1.6 Drugs

## Learning objectives

After this topic you will be able to:

- describe the difference between recreational and medicinal drugs
- describe the effects of drugs on health and behaviour.

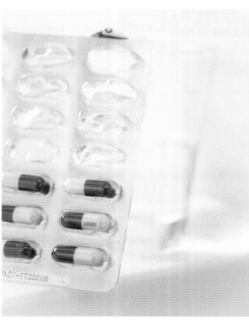

▲ Antibiotic pills are used to treat bacterial infections.

## Key Words

drug, medicinal drug, recreational drug, addiction, withdrawal symptoms

**Some drugs can seriously damage your health, or even be deadly. Some can save your life, and are used widely in medicine. So what's the difference?**

### What are drugs?

**Drugs** are chemical substances that affect the way your body works. They alter the chemical reactions that take place inside your body. Sometimes these changes are helpful but in many cases they are harmful.

There are two types of drugs – **medicinal drugs** and **recreational drugs**.

**A** State what is meant by a drug.

### What are medicinal drugs?

Medicinal drugs are used in medicine. They benefit your health in some way. They may be used to treat the symptoms of a condition; for example, paracetamol is taken to relieve pain. Other drugs can cure an illness. For example, antibiotics are often used to treat chest infections.

However, even medicinal drugs can cause harm if you do not take them in the right way. Some medicinal drugs also have unwanted side effects. When prescribing drugs, doctors have to weigh up the benefits of a person taking a drug over any possible risks.

**B** State what is meant by a medicinal drug.

### What are recreational drugs?

Recreational drugs are drugs that people take for enjoyment, to help them relax, or to help them to stay awake. Recreational drugs normally have no health benefits and in many cases are harmful.

**C** State what is meant by a recreational drug.

Recreational drugs are not prescribed by a doctor. Many are illegal – this means that you are breaking the law if you take them. Even very small amounts of these drugs can damage your body. Examples of these drugs include heroin, cocaine, cannabis, and ecstasy.

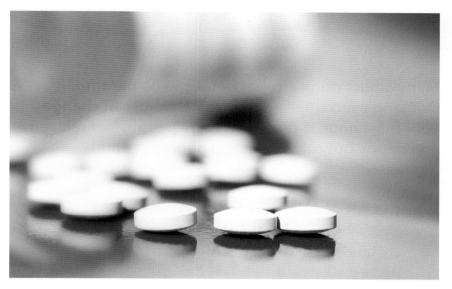

▲ Many recreational drugs are illegal.

▲ Caffeine is a recreational drug that speeds up your nervous system.

**D** Name three illegal drugs.

Some recreational drugs are legal to use. They can still be harmful. These include:

- alcohol – drinking alcohol affects your nervous system and damages your liver.
- tobacco – smoking significantly increases your risk of cancer, as well as lung and heart disease.

## Drug addiction

If your body gets used to the changes caused by a drug, it may become dependent on the drug. This means that you need to keep taking the drug to feel normal. If this happens you have an **addiction**. If a person with an addiction tries to stop taking the drug, they may suffer **withdrawal symptoms**. These can be very unpleasant and make it even harder to give up the drug. Withdrawal symptoms include headaches, anxiety, and sweating.

**E** State what is meant by an addiction.

### Drug factsheet

Produce a factsheet about one of the following drugs to share with other members of your class:
cannabis, cocaine, ecstasy, heroin

## Summary Questions

1 Copy and complete the sentences below.

Drugs are _____ that affect the way your body works.

_____ drugs are taken for enjoyment. _____ drugs benefit health.

If you take drugs too often you may develop an _____. When addicted people stop taking drugs, they suffer _____ _____, which can make it harder to give up.

*(5 marks)*

2 Describe three differences between medicinal drugs and recreational drugs.

*(3 marks)*

3 Compare the effects of different types of drug on health and behaviour.

*(6 marks)*

# 1.7 Alcohol

## Learning objectives

After this topic you will be able to:

- describe the effect of alcohol on health and behaviour
- describe the effect alcohol has on conception and pregnancy.

Many adults drink alcohol but it can be harmful. Drinking even small amounts of alcohol can change your behaviour. It can make some people feel relaxed and happy but others can feel aggressive and depressed.

## What is alcohol?

Alcohol contains the drug **ethanol**. When you drink alcohol, ethanol is absorbed into your bloodstream. It then travels to your brain, where it affects your nervous system. This chemical is called a **depressant** because it slows down your body's reactions.

**A** Name the drug found in alcoholic drinks.

If people drink a lot of alcohol regularly, they may need to drink greater and greater amounts to cause the same effect on their body. They may become addicted. People who have an addiction to alcohol are called **alcoholics**.

**B** State what is meant by the word alcoholic.

## How much alcohol can you drink safely?

Different alcoholic drinks contain different amounts of alcohol. For example, spirits such as vodka and whisky contain more alcohol than beer.

To lower the risk of damage to your body from drinking alcohol, the government recommends that adult women drink a maximum of two **units of alcohol** per day (14 units per week) and adult men a maximum of three units per day (21 units per week). One unit of alcohol is 10 ml of pure alcohol.

However, these are only guidelines because height, weight, and gender affect the way people react to alcohol.

**C** State the recommended maximum number of alcohol units per week for adult women and for adult men.

no alcohol

**how a person would be affected**

generally relaxed and happy

increasing alcohol intake

drunk – person loses control of their muscles, making it difficult to walk and balance

slurred speech

blurred vision

unconsciousness

death

excessive alcohol

▲ This diagram shows what happens to a person as they increase their alcohol intake.

| pint of lager | alcopop | glass of wine | shot of vodka |
| 3 | 1.5 | 2 | 1 |

**units of alcohol**

▲ What is one unit of alcohol?

## Dangers of alcohol

Drinking large amounts of alcohol over a long time can cause stomach ulcers, heart disease, and brain and liver damage.

Your liver breaks down harmful chemicals (including ethanol) into harmless waste products, which are then excreted from your body. As a result of having to break down large amounts of ethanol the livers of heavy drinkers become scarred. This means their liver works less efficiently, taking longer to break down alcohol and other chemicals. This condition is called cirrhosis of the liver, and can result in death.

**D** Name three conditions that are more likely to occur if a person drinks a lot of alcohol for a long time.

## Should pregnant women drink?

The Department of Health recommends that pregnant women do not drink any alcohol. Drinking alcohol increases the risk of miscarriage, stillbirth, premature birth, and low-birth-weight babies.

When a pregnant woman drinks alcohol, it diffuses into the baby's bloodstream. It can then damage the developing organs and nervous system. Fetal Alcohol Syndrome (FAS) affects the way a baby's brain develops. It can result in children with learning difficulties, facial problems, and poor immune systems.

Alcohol can also reduce fertility in both men and women. This means they are less likely to conceive (get pregnant). For example, alcohol reduces the amount of sperm that a man produces.

### Units of alcohol

On drinks labels the alcohol content is given as a percentage of the whole drink. Wine that says "10%" on its label contains 10% pure alcohol. Calculate the number of units of alcohol in a 200 ml glass of wine. One unit = 10 ml of pure alcohol.

## Key Words

ethanol, depressant, alcoholic, unit of alcohol

▲ Look at the difference in appearance of a diseased liver (left) and a healthy liver (right).

## Summary Questions

1 🧪 Copy and complete the sentences below.

Alcoholic drinks contain the drug _____. This is a _____, because it affects the_____ system, slowing down your body's reactions. Drinking alcohol can lead to brain and _____ damage.

*(4 marks)*

2 🧪🧪 Explain why it is important that pregnant women avoid alcohol.

*(3 marks)*

3 🧪🧪🧪 Make a visual summary to show the effects of alcohol on behaviour, health, and life processes such as conception, growth, and development.

*(6 marks)*

# 1.8 Smoking

## Learning objectives

After this topic you will be able to:

- describe the effects of tobacco smoke on health
- describe the effects of tobacco smoke on pregnancy.

## Key Words

passive smoking, stimulant

▲ The chemicals in tobacco smoke can be deadly.

**Most people know that smoking harms your health, yet many people still smoke. Even breathing in the smoke of someone else's cigarette can affect your health.**

## Why is smoking dangerous?

Smoking increases your chances of developing conditions such as breathing problems, cancer, heart attacks, and strokes. Smokers are much more likely to die prematurely than non-smokers. For example, male smokers are over 20% more likely to die from lung cancer than non-smokers.

**A** Name three conditions that a smoker is more likely to suffer from.

As well as affecting their own health, smokers endanger the health of others. By breathing in other people's smoke, your risk of developing circulatory and respiratory conditions increases. This is known as **passive smoking**.

Smoking in pregnancy greatly increases the risk of miscarriage. It can also increase the risk of low-birth-weight babies and affects the fetus's development. Parents who smoke after a baby is born increase the risk of sudden-infant-death syndrome ('cot death') and respiratory illness, such as bronchitis and pneumonia.

**B** State what is meant by passive smoking.

## Deadly smoke

Use the graph to answer the following questions:

1 Which smoking-related diseases cause the greatest number of deaths?

2 How many more deaths occurred due to lung disease than heart disease?

3 How many times more likely is a smoker to die from lung and throat cancer, compared to a stroke?

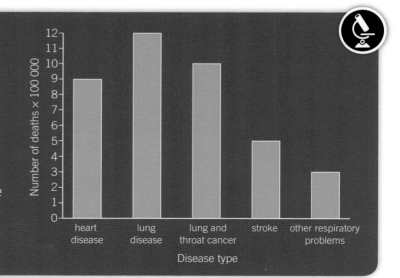

## What's in tobacco smoke?

Cigarettes contain tobacco. Tobacco smoke contains over 4000 chemicals, many of which are harmful. These include:

- tar – a sticky black material that collects in the lungs. It irritates and narrows the airways. Some of the chemicals it contains cause cancer.
- nicotine – an addictive drug that speeds up the nervous system. It is a **stimulant**, which makes the heart beat faster and narrows blood vessels.
- carbon monoxide – a poisonous gas that stops the blood from carrying as much oxygen as it should. It binds to the red blood cells in the place of oxygen.

**C** Name the addictive drug in tobacco smoke.

## How does smoking cause disease?

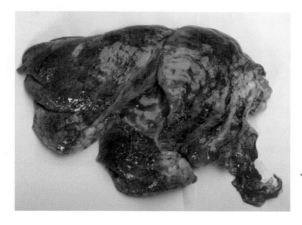

◀ This diseased lung is full of tar. Healthy lungs should be pink.

Some examples of the way smoking causes disease are listed below:

- Heart disease – smoking causes a person's arteries to become blocked. This prevents blood flowing properly, and can cause a heart attack or stroke.
- Emphysema (a lung disease) – chemicals in tobacco smoke affect the alveoli in your lungs. Their walls become weakened so they do not inflate properly when you inhale. They may also burst during coughing. This reduces the amount of oxygen that can pass into the blood, making the person breathless.
- Respiratory infections – the cells lining your windpipe produce mucus, which traps dirt and microorganisms. They also have cilia that sweep the mucus into your stomach, keeping your airways clean. Chemicals in tobacco smoke stop the cilia from moving. This allows mucus to flow into your lungs, making it harder to breathe and often causing infection. Smokers cough this mucus up, which can damage the lungs further.

According to the World Health Organisation, approximately one person dies every six seconds due to tobacco. Deaths caused by tobacco accounts for 10% of adult deaths.

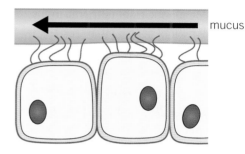

mucus

▲ Smoking makes it harder for ciliated cells to sweep mucus from your airways.

## Summary Questions

**1** 🧪 Match the chemicals in tobacco smoke to their harmful effect.

| | |
|---|---|
| **tar** | addictive and makes the heart beat faster |
| **nicotine** | reduces the amount of oxygen the blood can carry |
| **carbon monoxide** | contains chemicals that cause cancer |

*(3 marks)*

**2** 🧪🧪 Suggest why smokers often cough a lot when they first wake in the morning.

*(2 marks)*

**3** 🧪🧪 Describe how tobacco smoke can cause problems during pregnancy.

*(2 marks)*

**4** 🧪🧪🧪 Explain in detail three ways that smoking can damage your health.

*(6 marks)*

## Key Points

- Nutrients are essential substances that your body needs to survive. They are carbohydrates, lipids, proteins, vitamins, mineral, water, and fibre.
- Food tests are used to find out which nutrients a food contains.
- To remain healthy you must eat a balanced diet. This means eating food containing the right nutrients in the correct amounts.
- Underweight people often lack energy. They may also suffer from a vitamin or mineral deficiency, which can cause problems like a poor immune system.
- Overweight people have an increased risk of heart disease, stroke, diabetes, and some cancers.
- During digestion large molecules like lipids and proteins are broken down into small molecules. They can then pass into the blood where they are used by the body.
- Enzymes are proteins that can break large molecules into small molecules. They are biological catalysts – they speed up digestion without being used up.
- Drugs are substances that alter the chemical reactions that take place inside your body. Medicinal drugs have health benefits. Recreational drugs are taken for enjoyment.
- If a person becomes dependent on a drug, they have an addiction.
- A person with an addiction can suffer withdrawal symptoms if they stop taking the drug.
- Alcoholic drinks contain the drug ethanol. This is a depressant, which slows down the nervous system.
- Drinking large amounts of alcohol over a long time can cause stomach ulcers, heart disease, and brain and liver damage. A person with an alcohol addiction is called an alcoholic.
- Smoking tobacco causes breathing problems, cancer, heart attacks, and strokes.
- Tobacco smoke contains nicotine. This is a stimulant, which speeds up the nervous system. It is also addictive.

## Key Words

nutrients, carbohydrate, lipids, protein, vitamin, mineral, fibre, balanced diet, food test, hypothesis, malnourishment, starvation, deficiency, obese, digestive system, digestion, gullet, stomach, small intestine, large intestine, rectum, anus, villi, feces, enzyme, catalyst, carbohydrase, protease, lipase, bile, drug, medicinal drug, recreational drug, addiction, withdrawal symptom, ethanol, alcoholic, depressant, unit of alcohol, stimulant, passive smoking, hypothesis

## BIG Write

### Say no to drugs

You work for the NHS as a communications officer. You have been asked to produce an antidrugs leaflet. It will be given to all teenagers as part of an antidrugs campaign.

### Task

Write the text that will appear in the leaflet. It should contain information on smoking, alcohol, and illegal recreational drugs.

### Tips

- Make sure your points are clear, concise, and convincing – back up your arguments with scientific facts.
- Keep your audience in mind – your leaflet needs to appeal to teenagers and all scientific concepts must be explained clearly.

# End-of-chapter questions

1 ⚗ To remain healthy you must eat a balanced diet. Draw a line to match the nutrient to its function in the body.

| | |
|---|---|
| **carbohydrates** | used for growth and repair |
| **lipids** | needed in small amounts to keep you healthy |
| **proteins** | provide energy |
| **vitamins and minerals** | provide a store of energy and are used to insulate the body |

*(4 marks)*

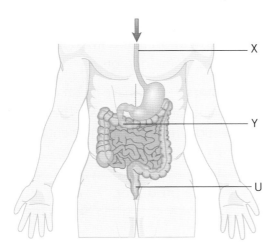

2 ⚗ The diagram above shows your digestive system.
  a Name structure X. *(1 mark)*
  b State what happens in structure Y. *(1 mark)*
  c Which letter represents the structure that stores feces until it leaves the body?
  *(1 mark)*
  d Describe the role of the stomach in digestion. *(2 marks)*
  *(5 marks)*

3 ⚗⚗ A student wants to do a food test to find out which nutrients are in crisps. She starts by making a solution of the crisps.

  a Name the piece of equipment she should use to break the crisps into small pieces.
  *(1 mark)*
  b Suggest **two** safety precautions the student should take before beginning the test. *(2 marks)*
  c Describe how the student should test the food solution for protein. *(3 marks)*
  *(6 marks)*

4 ⚗⚗ People take drugs for a number of reasons.
  a Describe the difference between medicinal drugs and recreational drugs.
  *(2 marks)*
  b State how a drug causes an effect on the body. *(1 mark)*
  c State the difference between a stimulant and a depressant. Give an example of each type of drug. *(4 marks)*
  *(7 marks)*

5 ⚗⚗⚗ Enzymes are special proteins that play a crucial rule in digestion.
  a Describe the role of enzymes in digestion.
  *(1 mark)*
  b Explain why enzymes are called catalysts.
  *(2 marks)*
  c Compare how and where carbohydrates and proteins are digested. *(4 marks)*
  d Explain how lipids are broken down and digested. *(3 marks)*
  *(10 marks)*

6 ⚗⚗⚗ Alcohol contains the drug ethanol and can have damaging effects on health.

  Explain why a couple should avoid alcohol when trying to conceive, and why a pregnant woman should not drink any alcohol during pregnancy.
  *(6 marks)*

# 2.1 Photosynthesis

## Learning objectives

After this topic you will be able to:

- describe the process of photosynthesis
- state the word equation for photosynthesis.

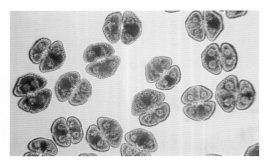
▲ Algae live in water.

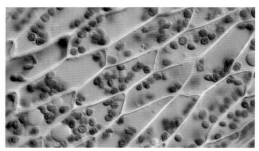
▲ Photosynthesis takes place inside chloroplasts in leaf cells.

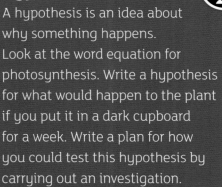

### Hypothesis

A hypothesis is an idea about why something happens. Look at the word equation for photosynthesis. Write a hypothesis for what would happen to the plant if you put it in a dark cupboard for a week. Write a plan for how you could test this hypothesis by carrying out an investigation.

Unlike animals, plants do not have to eat other organisms to survive. Instead they make their own food using sunlight. How do they do this?

## What is a producer?

Plants and **algae** are called **producers** because they make their own food. They convert materials found in their environment into glucose, a carbohydrate, using sunlight.

Algae are like plants because they are green organisms that make their own food. However, they differ from plants in the following ways:

- They can be unicellular or multicellular organisms.
- They live underwater while most plants live on land.
- Algae do not have leaves, stems, or roots.

Animals are called **consumers** as they have to eat other organisms to survive. These can be plants or other animals. They break down the organism during digestion. This releases nutrients, which are then used by the body.

**A** State what is meant by a producer.

## What is photosynthesis?

Plants make food through the process of **photosynthesis**. Photosynthesis is a chemical reaction in which plants take in carbon dioxide and water and change them into glucose. This provides the plant with food. Oxygen is also made. Oxygen is a waste product of the reaction. Oxygen is released back into the atmosphere. Plants need to use light from the Sun in this chemical reaction.

The word equation below shows the process of photosynthesis.

$$\text{carbon dioxide} + \text{water} \xrightarrow{\text{light}} \text{glucose} + \text{oxygen}$$
$$\text{(reactants)} \qquad\qquad\qquad \text{(products)}$$

**B** State the word equation for photosynthesis.

## Where does photosynthesis occur?

Photosynthesis mainly takes place in chloroplasts in the leaf cells, though a small amount happens in the stem. Leaves and stems are green because they contain the green pigment **chlorophyll**. Chlorophyll uses light from the Sun. The energy transferred from the Sun is needed for the plant to change carbon dioxide and water into glucose and oxygen.

**C** Name the part of the cell where photosynthesis occurs.

## How does water get into a plant?

Water diffuses into the root hair cells. It is then transported around the plant in tubes, called xylem tubes. As the water evaporates from the leaves, more water is drawn up through the plant. It is a bit like sucking on a straw!

## How do gases get into and out of a plant?

On the underside of the leaf there are tiny holes. These allow gases to diffuse into the leaf. Carbon dioxide diffuses into the leaf, and oxygen diffuses out.

The diagram below represents what happens during photosynthesis.

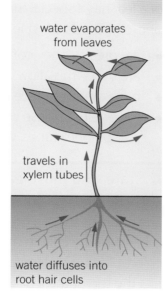

water evaporates from leaves

travels in xylem tubes

water diffuses into root hair cells

▲ Water enters the plant through the roots, then travels through the plant in the xylem tubes.

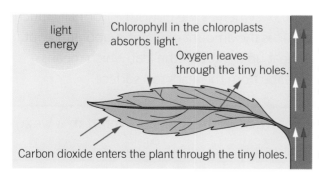

light energy

Chlorophyll in the chloroplasts absorbs light.

Oxygen leaves through the tiny holes.

Carbon dioxide enters the plant through the tiny holes.

Glucose is transported to all the parts of the plant. Water is transported from the roots to the stem and leaves.

## Key Words

algae, producer, consumer, photosynthesis, chlorophyll

## Link

You can learn more about diffusion in B1 1.4 Movement of substances

## Summary Questions

**1** 🧪 Copy and complete the sentences below.

Plants and _____ are _____. They use _____ to make their own food. They use _____ and water to make _____ and oxygen using _____ energy.

*(6 marks)*

**2** 🧪🧪 Explain why photosynthesis is important for all life.

*(3 marks)*

**3** 🧪🧪 State and explain whether photosynthesis would occur in the following situations:

  **a** a bright sunny day   *(1 mark)*

  **b** at night   *(1 mark)*

  **c** in the root hair cells   *(2 mark)*

**4** 🧪🧪🧪 Explain how the reactants of photosynthesis get into the leaf cells and what happens to the products of photosynthesis.

*(6 marks)*

## Definitions

Using the information in the text to write a definition of the following words – producer, consumer, photosynthesis.

# 2.2 Leaves

## Learning objectives

After this topic you will be able to:

- describe the structure and function of the main components of a leaf
- explain the distribution of chloroplasts in a leaf.

▲ Leaves come in all shapes and sizes.

**Leaves come in all shapes and sizes. Most are green because they contain lots of chlorophyll but have you ever looked closely at a leaf? Some, like stinging nettles, are covered in tiny hairs.**

## Structure of a leaf

Leaves are specially adapted for photosynthesis. Each component of a leaf has a special function that helps it to carry out photosynthesis. Most leaves:

- are green – they contain chlorophyll, which absorbs sunlight
- are thin – this allows gases to diffuse in and out of the leaf easily
- have a large surface area – to absorb as much light as possible
- have veins – these contain xylem tubes, which transport water, and phloem tubes, which transport glucose.

**A** State why most leaves are green.

The underneath of a green leaf is lighter than the top. This is because the cells in the bottom of the leaf contain fewer chloroplasts, which means there is less chlorophyll. Most sunlight hits the top of the leaf so this is where the chloroplasts need to be to absorb as much sunlight as possible.

**B** State which part of the leaf contains the most chloroplasts.

The top of the leaf feels waxy, whereas the bottom is normally much drier. This waxy layer reduces the amount of water evaporating out of the leaf. The Sun will heat up the top of the leaf, which means more water will try to escape from the leaf's top surface.

**C** State why the top surface of the leaf is covered in a waxy layer.

## Link

You can learn more about evaporation in C1 1.5 More changes of state

**Observing stomata**

Draw a detailed diagram of the underside of a leaf, labelling the key structures.

## How do gases get into and out of the leaf?

The tiny holes found on the bottom surface of the leaf are called **stomata** (singular: stoma). Their function is to allow gases to diffuse into and out of the leaf:

- Carbon dioxide diffuses in. Carbon dioxide is a reactant in photosynthesis.
- Oxygen and water vapour diffuse out. Oxygen and water are products of photosynthesis.

Stomata are opened and closed by guard cells. These cells open the stomata during the day, and close them at night.

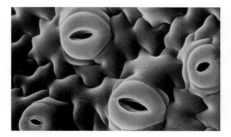

▲ Open stomata.    ▲ Closed stomata.

**D** State the function of stomata.

▲ The top and bottom surfaces of the leaf are normally quite different.

**Key Words**

stomata

## What does the inside of a leaf look like?

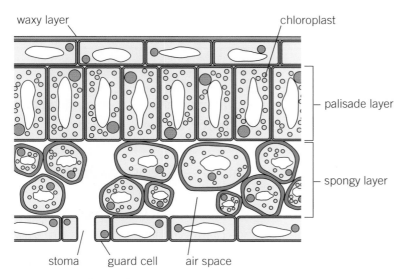

waxy layer — chloroplast — palisade layer — spongy layer

stoma    guard cell    air space

▲ Cross section of a leaf.

The leaf is divided into two main layers:

- palisade layer – contains cells packed with chloroplasts. This is where most of a plant's photosynthesis occurs.
- spongy layer – contains air spaces, allowing carbon dioxide to diffuse throughout the leaf. Oxygen diffuses out of the leaf.

**Summary Questions**

**1** Match the part of a leaf to its function.

| | |
|---|---|
| stomata | reduces amount of water evaporating |
| waxy layer | main site of photosynthesis |
| guard cells | transport water to cells in leaf |
| veins | open and close stomata |
| cells in palisade layer | allow gases to diffuse into and out of the leaf |

(5 marks)

**2** Suggest why stomata may close during hot weather.

(1 mark)

**3** Explain in detail how leaves are adapted for photosynthesis.

(6 marks)

## Learning objectives

After this topic you will be able to:

- describe how a plant uses minerals for healthy growth
- explain the role of nitrates in plant growth.

### Link

You can learn more about the importance of minerals in B2 1.1 Nutrients

**Farmers and gardeners regularly check their plants for signs of poor health. If your plants start to wilt they need watering. What does it mean if the leaves turn yellow? Just like people, plants need minerals for healthy growth.**

## What minerals do plants need?

For healthy growth, plants need four important minerals:

- **nitrates** (contain nitrogen) – for healthy growth
- **phosphates** (contain phosphorus) – for healthy roots
- **potassium** – for healthy leaves and flowers
- **magnesium** – for making chlorophyll.

**A** Name four minerals that plants need for healthy growth.

## Where do plants get minerals from?

Plants get the minerals they need from the soil. The minerals are dissolved in soil water. They are absorbed into the root hair cells, and are then transported around the plant in the xylem tubes.

**B** State how minerals enter plants.

## Mineral deficiency

If a plant does not get enough minerals, its growth will be poor. This is called a mineral **deficiency**. Different mineral deficiencies have different symptoms:

- nitrate deficiency – plant will have poor growth and older leaves are yellowed
- magnesium deficiency – plant leaves will turn yellow
- phosphorus deficiency – plant will have poor root growth, and younger leaves look purple
- potassium deficiency – has yellow leaves, with dead patches.

**C** State what is meant by a mineral deficiency.

▲ A nitrate deficiency results in poor growth.

## Mineral deficiency

Produce a leaflet for farmers that could help them to decide which mineral their plant is missing. You should include an image of a healthy plant that farmers can compare to their own.

▲ Magnesium deficiency results in yellow leaves.

The chlorophyll molecule, which makes plants green, contains magnesium. If a plant does not get enough magnesium it can't make as much chlorophyll as it needs. This results in yellow leaves.

Nitrates are involved in making amino acids. The amino acids join together to form proteins. These proteins are needed for cell growth, to grow leaves and shoots.

## Why do farmers use fertilisers?

When crops are harvested, minerals are removed from the ground. These would normally be replaced when the plant dies, or when leaves are shed. To prevent future crops suffering from a mineral deficiency, farmers add chemicals to the soil to replace missing minerals – these chemicals are called **fertilisers.**

**D** State what is meant by a fertiliser.

NPK is a common fertiliser. It contains three of the important minerals needed for healthy plant growth: nitrogen (N), phosphorus (P), and potassium (K).

▲ Farmers use fertilisers to add minerals to their crops.

## Key Words

nitrates, phosphates, potassium, magnesium, deficiency, fertiliser

## Summary Questions

**1** 🝪 Copy and complete the sentences below.

To remain healthy, plants need to absorb _____ from the soil. They are absorbed through the root _____ cells and then travel around the plant in the _____ tubes.

The mineral _____ is needed to make chlorophyll, and _____ are needed to make amino acids.

*(5 marks)*

**2** 🝪🝪 Explain the role of nitrates in plant growth.

*(3 marks)*

**3** 🝪🝪🝪 Explain in detail why farmers have to add to fertiliser to soil to ensure good crop yields year after year.

*(6 marks)*

# 2.4 Chemosynthesis

## Learning objectives

After this topic you will be able to:

- describe where chemosynthesis takes place
- describe the process of chemosynthesis.

## Key Words

chemosynthesis

**All living organisms need food to survive. Animals are consumers but plants and some microorganisms have to produce their own food. Plants use light to photosynthesise. How do microorganisms that live in the dark make their own food?**

### What is chemosynthesis?

Some species of bacteria use a variety of chemical reactions to make glucose. Glucose is a carbohydrate. This process is known as **chemosynthesis**.

**A** State what is meant by chemosynthesis.

You know the word equation for photosynthesis. There is no general word equation for chemosynthesis, as the chemical reaction depends on the chemical involved. Chemosynthesis reactions:

- use chemicals as their source of energy
- often use carbon dioxide as a reactant
- have glucose as a product.

**B** Name the gas that is often used in chemosynthesis.

### Where do bacteria live?

Bacteria that perform chemosynthesis are called chemosynthetic. They live in places without light.

- Sulfur bacteria are found at the bottom of the sea near volcanic vents. Hydrogen sulfide pours out of the vents. The sulfur bacteria turn the hydrogen sulfide into sulfur by chemosynthesis. This produces organic molecules, which they use as nutrients.
- Nitrogen bacteria perform chemosynthesis using nitrogen compounds. They live in the soil and roots of some plants.

**C** Name two types of bacteria that perform chemosynthesis.

▲ Nitrogen bacteria live on plant roots.

## Chemosynthesis in other organisms

Some chemosynthetic bacteria live within animals. For example, tubeworms, which live close to deep sea vents, have no stomach. Instead, chemosynthetic bacteria live within the tubeworm. The bacteria use chemicals from the tubeworms to make food. In return, the tubeworms feed off the substances made by the bacteria.

This type of biological relationship between organisms, where each organism benefits the other, is known as a symbiotic or mutualistic relationship.

▲ Tubeworms on a deep sea vent.

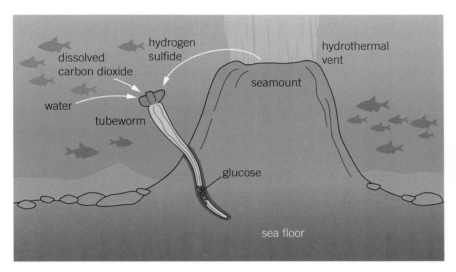

▲ Chemosynthetic bacteria live within tubeworms, close to volcanic vents on the ocean floor. They produce sulfur, which is used to make nutrients needed by the tubeworms.

### Interesting organisms
Find out about one organism that performs chemosynthesis. Share your findings with your partner.

## Photosynthesis and chemosynthesis
The table below shows the similarities and differences between photosynthesis and chemosynthesis.

|  | Photosynthesis | Chemosynthesis |
|---|---|---|
| Energy required | yes | yes |
| Energy source | light | chemical |
| Water required? | yes | not always |
| Carbon dioxide required? | yes | usually |
| Glucose produced? | yes | yes |

## Summary Questions

1 🧪 Copy and complete the sentences below.

Some species of _____ use energy released by chemical _____ to make _____ .

This process is known as _____ .

*(4 marks)*

2 🧪🧪

a Name one organism that produces glucose through the process of chemosynthesis.

*(1 mark)*

b For the example you have chosen, explain why it cannot produce glucose using photosynthesis. *(1 mark)*

3 🧪🧪🧪 Seaweed is a plant. Tubeworms contain bacteria that perform chemosynthesis. Compare the way in which glucose is produced in seaweed and tubeworms.

*(6 marks)*

# 2.5 Aerobic respiration

## Learning objectives

After this topic you will be able to:

- state the word equation for aerobic respiration
- describe the process of aerobic respiration.

### Key Words

aerobic respiration, plasma, haemoglobin

### Defining respiration

Read through the information about respiration on these pages for three minutes. Close the book, and produce a definition and description of aerobic respiration. Swap your ideas with a partner. Together can you improve your definition?

### Link

You can learn more about mitochondria in B1 2.2 Plant and animal cells

**You now know how organisms consume or produce glucose, but what happens next? Glucose is the key chemical that your body needs.**

### How do cells transfer energy?

Your body needs energy for everything it does. You need energy to move, to grow, and to keep warm. Energy is being used constantly (even when you are asleep!) to keep your body functioning.

You get your energy from organic molecules in the food you eat. To transfer the energy stored in food, glucose reacts with oxygen in a chemical reaction called **aerobic respiration**. This reaction transfers energy to your cells. The waste products carbon dioxide and water are also produced.

**A** Name the chemical reaction that transfers energy from glucose.

The word equation for aerobic respiration is:

$$\text{glucose} + \text{oxygen} \longrightarrow \text{carbon dioxide} + \text{water} (+ \text{energy})$$

(reactants)             (products)

**B** State the word equation for aerobic respiration.

▲ Physically active people like athletes need to eat lots of high-energy foods, as their bodies require energy to be transferred quickly.

## Where does respiration happen?

Respiration happens inside tiny structures inside your cells called mitochondria. All cells contain mitochondria but different cells contain different amounts. Muscle cells carry out lots of respiration, so they contain large amounts of mitochondria.

**C** State where in a cell respiration occurs.

## How does glucose get into cells?

Glucose is a carbohydrate found in food. Digestion breaks down food into small molecules, releasing glucose molecules. These molecules are absorbed by the wall of the small intestine, into the bloodstream.

Glucose is transported around your body in your blood. It dissolves in the liquid part of your blood called **plasma**. The dissolved glucose can diffuse into the cells that need it for respiration.

## How does oxygen get into cells?

When you breathe in, oxygen fills the alveoli in your lungs. The oxygen then diffuses into your bloodstream.

Oxygen is carried by the red blood cells in your body. Red blood cells contain **haemoglobin** (the substance that makes them red). Oxygen joins to the haemoglobin, and gets carried around the body in the blood vessels. When it reaches a cell requiring oxygen, the oxygen diffuses into the cell.

**D** Name the component of blood that carries oxygen around the body.

## How does carbon dioxide leave the body?

If carbon dioxide remained in your body it would build up to a harmful level. You get rid of carbon dioxide when you exhale. Carbon dioxide produced during respiration diffuses out of your cells and into the blood plasma. The blood transports it to the lungs, where it diffuses into the air sacs, and is then exhaled.

**E** Name the component of blood that transports carbon dioxide.

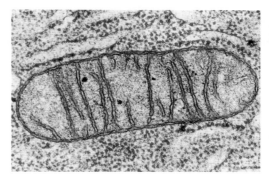

▲ A mitochondrion.

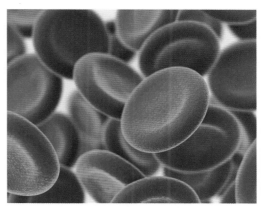

▲ Red blood cells carry oxygen to cells.

## Summary Questions

**1** 🧪 Copy and complete the sentences below.

Energy is released in _____ inside your cells by the process of _____. _____ and oxygen react together to release _____. Carbon dioxide and _____ are produced as waste products.

*(5 marks)*

**2** 🧪🧪 Describe where and how respiration takes place.

*(4 marks)*

**3** 🧪🧪🧪 Explain in detail how the reactants of respiration get into the cells and what happens to the products of respiration.

*(6 marks)*

## Learning objectives

After this topic you will be able to:

- state the word equation for anaerobic respiration
- describe the differences between aerobic and anaerobic respiration.

▲ After heavy exercise you will breathe heavily, to break down lactic acid in your muscles.

### Key Words

anaerobic respiration, oxygen debt, fermentation

### Useful microorganisms

Using the information on this page, write a paragraph explaining how anaerobic respiration is used to produce a useful product.

**During a sprint race athletes have very little time to breathe. Respiration must constantly supply your body with energy, even when you are unable to breathe.**

### How do you respire without oxygen?

**Anaerobic respiration** is a type of respiration that does not use oxygen. Your body uses this type of respiration to transfer energy from glucose when there is not enough oxygen for aerobic respiration to take place.

Anaerobic respiration often happens during strenuous exercise, as the body requires extra energy to be produced quickly. The body can transfer this extra energy for short periods of time without oxygen.

The word equation for anaerobic respiration is:

$$\text{glucose} \longrightarrow \text{lactic acid (+ energy)}$$

(reactant)           (products)

---

**A** State the word equation for anaerobic respiration.

---

There are two reasons why the body normally respires aerobically:

1 Aerobic respiration transfers more energy per glucose molecule than anaerobic respiration.

2 The lactic acid produced from anaerobic respiration can cause painful cramps in your muscles.

When you have finished exercising you keep on breathing heavily. The extra oxygen you inhale breaks down the lactic acid. The oxygen needed for this process is called the **oxygen debt**.

---

**B** State two reasons why the body normally respires aerobically.

---

### Do other organisms perform anaerobic respiration?

Other animals also use anaerobic respiration when they require a lot of energy quickly. For example, when a fox chases a rabbit, both organisms are likely to respire anaerobically.

Anaerobic respiration also takes place in plants and some microorganisms when there is no oxygen available. For example, the roots of plants in waterlogged soils respire anaerobically.

## Fermentation

Anaerobic respiration in some microorganisms produces ethanol and carbon dioxide instead of lactic acid. This process is called **fermentation**. Fermentation is a type of anaerobic respiration, as the microorganism respires without oxygen.

The word equation for fermentation is:

$$\text{glucose} \longrightarrow \text{ethanol} + \text{carbon dioxide} (+ \text{energy})$$

(reactant)                    (products)

**C** State the word equation for fermentation.

Yeast is an important microorganism in food production. It is needed to make bread, beer, and wine. These products are made using fermentation.

**D** State three products that are made using fermentation.

### How do you make bread?

To make bread, bakers mix together flour, water, and yeast to make dough. The yeast ferments the carbohydrates in the flour into ethanol and carbon dioxide. The gas is trapped inside the dough and makes it rise. When the dough is baked the ethanol evaporates, and the dough becomes bread.

### How do you make beer and wine?

Beer is made by fermenting barley grains; wine is made by fermenting grapes. In both cases, yeast ferments sugar into alcohol.

▲ Yeast ferments the carbohydrates in flour to help the bread rise.

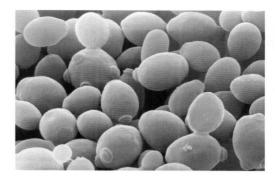

▲ Yeast is a type of fungus.

## Fantastic Fact

The world record for the longest loaf of bread is 1211.6 m. It was baked in Portugal in 2005 during the Bread and Bakers' Party.

## Summary Questions

**1** 🧪 Copy and complete the sentences below.

_____ respiration is a type of respiration that does not use _____. Anaerobic respiration in humans causes _____ to be released from glucose. _____ is produced as a waste product, which can build up in muscles and cause _____.

Some microorganisms carry out a type of anaerobic respiration called _____. In this reaction carbon dioxide and _____ are produced.

*(7 marks)*

**2** 🧪🧪 Describe the main differences between anaerobic and aerobic respiration.

*(3 marks)*

**3** 🧪🧪🧪 Imagine you are an athletics coach. Explain to a sprinter why they use anaerobic respiration during a race but marathon runners use aerobic respiration.

*(6 marks)*

# 2.7 Food chains and webs

## Learning objectives

After this topic you will be able to:

● describe what food chains show
● describe what food webs show.

To survive you need to transfer energy from food to your cells. You need to eat plants or other animals. Some of the animals you eat may have to eat other animals to survive. We can represent this information in diagrams called **food chains** and **food webs**.

### What is a food chain?

A **food chain** is a diagram that shows what an organism eats. It shows the transfer of energy between organisms.

**A** State what a food chain is.

Food chains have the following features:

● The first organism is a producer. Energy is transferred from the Sun to the organism and is changed into glucose by photosynthesis.
● The second organism is a herbivore. This is an animal that only eats plants.
● The third organism is a carnivore. This is an animal that eats other animals.
● Arrows show the transfer of energy (stored in food) from one organism to the next.

▲ A human is an omnivore. This means we eat both plants and other animals.

**B** State the difference between a herbivore and a carnivore.

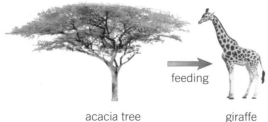

acacia tree          giraffe          lion

feeding          feeding

An example of a food chain from Africa is shown opposite.

In this example the acacia tree is a producer, the giraffe is a herbivore, and the lion is a carnivore.

A giraffe is also a **prey** organism. This means that it is eaten by another animal. The lion is a **predator**. This means it eats other animals.

**C** State the difference between a predator and a prey organism.

### Do all food chains have three links?

Most food chains have only four or five links. If there were more, too little energy would be transferred to organisms at the top of the chain. As energy is transferred along the food chain some is

## Key Words

food chain, predator, prey, food web

transferred to the surroundings by heating and as waste products. This means that at each level of the food chain less energy is transferred to the organism in the level above.

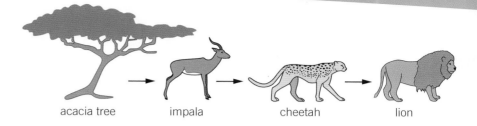

acacia tree      impala      cheetah      lion

The food chain opposite has four links:

The lion can is called the top predator – this means it is not eaten by any other animals. The top predator is always the last link in the food chain.

## How much energy?
Around 10% of the energy available at one level of a food chain is transferred to the next level. If 1000 kJ of energy enters a food chain that has three links, how much energy would be transferred to the top predator?

## What is a food web?
Most animals eat more than one type of organism. For example, lions eat giraffes, cheetahs, leopards, and zebras. Scientists show this in **food webs**. A food web is a set of linked food chains. Food webs show the feeding relationships of organisms more realistically than food chains.

**D** State what a food web is.

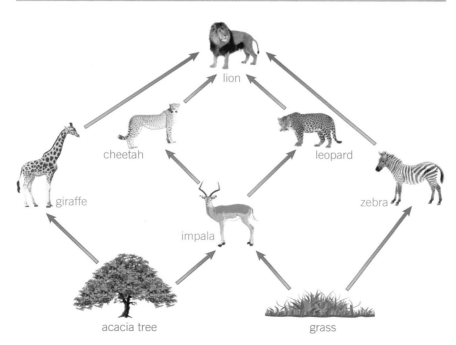

▲ A food web showing feeding relationships in Africa.

## Summary Questions

**1** 🧪 Match the following definitions to their meanings.

| | |
|---|---|
| food chain | diagram showing linked food chains |
| food web | animal that is eaten |
| predator | animal that eats another animal |
| prey | diagram showing the transfer of energy between organisms |

*(4 marks)*

**2** 🧪🧪 Use the food web on this page to answer the questions below.

  **a** Name a herbivore.  *(1 mark)*

  **b** Name a producer.  *(1 mark)*

  **c** State what the giraffe eats.  *(1 mark)*

  **d** Draw a food chain that has four links.  *(2 marks)*

**3** 🧪🧪🧪 Using scientific terms, describe the feeding relationships between the organisms in the following food chain.

grass → grasshopper → field mouse → owl

5000 kJ of energy is available in the grass.

*(6 marks)*

## Learning objectives

After this topic you will be able to:

- describe the interdependence of organisms
- describe how toxic materials can accumulate in a food web.

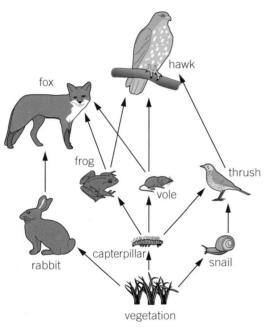

▲ The organisms in this food web are interdependent.

Some crops, including many fruits and vegetables, depend on bees to pollinate their flowers in reproduction. Bees depend on flowers as they feed on their nectar to survive. Bees and flowers are said to be interdependent – they each depend on the other for survival.

**Interdependence** is the way in which living organisms depend on each other to survive, grow, and reproduce.

**A** State what is meant by interdependence.

## Interdependence in food webs

The organisms in a food web depend on each other for survival. They are interdependent.

The number of animals or plants of the same type that live in the same area is called a **population**. In a food web, the populations of organisms are constantly changing. The population size of one type of organism has a direct effect on the size of another type of population.

The food web opposite shows the feeding relationships of organisms living in a field.

There are many food chains within this web. Some organisms, like the rabbit, have just one predator. Its predator is a fox. If the number of rabbits decreased due to a disease, the number of foxes would also decrease as they would have less to eat.

**B** Write down the meaning of the word population.

## Producer population

Grass is the producer. If there was no grass there would be no food for the snails, caterpillars, or rabbits. These organisms would die (unless they travelled to another area). All the other animals in the food web would also die as their food source has gone. If the population of the producer falls then the populations of the consumers also fall.

**C** State what happens to the population of consumers if the population of the producer decreases.

## Interpreting food webs

In small groups discuss what would happen to the other organisms in the food web above if disease reduced the population of voles.

## Consumer population

If the snail population decreased, the thrush population would also decrease. This may reduce the population of hawks. However, the hawk population would not decrease if they could gain enough energy from eating more frogs and voles. If this happened the population of frogs and voles would decrease.

## Bioaccumulation

It is not only energy that transfers along a food chain. Some chemicals can also be passed on. One example is insecticides. These are chemicals that some farmers use to kill insects that eat their crops.

Some insecticides are washed into rivers and end up in the sea. Fish absorb small amounts of these chemicals and store them in their body. Seals eat the fish, and the insecticide passes into their body. The levels of the chemical accumulate (build up) in the seals because one seal eats lots of fish. This process is called **bioaccumulation**.

Polar bears eat seals. One polar bear eats a lot of seals and so the insecticide accumulates into dangerous levels in the polar bear's body. This makes the bear ill and can cause death.

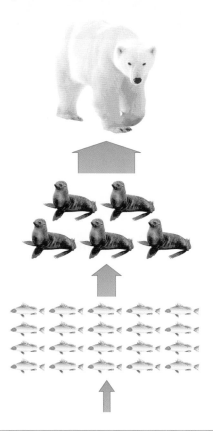

◄ This food chain shows the bioaccumulation of insecticides.

**D** State what is meant by bioaccumulation

### Key Words

interdependence, population, bioaccumulation

### Summary Questions

1  🧪 Copy and complete the sentences below.

   If two organisms both depend on each other for something, this is called _____.

   In a food web if the producer population decreases the consumer population will _____.

   Toxic chemicals can build up in organisms through a food chain. This is known as _____.

   *(3 marks)*

2  🧪🧪 Using the food web on this page:

   a Explain what would happen to the population of rabbits if all the foxes died. *(2 marks)*

   b Explain what would happen to the populations in the food web if all the frogs died. *(4 marks)*

3  🧪🧪🧪 DDT is an insecticide that was once used to kill insects. It is no longer used, as it killed many fish-eating birds. The fish fed on plankton, which absorbed the insecticide from rivers. Draw a food chain to show this and explain how the insecticide killed the birds but not the fish.

   *(6 marks)*

# 2.9 Ecosystems

**Learning objectives**

After this topic you will be able to:

- describe how different organisms co-exist within an ecosystem
- identify niches within an ecosystem.

In a coral reef, there are many types of fish that live together. They can do this because they all require slightly different things from the reef and they each perform different roles.

▲ Many species of fish live together in the coral reef.

## What is an ecosystem?

An **ecosystem** is the name given to the plants and animals that are found in a particular location, and the area in which they live. These plants and animals depend on each other to survive.

**A** State what is meant by an ecosystem.

The organisms in an ecosystem are known as a **community**. The area they live in is called a **habitat**.

For example, in a pond ecosystem:

- habitat – pond
- community – water plants, microorganisms, insects, fish, and fish-eating birds.

The plants and animals in a community and a habitat **co-exist**. This means they live in the same place at the same time.

**B** State what is meant by a habitat.

**Link**

You can learn more about the relationships between different organisms in B2 3.1 Competition and adaptation

# Co-existing in an ecosystem

leaf canopy
bees, wasps, moths,
squirrels, sparrows,
and hawks

trunk
insects and larvae

roots and leaf litter
bacteria, earthworms,
wood lice, and fungi

▲ An oak-tree ecosystem.

The diagram above shows an oak-tree ecosystem. There are lots of living organisms that live in or close to the tree but not every organism lives in the same part of the tree:

- Roots and leaf litter – microorganisms, woodlice, and earthworms live at the base of the tree. They break down the old leaves, releasing nutrients that the tree can then absorb and use for new growth.
- Trunk – the tree trunk provides food or shelter for a number of insects and caterpillars.
- Tree canopy – many organisms live amongst the branches and leaves of the tree. For example, bees gather pollen and nectar when the tree is in blossom. Fungi may grow on the leaves. Squirrels gather acorns and moths lay their eggs. Small birds such as sparrows eat the moth larvae. Sparrow hawks feed on the sparrows.

## What is a niche?

Each of the organisms living in the oak-tree ecosystem has its own **niche**. A niche is a particular place or role that an organism has within an ecosystem. For example, they may live in a particular part of the tree or have a particular food source.

***

**C** State what is meant by a niche.

***

Sparrows and squirrels both live in the tree canopy but they do not compete for food. Squirrels feed on acorns, while sparrows feed on moth larvae and caterpillars. The sparrows and squirrels have similar but slightly different niches.

## Scientific glossary

There have been lots of new words introduced in this chapter. Produce a scientific glossary of all the key terms covered in this chapter. Where possible, use examples to illustrate your answer.

## Key Words

ecosystem, community, habitat, co-exist, niche

## Summary Questions

**1** Match the words below to their definitions.

| | |
|---|---|
| ecosystem | plants and animals found in a particular habitat |
| community | particular place or role that an organism has in an ecosystem |
| habitat | living organisms in a particular area, and the habitat they live in |
| niche | place where a plant or animal lives |

*(4 marks)*

**2** Explain how bees and birds can both live within the canopy of a tree.

*(2 marks)*

**3** Describe in detail how the different niches occupied by three organisms in a habitat mean that organisms can co-exist.

*(6 marks)*

## Key Points

- Plants and algae are producers – they make their own food by photosynthesis.
- Photosynthesis: carbon dioxide + water $\rightarrow$ glucose + oxygen
- Photosynthesis takes place in chloroplasts. Chloroplasts contain chlorophyll, which traps the light needed for photosynthesis.
- Stomata allow gases to enter and leave a leaf. Guard cells open the stomata during the day and close them at night.
- Plants need minerals for healthy growth. For example, nitrates are needed to make amino acids. Amino acids join together to form proteins, which are used for growth.
- To transfer energy from glucose, aerobic respiration takes place inside mitochondria.
- Aerobic respiration: glucose + oxygen $\rightarrow$ carbon dioxide + water (+ energy)
- If no oxygen is present, energy can be transferred from glucose using anaerobic respiration.
- Anaerobic respiration: glucose $\rightarrow$ lactic acid (+ energy)
- Fermentation is a type of anaerobic respiration performed by microorganisms. It is used in bread- and beer-making.
- Fermentation: glucose $\rightarrow$ ethanol + carbon dioxide (+ energy)
- Food chains show the transfer of energy between organisms. A food web is a set of linked food chains.
- Toxic chemicals can build up in organisms in a food chain until they reach harmful levels. This is called bioaccumulation.
- Interdependence is the way in which organisms depend on each other to survive, grow, and reproduce.
- Organisms can co-exist within a habitat as they each have a different niche.

## BIG Write

### Banana power
Many tennis players eat a banana during a match to give them a boost of energy. The energy transferred to them from the banana has started off in the Sun. Almost all life on Earth depends on the transfer of the Sun's energy to plants and algae in photosynthesis.

### Task
Write a short essay explaining how the energy was transferred into the banana from the Sun, and what happens inside the tennis player's body to transfer this energy to his muscles.

### Tips
- Make sure you use as many scientific terms as possible.
- Use word equations to represent reactions that take place.

## Key Words

algae, producer, consumer, photosynthesis, chlorophyll, stomata, mineral, nitrates, phosphates, potassium, magnesium, deficiency, fertiliser, chemoynthesis, aerobic respiration, plasma, haemoglobin, anaerobic respiration, oxygen debt, fermentation, food chain, predator, prey, food web, interdependence, population, bioaccumulation, ecosystem, community, habitat, co-exist, niche

# End-of-chapter questions

**1** 🔬
  **a** Name the reaction that your body uses to transfer energy from glucose. *(1 mark)*
  **b** State where in a cell this reaction happens. *(1 mark)*
  **c** Complete the word equation below to represent this process:

glucose + _____ → _____ water (+ energy)
*(2 marks)*
*(**4 marks**)*

**2** 🔬
  **a** Re-arrange the following organisms into a food chain:
  owl    mouse    corn    *(1 mark)*
  **b** Name the producer.    *(1 mark)*
  **c** Describe the difference in how energy is transferred to producers and consumers. *(2 marks)*
  **d** Describe what would happen to the number of mice if a disease killed all of the owls. *(2 marks)*
*(**6 marks**)*

**3** 🔬🔬 This equipment can be used to study photosynthesis.

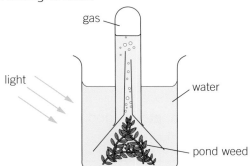

  **a** Name the gas given off by the plant. *(1 mark)*
  **b** State the **two** reactants needed for photosynthesis. *(2 marks)*
  **c** Explain what would happen to the number of bubbles if the plant was placed in the dark. *(3 marks)*
  **d** Describe the role of stomata in photosynthesis. *(2 marks)*
*(**8 marks**)*

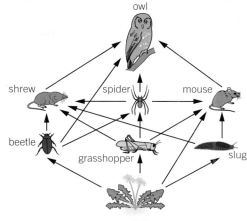

**4** 🔬🔬 This food web shows the feeding relationships between organisms in a garden.
  **a** State and explain what would happen to the spider population if all the owls were removed from the area. *(2 marks)*
  **b** State and explain what would happen to the grasshopper population if all the beetles died. *(2 marks)*
  **c** Mice and shrews are very similar organisms. Explain why they can both successfully survive in the same habitat. *(2 marks)*
  **d** A toxic chemical was used to kill all the dandelions. Explain how this could eventually result in the death of the owls. *(3 marks)*
*(**9 marks**)*

**5** 🔬🔬🔬 To remain healthy plants need minerals.
  **a** Explain how a plant absorbs minerals and transports them to different parts of the plant. *(3 marks)*
  **b** Plants lacking in magnesium have yellow leaves. Explain why this means they carry out less photosynthesis. *(2 marks)*
  **c** Explain how the structure of a leaf is adapted to maximise sunlight absorption. *(3 marks)*
*(**8 marks**)*

**6** 🔬🔬🔬 Explain how fermentation is used in food production. *(**6 marks**)*

## Learning objectives

After this topic you will be able to:

- describe some resources that plants and animals compete for
- describe how organisms are adapted to their environments.

▲ Birds competing for food.

## Link

You can learn more about how organisms are adapted in B2 3.2 Adapting to change

## Fantastic Fact

The Scimitar-horned oryx can survive for up to 10 months without drinking water. They get the moisture they need to survive from their food.

**If you have ever put food out for birds, you might see the birds 'fighting' over the food. Often, smaller species are scared off by larger birds. In the wild, all animals have to compete for resources.**

## What do animals compete for?

In a habitat there is a limited supply of resources, such as food, water, and space. To survive, animals compete with each other to get enough of these resources. This is known as **competition**.

Animals compete for:

1 food

2 water

3 space – to hunt and for shelter

4 mates – to reproduce.

**A** State four resources that animals compete for.

## What do plants compete for?

Plants also compete for resources in their environment. Plants compete for:

1 light

2 water

3 space

4 minerals – plants do not compete for food, as they produce their own through photosynthesis.

**B** State four resources that plants compete for.

## Who are the best competitors?

When competing with other animals for food the best predators will be fast, strong, and quick to spot their prey. These abilities allow them to sense their prey quickly and react before others, making sure that they get the food. Spotting their prey may require good eyesight or hearing. These features are known as **adaptations** – they are characteristics that enable an organism to be successful, and so survive.

◄ A cheetah is the fastest land animal – this adaptation of speed makes it a very successful predator.

**C** State what is meant by the term adaptation.

## How can animals live in a desert?

The desert is one of the harshest habitats to live in as food and water are scarce. Temperatures are also extremely hot during the day. Most desert animals are small and hide away in burrows to avoid the daytime heat. Only a few large mammals, such as camels and oryx, can survive. They travel long distances to find food, and can survive for long periods of time without drinking.

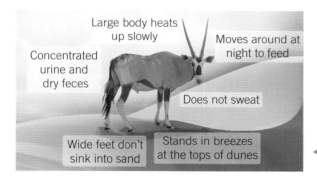

Large body heats up slowly

Concentrated urine and dry feces

Moves around at night to feed

Does not sweat

Wide feet don't sink into sand

Stands in breezes at the tops of dunes

◄ Adaptations of an oryx.

## How can plants live in a desert?

Plants in the desert have a number of adaptations to enable them to survive with very little water. These include:

- a waxy layer that covers the plant – this reduces water escaping from the plant
- stems that can store water
- widespread roots – to collect water from a large area
- spines instead of leaves – this gives a smaller surface area to reduce water loss. Spines also prevent the plant being eaten.

### Nocturnal animals

Find out about the adaptations of a nocturnal animal. These animals reduce competition with other animals by being active at night. Produce an information poster about your chosen animal, labelling its features with as many scientific terms as possible.

▲ Cacti are very well adapted to surviving in a desert.

## Key Words

competition, adaptation

## Summary Questions

1 Copy and complete the sentences below.

Plants and animals _____ for a number of _____. These include water and space.

Animals also compete for food and for _____ to reproduce. Plants make their own food by photosynthesis so they compete for _____.

Organisms have a number of _____ that enable them to survive in their habitat.

*(5 marks)*

2 Describe three ways that a cactus is adapted to prevent water loss.

*(3 marks)*

3 Explain in detail how the adaptations and behaviour of an oryx allow it to survive in the desert.

*(6 marks)*

# 3.2 Adapting to change

## Learning objectives

After this topic you will be able to:

- describe how organisms adapt to environmental changes
- describe how competition can lead to adaptation.

▲ Deciduous trees lose their leaves in winter.

▲ The snowshoe hare. Its predator is the Canadian lynx.

**You can usually tell what season it is by observing leaves on trees. If the leaves are in bud it is spring, green leaves mean it is summer, shades of orange and brown mean autumn, and when the tree is bare it is winter. Losing leaves is one way that trees change with their environment.**

### How do trees cope with the seasons?

Plants and animals have to cope with changes in their environment. For example, deciduous trees look different in each season. They grow rapidly during the spring when the weather is wet and warm but lose their leaves in winter. This saves energy. The fallen leaves provide a layer of warmth and protection around the base of the tree. The tree can reuse the nutrients from these leaves too.

**A** State two advantages of trees losing their leaves in winter.

### How do animals cope with the seasons?

Animals have a number of ways of coping with cold winter temperatures, such as:

- hibernation – animals like bears find somewhere warm to sleep through the winter
- migration – animals like birds move somewhere warmer, or somewhere with more food
- grow thicker fur – animals like sheep are kept warm by their thick coat.

**B** Name three ways that different animals adapt to the winter.

### The snowshoe hare

During the winter, snowshoe hares have white fur, which helps them blend in with the snow. When the seasons change to spring and summer, the snowshoe hare's fur turns a reddish-brown. This helps them to blend in with rocks and earth in mountain forests. When they are blended in with their environment it is harder for a predator to see them. This increases their chances of survival.

## Predator–prey relationships

Animals have to adapt to changes in their food supply. Only the best competitors will survive to reproduce.

When a predator feeds on just one type of prey, there is an **interdependence** between the predator population and the prey population. This means that changes in the population of one animal directly affects the population of the other. When plotted on a graph this relationship shows a clear pattern.

**C** State what is meant by interdependence.

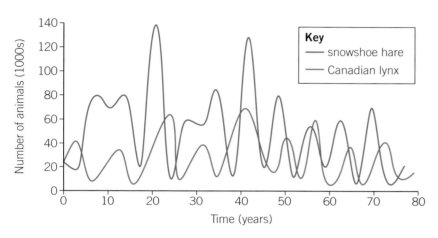

▲ Predator–prey graph showing the interdependence of the lynx and the hare.

- When the prey population (hare) increases, the predators (lynx) have more to eat. The lynx survive longer and reproduce more.
- This increases the number of predators.
- The growing predator population eats more prey. The prey numbers fall.
- Eventually there is not enough food for all the predators so their numbers decrease.
- There are now fewer lynx feeding on the hares. The hare population increases, and the cycle starts again.

## How do organisms cope with change?

Plants and animals can lose their habitat through fire or climate change. Food supplies may also be reduced by disease. Sudden changes result in increased competition for survival. The organisms best adapted to the change will survive and reproduce, increasing the population of that species. Organisms that are not very well adapted will have to move to another habitat, or die.

---

### Predator–prey graphs

Foxes are predators that eat rabbits. Sketch a graph showing how the fox and rabbit populations change over time.

### Key Words

interdependence

---

## Summary Questions

**1** Copy and complete the sentences below.

A predator–prey relationship shows how the _____ of a predator and its prey are linked. When there are lots of prey, the population of _____ increases. However, a large predator population will cause the _____ population to _____. There is not enough food for all the predators so its population decreases. As a result, the prey population will _____, and the cycle starts again.

*(5 marks)*

**2** Describe how competition can lead to adaptation.

*(3 marks)*

**3** Ladybirds with seven spots have spread to the UK from Europe. They are more successful than native UK ladybird, as they eat more aphids and reproduce faster. They also eat other ladybird species. Explain in detail how the population of seven-spotted ladybirds will vary over time. Draw a predator–prey graph as part of your answer.

*(6 marks)*

# 3.3 Variation

## Learning objectives

After this topic you will be able to:

- describe how variation in species occurs
- describe the difference between environmental and inherited variation.

▲ There is a lot of variation between types of dog.

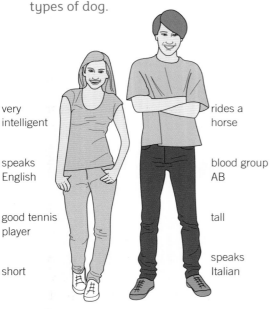

very intelligent

speaks English

good tennis player

short

rides a horse

blood group AB

tall

speaks Italian

### Link

You can learn more about how characteristics are inherited in B2 3.5 Inheritance

**If you imagine your friends and family, you will picture people who look quite different to each other. For example, people may vary in height and have different colour hair. They have different characteristics.**

## How do organisms vary?

Differences in characteristics are known as **variation**.

**A** State what is meant by variation.

It is easy to tell the difference between a dog and a fish. For example, a fish has fins and gills; a dog has four legs and is covered in fur. This is because these organisms belong to different **species**. They have lots of different characteristics.

**B** State what is meant by a species.

However, it is more difficult to tell the difference between two fish. This is because organisms of the same species have lots of similar characteristics. They can mate to produce fertile offspring.

Sometimes a species can be further grouped into types or breeds. These may look quite different but the individuals still belong to the same species. For example, different breeds of dog show great variation but they are all dogs.

## How do humans vary?

Every human in the world is different – even identical twins differ in some ways. The image opposite shows some of the ways people may vary.

## What causes variation?

Some variation is from characteristics the people have inherited from their parents, such as their eye colour. This is known as **inherited variation**.

Children usually share some characteristics with their mother and some with their father. They are not identical to either of their parents, as they get a mixture of their parents' features. An example of inherited variation is lobed or lobeless ears.

lobed ear          lobeless ear

◀ Whether you have lobed or lobeless ears depends on your parents.

**C** State what is meant by inherited variation.

### Environmental variation

Variation caused by your surroundings and what happens to you is called **environmental variation**. For example, your characteristics can be affected by factors such as your diet, education, and lifestyle. A person with dyed hair, for example, has environmental variation.

**D** State what is meant by environmental variation.

Many characteristics are affected by both inherited and environmental variation. For example, you might inherit the characteristic to be tall from your father. However, if you eat a poor diet your rate of growth may be reduced.

Inherited characteristics that are not affected by environmental variation include:

- eye colour
- blood group
- genetic diseases.

### Spelling key terms

There are a lot of long scientific words in this chapter. Can you spell them all correctly? Look carefully at the spelling of the following words for two minutes: species, variation, adaptation, inherited, environmental. Cover the words and ask a partner to test your spelling.

## Key Words

variation, species, inherited variation, environmental variation

▲ These people have environmental variation.

## Summary Questions

**1** 🧪 Copy and complete the sentences below.

The organisms in a _____ share many of the same _____. They can reproduce to produce fertile _____.

Differences in characteristics within a species are known as _____.

Variation can be a result of _____ factors or through _____ factors.

*(6 marks)*

**2** 🧪🧪 Copy and complete the table using the words below.

**body mass   intelligence   tattoo
blood group   eye colour   scar**

| Environmental variation | Inherited variation | Both |
|---|---|---|
|  |  |  |
|  |  |  |

*(6 marks)*

**3** 🧪🧪 Explain why identical twins are the best people to study if you want to find out how the environment influences characteristics.

*(2 marks)*

**4** 🧪🧪🧪 Explain in detail the difference between inherited and environmental variation.

*(6 marks)*

# 3.4 Continuous and discontinuous

## Learning objectives

After this topic you will be able to:

- describe the difference between continuous and discontinuous variation
- represent variation within a species using graphs.

## Fantastic Fact

The tallest ever person was Robert Wadlow. He grew to a height of 2.72 m. He could not fit into many houses without ducking!

## Key Words

discontinuous variation, continuous variation.

If you look around your classroom at the other students, you will see that some students share the same eye colour but very few are exactly the same height. This is because there are different types of variation.

## What is discontinuous variation?

Characteristics that can only result in certain values show **discontinuous variation**. For example, gender shows discontinuous variation. There are only two possible values: you are either male or female.

Other characteristics that show discontinuous variation are your blood group and eye colour.

**A** State what is meant by discontinuous variation.

## What is continuous variation?

A characteristic that can take any value within a range is said to show **continuous variation**. For example, the height of the population ranges from the shortest person in the world to the tallest person. Everyone else's height can be any value in between. This is an example of continuous variation.

Other characteristics that show continuous variation are your body mass, hair length, and arm span.

**B** State what is meant by continuous variation.

## Patterns of variation

To study variation, scientists take measurements of different characteristics within the species. To come up with conclusions, they need to collect measurements from large numbers of the population. This data is then plotted on a graph so that patterns in the data can be easily spotted.

## Plotting discontinuous variation

Characteristics that show discontinuous variation should be plotted on a bar chart.

For example, a person can only have one of four blood groups – A, B, AB, or O. These are the only values that a blood group can be, so you should plot a graph with four bars.

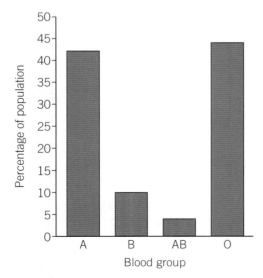

▲ Discontinuous data is always plotted on a bar chart.

Characteristics that occur only as result of inherited variation normally show discontinuous variation.

**C** State the type of graph that should be used to plot discontinuous data.

## Plotting continuous variation

Characteristics that show continuous variation should be plotted on a histogram. A line is then often added to the chart to make it easier to see the shape of the graph.

Within a population, characteristics that show continuous variation will display a range of measurements from one extreme to another.

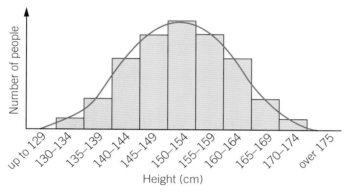

▲ Continuous data is always plotted on a histogram.

This type of variation usually produces a curve, which is known as a normal distribution.

Characteristics that occur as a result of both environmental and inherited variation usually show continuous variation.

**D** State the type of graph that should be used to plot continuous data.

### Which graph?

Which type of graph – a bar chart or histogram – would you use for the sets of data below?

**a** members of your class who have lobed, or lobeless ears

**b** the length of feet of each of your teachers

**c** the height of a group of seedlings, planted for a germination experiment

**d** the number of strawberries per plant, from a sample of 25 plants.

## Summary Questions

**1** 🧪 Copy and complete the sentences below.

Characteristics that can only result in certain values show _____ variation. Characteristics that can have any value within a range show _____ variation.
The range of values of a characteristic from a sample can be displayed using a _____.
A characteristic such as eye colour should be displayed using a _____.
Characteristics showing continuous variation, such as body mass, should be shown using a _____.

*(5 marks)*

**2** 🧪🧪 Classify each of these characteristics into continuous variation and discontinuous variation.

**length of arm, hair colour, maximum sprinting speed, shoe size, average leaf size**

*(5 marks)*

**3** 🧪🧪

**a** Look at the graph of the variation in heights on this page. Describe the pattern that this variation shows. *(3 marks)*

**b** Explain whether this variation is a result of environmental factors, inherited factors, or both. *(3 marks)*

**4** 🧪🧪🧪 Explain in detail the difference between continuous and discontinuous variation, using examples of features from the human body.

*(6 marks)*

# 3.5 Inheritance

## Learning objectives

After this topic you will be able to:

- describe how characteristics are inherited
- describe how scientists worked together to develop the DNA model.

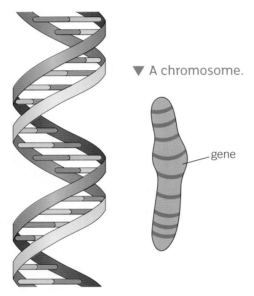

▼ A chromosome.

gene

▲ The shape of DNA is a double helix – a bit like a twisted ladder.

### DNA timeline

Carry out some research to produce a timeline, showing the key steps in scientists' understanding of DNA.

### Link

You can learn more about DNA in B3 2.5 DNA

**You can often tell if people are members of the same family, as they look alike. The children have inherited some characteristics from each of their parents. Brothers and sisters do not look completely the same, as they each inherit a different mixture of characteristics.**

## How do you inherit characteristics?

You inherit characteristics from your parents through genetic material stored in the nucleus of your cells. This material is a chemical called **DNA** (deoxyribonucleic acid). DNA contains all the information needed to make an organism.

**A** State what DNA is.

## Chromosomes

Inside the nucleus, your DNA is arranged into long strands called **chromosomes**. Different species have a different number of chromosomes in their nucleus. Humans have 46 chromosomes; cats have 38 chromosomes.

You inherit half of your chromosomes from your mother and half from your father. This is why you share some of your characteristics with your mother and some with your father.

**B** State what a chromosome is.

## Genes

Each chromosome is divided into sections of DNA. The sections that hold the information to produce a characteristic are called **genes**. For example, one gene contains the information that sets your eye colour, while a different gene sets your hair colour. Each chromosome contains thousands of genes.

**C** State what a gene is.

## How is genetic material inherited?

Inside the nucleus of your cells, the 46 chromosomes are arranged into 23 pairs. One copy of the chromosome of each pair comes from your mother, and the other comes from your father.

Egg and sperm cells are the only cells to contain 23 chromosomes. They only have one copy of each chromosome. During fertilisation, the egg and sperm cells join together. When their nuclei join, their chromosomes pair up, producing an embryo with 46 chromosomes.

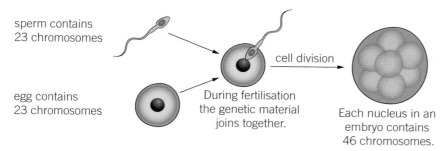

sperm contains
23 chromosomes

cell division

During fertilisation
the genetic material
joins together.

egg contains
23 chromosomes

Each nucleus in an
embryo contains
46 chromosomes.

▲ You get half of your genetic material from your mother, and half from your father.

**D** State the number of chromosomes present in a normal human body cell.

## Discovering DNA

Four scientists worked together to produce a model of the structure of DNA.

In the early 1950s two scientists, Rosalind Franklin and Maurice Wilkins, used X-rays to investigate the structure of DNA. The image they produced is shown above.

James Watson and Francis Crick, scientists working at another university, were also studying DNA. When they saw this image it told them that DNA had a helical shape. Through further investigations, Watson and Crick worked out that the structure of DNA is like a twisted ladder. This is known as a double helix.

In 1962 Crick and Watson, along with Wilkins, won the Nobel Prize for Medicine for their discovery. Franklin died in 1958; some people say that at the time her role in this famous discovery wasn't recognised.

### Team work

The scientists who discovered the structure of DNA did so by working together. Communication is very important so that scientists can share their ideas and carry out investigations. Watson and Crick were able to work out the structure of DNA by building on the work of Franklin and Wilkins.

◀ The first image of DNA, produced using X-rays.

## Key Words

DNA, chromosome, gene

## Summary Questions

**1** 🔬 Copy and complete the sentences below.

Genetic material in the body is stored in the _____ of a cell.

_____ is the name of the chemical that contains the instructions needed to make an organism.

_____ are made of long strands of DNA.

The sections of DNA that hold the information for a _____ are called _____ .

*(5 marks)*

**2** 🔬🔬 Arrange these objects in order of size, starting with the smallest.

**cell chromosome gene DNA nucleus**

*(2 marks)*

**3** 🔬🔬 Describe how scientists worked together to discover the structure of DNA.

*(2 marks)*

**4** 🔬🔬🔬 Explain in detail why you share some characteristics with your mother and some with your father.

*(6 marks)*

# 3.6 Natural selection

## Learning objectives

After this topic you will be able to:

- describe the process of natural selection
- describe how organisms evolve over time.

## Fantastic Fact

More proof for evolution comes from your DNA. You share about 97% of your DNA with a gorilla and 50% with a banana! This is evidence that all living things evolved from the same ancestor.

## Key Words

evolution, fossil, natural selection

## Evolution cartoon

Produce a cartoon strip showing the evolution of an organism of your choice – this could be a real organism or a made-up one.

**Have you heard the phrase 'survival of the fittest'? It means that organisms that are best adapted to a situation will survive, and those that are not will die. This is how scientists think that all organisms on Earth have developed.**

## What is evolution?

Scientists have shown that the species we see on Earth today have gradually developed over millions of years. This process is called **evolution**.

Evolution started with unicellular organisms. These organisms, similar to bacteria, lived in water more than three billion years ago. Over time they evolved to become multicellular organisms. Eventually, this process resulted in organisms that could live on land and in the air.

**A** State what is meant by evolution.

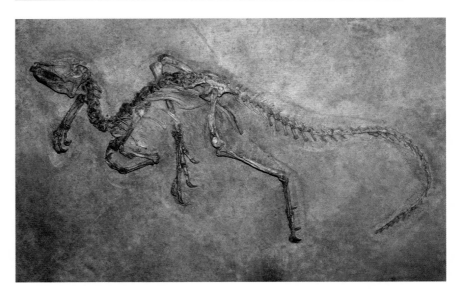

▲ A dinosaur fossil.

The **fossil** record provides most of the evidence for evolution. Fossils are the remains, or traces, of plants or animals that lived many years ago. They have been preserved by natural processes. The fossil record provides evidence of species that no longer exist, such as dinosaurs.

**B** Describe what a fossil is.

## How do organisms evolve?

Organisms evolve through the process of **natural selection**. They change slowly over time, to become better adapted to their environment. The process takes many years, sometimes millions, as it happens over a number of generations.

**C** Describe the process of natural selection.

### Peppered moths

Living organisms are continually evolving to adapt to their environment. Evolution usually happens slowly over many years. However, dramatic changes in an organism's environment can result in evolution happening quickly. Peppered moths evolved in this way during the 19th century.

Before the Industrial Revolution, most peppered moths in Britain were pale coloured. This was helpful to the moths, as they blended in with tree bark. A few peppered moths were dark coloured. This was a disadvantage, as they were easily seen by birds, and eaten. The pale moths were more likely to survive and reproduce, so most of the peppered-moth population was pale coloured.

After the Industrial Revolution many trees were covered in soot, turning the bark black. This meant that the dark moths were camouflaged. More dark peppered moths survived and reproduced than pale moths. After several years, the population of dark peppered moths in towns and cities became much higher than the population of pale peppered moths.

▲ Before the Industrial Revolution, pale peppered moths were highly camouflaged against tree bark. Dark moths were easily seen.

▲ After the Industrial Revolution, dark peppered moths were more camouflaged against soot-blackened trees and pale moths were easily seen.

**Natural selection**

Organisms in a species show variation – this is caused by differences in their genes.

The organisms with the characteristics that are best adapted to the environment survive and reproduce. Less well adapted organisms die. This process is known as 'survival of the fittest'.

Genes from successful organisms are passed to the offspring in the next generation. This means the offspring are likely to possess the characteristics that made their parents successful.

This process is then repeated many times. Over a period of time this can lead to the development of a new species.

## Summary Questions

**1** 🧪 Copy and complete the sentences below.

All living organisms have _____ from a common ancestor. This process has taken _____ of years.

_____ provide evidence for evolution. These are the _____ of plants or animals that died long ago, which have turned to _____ .

*(5 marks)*

**2** 🧪🧪 Describe the process of natural selection.

*(3 marks)*

**3** 🧪🧪🧪 Explain in detail how peppered moths evolved as a result of the Industrial Revolution.

*(6 marks)*

## Learning objectives

After this topic you will be able to:

- describe some factors that may lead to extinction
- describe the purpose of gene banks.

▲ An ammonite fossil. These animals lived in the sea and could grow up to 2 m wide.

▲ The dodo was a large, flightless bird.

**Key Words**

extinct, biodiversity, endangered, gene bank

**Can you think of any species that no longer live on the Earth? You might think of dinosaurs; millions of years ago these organisms were found all over the Earth. There are many other animal and plant species that have completely died out.**

## What does extinction mean?

If a species is not adapted to its environment, it will not survive. Organisms will die before reproducing. Eventually the species becomes **extinct**. A species becomes extinct when there are no more individuals of that species left anywhere in the world. An extinct species has gone forever; no new organisms can be created.

**A** State what is meant by the word extinct.

## How do we know other species existed?

The fossil record shows that many species have become extinct. For example, you may have seen the fossils of ammonites. These animals existed at around the same time as the dinosaurs. They had spiral shells and could be up to 2 m wide.

## How do organisms become extinct?

There are a number of factors that can cause a species to become extinct, including:

- changes to the organism's environment
- destruction of habitat
- outbreak of a new disease
- introduction of new predators and competitors.

**B** State three causes of extinction.

Extinction occurs naturally. For example, most scientists believe that dinosaurs became extinct due to a dramatic change in the Earth's climate, after a meteor hit the Earth. Dinosaurs could not adapt to these changes in their environment and died out.

Humans can make extinction more likely. For example, the dodo lived on island of Mauritius, which was an uninhabited island. It had no natural predators. In the 17th century people arrived on the island,

and dodos were hunted for food. Rats that came on the ships ate the dodos' eggs. In less than a century, the dodo became extinct.

Climate change has resulted in many organisms losing their habitat. For example, the size of the polar ice caps is shrinking. If a species that lives in these habitats cannot adapt successfully, or find somewhere else to live, it could become extinct.

When a species becomes extinct, **biodiversity** is reduced. Biodiversity is the range of organisms living in an area.

**C** Name two organisms that have become extinct.

▲ The black rhino has become endangered due to poachers killing them for their horns.

## How can we prevent extinction?

Species of plants and animals that have only a small population in the world are said to be **endangered**.

Scientists are trying to help prevent these species becoming extinct, and therefore maintain biodiversity. One way is by using **gene banks**. Gene banks store genetic samples from different species. In the future they can be used for research, or to produce new individuals.

There are a number of different types of gene bank. These include:

- seed banks – dried seeds of plants are stored at low temperatures
- tissue banks – buds and other cells from plants are stored
- cryobanks – a seed or embryo is preserved at very low temperatures, normally in liquid nitrogen; sperm and egg cells from animals can also be stored in this way
- pollen banks – pollen grains are stored.

▲ A seed bank.

**D** State what is meant by a gene bank.

### Extinction

Find out about an organism that has become extinct. Write a newspaper article that describes how and why the organism became extinct.

## Summary Questions

**1** 🧪 Copy and complete the sentences below.

A species becomes _____ when there are no more individuals of that species left _____ in the world.

Changes in a species' _____ or the introduction of new _____ can cause a species to become extinct.

Gene banks store genetic samples from organisms, which can be used for _____ and to create new individuals.

*(5 marks)*

**2** 🧪🧪 Describe the role of gene banks in preventing extinction.

*(3 marks)*

**3** 🧪🧪🧪 Explain in detail how a species could become extinct.

*(6 marks)*

## Key Points

- Animals compete for food, water, mates, and space. Plants compete for light, water, space, and minerals.
- Adaptations are characteristics that help an organism to survive and reproduce.
- Predator and prey species are interdependent – a change in the population of one animal directly affects the population of the other.
- Differences in characteristics within a species are known as variation. Inherited variation comes from characteristics inherited from your parents. Variation caused by your surroundings is called environmental variation. Many characteristics are affected by both.
- Characteristics that can only have certain values show discontinuous variation.
- Characteristics that can be any value within a range show continuous variation.
- You inherit characteristics from your parents in your DNA.
- DNA is arranged into long strands called chromosomes. Each chromosome is divided into sections of DNA. The sections of DNA that contain the information to produce a characteristic are called genes.
- Watson, Crick, Franklin, and Wilkins worked together to produce a model of the structure of DNA.
- All living organisms have evolved from a common ancestor, through the process of natural selection.
- Fossils provide evidence for evolution.
- If a species is not adapted to its environment, it will not survive. Eventually a species can become extinct.
- Gene banks store genetic samples from organisms. This may help to prevent extinction.

# BIG Write

**Explaining natural selection**

Imagine that you have to teach the process of natural selection to other members of your year group.

**Task**

Produce a presentation that explains how peppered moths evolved as a response to the Industrial Revolution. You need to explain what genes are, and how they are passed on.

**Tips**
- Make sure your slides are clear and cover topics in a logical order.
- Remember to explain all scientific terms clearly.

## Key Words

competition, adaptation, interdependence, variation, species, continuous variation, discontinuous variation, DNA, chromosome, gene, evolution, fossils, natural selection, extinct, biodiversity, endangered, gene bank

# End-of-chapter questions

**1** 🧪 This is a polar bear. It has lots of adaptations to survive in its habitat.

**a** Name the habitat in which the polar bear lives. *(1 mark)*

**b** Match the adaptation to how it helps the polar bear to survive. *(4 marks)*

| | |
|---|---|
| white fur | insulation |
| thick fur | camouflage |
| large feet | to stop the bear sinking into snow |
| sharp claws and teeth | to catch and eat prey |

*(**5 marks**)*

**2** 🧪 A student studied the small insects living in a log pile.

**a** State the resource that the insects use the logs for. *(1 mark)*

**b** Apart from your answer to part a, state **one** other resource that all animals need for survival. *(1 mark)*

**c** Explain why plants don't compete for food. *(2 marks)*

**d** State **one** resource that plants compete for that animals don't compete for. *(1 mark)*

*(**5 marks**)*

**3** 🧪🧪 Characteristics are passed on from parents to their children through genetic material.

**a** Name the cell component that stores genetic material. *(1 mark)*

**b** Name the chemical that contains all the information needed to make an organism. *(1 mark)*

**c** Describe the difference between a gene and a chromosome. *(2 marks)*

**d** Describe how genetic material is passed from parents to their children. *(4 marks)*

*(**8 marks**)*

**4** 🧪🧪 Dinosaurs were animals that lived on Earth millions of years ago.

**a** State **one** piece of evidence that proves dinosaurs existed. *(1 mark)*

**b** State what is meant by the word extinction. *(1 mark)*

**c** State and explain **two** reasons that could cause an organism to become extinct. *(4 marks)*

**d** Describe the role of gene banks in helping to prevent extinction. *(3 marks)*

*(**9 marks**)*

**5** 🧪🧪🧪 Charlie was investigating variation within his class. He decided to investigate the differences in body mass between students.

**a** State what is meant by variation. *(1 mark)*

**b** Name the piece of equipment Charlie should use to measure body mass. *(1 mark)*

Charlie found that everybody in the class had a different body mass.

**c** Name the type of graph Charlie should use to display his results. *(1 mark)*

**d** Sketch and label the axes he should use to plot his results. *(2 marks)*

**e** Explain why body mass is an example of continuous variation. *(1 mark)*

**f** Explain how the variation in students' body mass is caused. *(4 marks)*

*(**10 marks**)*

**6** 🧪🧪🧪 Explain the process of natural selection and the role it plays in the evolution of species. *(**6 marks**)*

# Chemistry 2

Where do we get the materials we need? In this unit you will learn about the structure of the Earth, and the rocks of its crust. You will discover how we separate mixtures, and use chemical reactions, to obtain the materials we need from the Earth and its atmosphere.

You will also explore patterns in chemical reactions. You will identify patterns in the properties of elements, and learn how to use the Periodic Table to predict properties.

**Q**

Write the names of ten elements.

## You already know

- Dissolving, mixing, and changes of state are reversible changes.
- Some changes result in the formation of new materials and are not reversible.
- Techniques such as filtering, sieving, and evaporating can be used to separate mixtures.
- You can classify rocks according to their properties.
- The properties of rocks depend on how they were formed.
- Different materials have different properties.
- All materials are made up of one or more elements.
- There are 92 naturally occurring elements.
- All the elements are listed in the Periodic Table.

## BIG Questions

- How do we obtain the materials we use?
- How does the Periodic Table help us predict element properties?
- What are the patterns in the properties of metals?

Can you solve this Picture Puzzler?

The first letter of each of these images spells out a science word that you will come across in this unit.

*Can you tell what this zoomed-in picture is?*

**Clue**: *Made of lots of layers.*

## Making connections

In **B2** you will learn about nutrition and lifestyle.

In **C2** you will learn about how we obtain the materials we need, and the patterns in properties of elements.

In **P2** you will learn about how we use energy and power.

# 1.1 Metals and non-metals

## Learning objectives

After this topic you will be able to:

- explain how elements are classified as metals and non-metals
- use patterns to classify an element as a metal or non-metal.

▲ In 1869 Russian scientist Dmitri Mendeleev used patterns in properties to create the first Periodic Table.

### Making predictions

When Mendeleev created the Periodic Table in 1869 there were only 60 known elements. Using patterns in the table he was able to predict that new elements would be discovered. He left gaps in the table so that new elements could be filled in.

There are 92 elements that exist naturally. Can you remember all their properties? Luckily, you don't need to. There are patterns in element properties. You can predict the properties of an element from its place in the Periodic Table.

▲ The Periodic Table. This version does not include every element.

☐ solids ☐ liquids ☐ gases at room temperature

### Metal or non-metal?

There are many ways of sorting elements. One classification has just two categories – **metals** and **non-metals**. In the Periodic Table, metals are on the left of the stepped line. Non-metals are on the right.

▲ Silver is a metal.

▲ Sulfur is a non-metal.

**A** State one way of sorting the elements in the Periodic Table.

How can you tell whether an element is a metal or a non-metal? You can examine its properties:

| Properties of a typical metal (when solid) | Properties of a typical non-metal (when solid) |
|---|---|
| good conductor of electricity | poor conductor of electricity |
| good conductor of heat | poor conductor of heat |
| shiny | dull |
| high density (heavy for its size) | low density (light for its size) |
| malleable (you can hammer it into different shapes) | brittle (breaks easily) |
| ductile (you can pull it into wires) | |
| sonorous (makes a ringing sound when hit) | not sonorous |

Most metals have high melting points. They are usually solid at 20 °C. Many non-metals have low boiling points. For example, oxygen and chlorine are gases at 20 °C.

**B** State six properties of a typical non-metal.

## Do all elements fit the pattern?

Most elements are easy to classify as metals or non-metals. But the system is not perfect. Mercury is a metal. It is liquid at 20 °C. Its melting point is lower than that of some non-metals.

The elements near the stepped line are **metalloids**. Their properties are between those of metals and non-metals.

## Do metals and non-metals react differently?

The properties in the table on the opposite page are **physical properties**. They describe things you can observe and measure.

Metals and non-metals also have different **chemical properties**. Chemical properties describe chemical reactions. Many metals and non-metals react with oxygen. The products are oxides. For example:

metal:          magnesium + oxygen → magnesium oxide

non-metal:      sulfur      + oxygen →   sulfur dioxide

Many non-metal oxides are gases at 20 °C. They dissolve in water to form acidic solutions. Sulfur dioxide and nitrogen dioxide are examples of acidic gases. They are formed when some fuels burn. They dissolve in rain to make rain acidic. **Acid rain** makes lakes acidic. It also damages trees.

Most metal oxides are solids at 20 °C. They are basic. If they dissolve in water, they form alkaline solutions.

**C** Describe one difference between metal oxides and non-metal oxides.

▲ Silicon is a metalloid. It is a semiconductor of electricity.

### Link

You can learn more about physical and chemical changes in C1 3.1 Chemical reactions

### Key Words

metal, non-metal, metalloid, physical property, chemical property, acid rain

### Summary Questions

**1** Sort these properties into two lists – properties of metals and properties of non-metals.

| | |
|---|---|
| sonorous | good conductor of electricity |
| low melting point | dull |
| high density | malleable |
| brittle | basic oxide |

*(8 marks)*

**2** Element A is on the left of the Periodic Table. Predict six of its properties.

*(6 marks)*

**3** Compare the properties of metals and non-metals.

*(6 marks)*

### Metal or non-metal?

Decide whether each element below is a metal or non-metal.

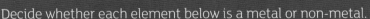

| | Element X | Element Y | Element Z |
|---|---|---|---|
| melting point (°C) | 3000 | −220 | 660 |
| relative electrical conductivity (the highest number is the best conductor) | 11 | 0 | 39 |
| oxide | basic | acidic | reacts with acids and bases |

# 1.2 Groups and periods

## Learning objectives

After this topic you will be able to:

- use patterns to predict properties of elements
- compare patterns in properties in the groups and periods of the Periodic Table.

▲ Palladium is an element. It is used in catalytic converters in cars, surgical instruments, and some flutes.

## Link

You can learn more about density in P2 3.3 Pressure in gases

## Key Words

group, density, period

**Palladium is metal. What can you predict about its properties? The picture shows that palladium is shiny. You might have predicted that it is a good conductor of heat and of electricity.**

If you find palladium in the Periodic Table, you can make even better predictions.

### What are groups?

In the Periodic Table, the vertical columns are called **groups**. The elements in a group have similar properties. Going down a group, there is a pattern in the properties such as melting point, boiling point, and **density**. Density is how much mass something has for its volume.

|   |   |   |   |   |   |   |   |   |   |   |   |   |   |   |   | group number | | 0 |
|---|---|---|---|---|---|---|---|---|---|---|---|---|---|---|---|---|---|---|
| 1 | 2 | | | H | | | | | | | | | 3 | 4 | 5 | 6 | 7 | He |
| Li | Be | | | | | | | | | | | | B | C | N | O | F | Ne |
| Na | Mg | | | | | | | | | | | | Al | Si | P | S | Cl | Ar |
| K | Ca | Sc | Ti | V | Cr | Mn | Fe | Co | Ni | Cu | Zn | | Ga | Ge | As | Se | Br | Kr |
| Rb | Sr | Y | Zr | Nb | Mo | Tc | Ru | Rh | Pd | Ag | Cd | | In | Sn | Sb | Te | I | Xe |
| Cs | Ba | La | Hf | Ta | W | Re | Os | Ir | Pt | Au | Hg | | Tl | Pb | Bi | Po | At | Rn |
| Fr | Ra | Ac | | | | | | | | | | | | | | | | |

▲ Some groups of the Periodic Table.

**A** State the name given to the vertical columns in the Periodic Table.

The tables show data for elements near palladium in the Periodic Table. Each table shows the elements in one group.

| Element | Melting point (°C) |
|---|---|
| iron | 1535 |
| ruthenium | 2500 |
| osmium | 3000 |

| Element | Melting point (°C) |
|---|---|
| cobalt | 1492 |
| rhodium | 1970 |
| iridium | 2440 |

| Element | Melting point (°C) |
|---|---|
| nickel | 1453 |
| palladium | |
| platinum | 1769 |

Sophie studies the data. She makes this prediction:

*For the groups headed by iron and cobalt, melting point increases from top to bottom. The nickel group is likely to show the same pattern. So I predict that the melting point of palladium is between 1453 °C and 1769 °C.*

A data book gives the melting point of palladium as 1550 °C. Sophie's prediction is correct.

## What are periods?

The horizontal rows of the Periodic Table are called **periods**. Going across a period, there are patterns in the properties of the elements.

The bar charts show the melting points of the Period 2 and Period 3 elements.

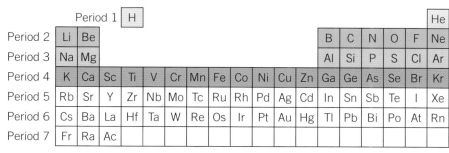

▲ Some periods of the Periodic Table.

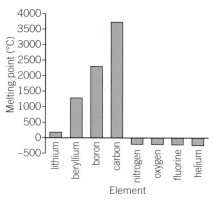

▲ The melting points of Period 2 elements.

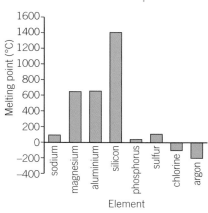

▲ The melting points of Period 3 elements.

Adam describes the patterns shown on the bar charts.

*For Period 2, the melting point increases from left to right for the first four elements. The melting points of the other elements are low. The pattern is similar for Period 3.*

**B** State the name given to the horizontal rows in the Periodic Table.

### Predictable patterns?

The tables show the sizes of atoms of the Period 2 and Period 3 elements. Draw bar charts to display these data. Write a sentence to compare the atom size patterns for Period 2 and Period 3.

| Period 2 | |
|---|---|
| Element | Atomic radius (nm) |
| lithium | 0.123 |
| beryllium | 0.089 |
| boron | 0.082 |
| carbon | 0.070 |
| nitrogen | 0.065 |
| oxygen | 0.066 |
| fluorine | 0.064 |

| Period 3 | |
|---|---|
| Element | Atomic radius (nm) |
| sodium | 0.157 |
| magnesium | 0.136 |
| aluminium | 0.125 |
| silicon | 0.117 |
| phosphorus | 0.110 |
| sulfur | 0.104 |
| chlorine | 0.099 |

### Fantastic Fact

The Periodic Table has this name because there is a repeating pattern of properties, like the repeating pattern of menstrual periods.

## Summary Questions

**1** Copy the sentences below, choosing the correct bold words.

The vertical columns of the Periodic Table are **groups/periods**. The horizontal rows are **groups/periods**. There are patterns in element properties **down/across** groups and **down/across** periods.

*(4 marks)*

**2** The tables give density data. Draw two bar charts to display the data. Use your bar charts, and the Periodic Table, to predict the density of palladium.

| Element | Density (g/cm³) | Element | Density (g/cm³) |
|---|---|---|---|
| cobalt | 8.9 | nickel | 8.9 |
| rhodium | 12.4 | palladium | |
| iridium | 22.5 | platinum | 21.4 |

*(3 marks)*

**3** Draw a big outline of the Periodic Table. Add labels to summarise the information on this spread.

*(6 marks)*

# The elements of Group 1

## Learning objectives

After this topic you will be able to:

- interpret data to describe patterns in properties of the Group 1 elements
- use patterns to predict properties of Group 1 elements.

▲ Sodium is a good conductor of heat. It is a coolant in nuclear power stations.

### Which conclusion?

The bar chart shows densities for Group 1 elements. Sam says there is no pattern. Ben says there is a pattern – overall, density increases down the group. Use the bar chart to work out an even better description of the pattern.

[Bar chart]
Density (g/cm³) vs Element
- lithium: ~0.5
- sodium: ~0.97
- potassium: ~0.83
- rubidium: ~1.5

## What do the pictures have in common?

▲ A mobile-phone battery.

▲ Engine-lubricating grease.

▲ Red fireworks.

They all rely on compounds of lithium. Lithium is in **Group 1**, on the left of the Periodic Table.

## Are Group 1 elements like other metals?

The Group 1 elements are to the left of the stepped line. This shows that they are metals. In many ways, Group 1 elements are like other metals:

- They are good conductors of electricity and heat.
- They are shiny when freshly cut.

In some ways, Group 1 elements are different to other metals. The table shows that Group 1 elements have lower melting points than other metals.

| Element | Is the element in Group 1? | Melting point (°C) |
|---|---|---|
| lithium | yes | 180 |
| sodium | yes | 98 |
| potassium | yes | 64 |
| rubidium | yes | 39 |
| copper | no | 1083 |
| platinum | no | 1796 |

Group 1 – the alkali metals

| H | | | | | | | | | | | | | | | | | He |
|---|---|---|---|---|---|---|---|---|---|---|---|---|---|---|---|---|---|
| Li | Be | | | | | | | | | | | B | C | N | O | F | Ne |
| Na | Mg | | | | | | | | | | | Al | Si | P | S | Cl | Ar |
| K | Ca | Sc | Ti | V | Cr | Mn | Fe | Co | Ni | Cu | Zn | Ga | Ge | As | Se | Br | Kr |
| Rb | Sr | Y | Zr | Nb | Mo | Tc | Ru | Rh | Pd | Ag | Cd | In | Sn | Sb | Te | I | Xe |
| Cs | Ba | La | Hf | Ta | W | Re | Os | Ir | Pt | Au | Hg | Tl | Pb | Bi | Po | At | Rn |
| Fr | Ra | Ac | Rf | Db | Sg | Bh | Hs | Mt | Ds | Rg | | | | | | | |

▲ The Group 1 elements.

**A** State one way in which Group 1 elements differ from other metals.

## Are there patterns in Group 1 properties?

The Group 1 elements show patterns in physical and chemical properties.

### Physical properties

The data on the opposite page shows that melting point decreases from top to bottom of Group 1. The data below shows that boiling point also decreases from top to bottom of Group 1.

| Element | Boiling point (°C) |
|---|---|
| lithium | 1330 |
| sodium | 890 |
| potassium | 774 |
| rubidium | 688 |

**B** State what happens to the boiling point as you move down Group 1.

### Chemical properties

The Group 1 elements are very **reactive**. This means that they easily take part in chemical reactions.

All the Group 1 elements have exciting reactions with water. The reactions make hydrogen gas. The gas moves the reacting element around on the water. The reactions also make alkaline solutions, so universal indicator turns purple.

lithium + water → lithium hydroxide + hydrogen

There is a pattern in the reactions. They all produce hydrogen and a metal hydroxide. The reactions get more vigorous going down the group.

 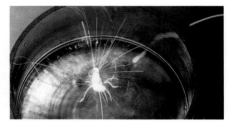

▲ Lithium, at the top of Group 1, reacts vigorously with water.   ▲ The reaction of potassium with water is very vigorous.

**C** Name the gas produced when Group 1 elements react with water.

**Key Words**

Group 1, reactive

## Summary Questions

**1** 🧪 Write five correct sentences from the sentence starters and enders.

| Sentence starters | Sentence enders |
|---|---|
| From top to bottom of Group 1… | …have low densities. |
| From bottom to top of Group 1… | …conduct electricity. |
| All Group 1 elements… | …melting point increases. |
| | …boiling point decreases. |
| | …react with water to make hydrogen and an alkaline solution. |
| | …the vigour of the reaction with water increases. |

*(5 marks)*

**2** 🧪🧪 The table gives hardness values for some Group 1 elements. The bigger the value, the harder the element.

| Element | Mohs hardness |
|---|---|
| lithium | 0.6 |
| sodium | 0.5 |
| potassium | |
| rubidium | 0.3 |
| caesium | 0.2 |

**a** Plot the hardness values on a bar chart. *(6 marks)*

**b** Describe the pattern in hardness. *(2 marks)*

**c** Predict the hardness of potassium. Explain your prediction. *(2 marks)*

**3** 🧪🧪🧪 Describe in detail patterns in the physical and chemical properties of the Group 1 elements.

*(6 marks)*

## Learning objectives

After this topic you will be able to:

- use patterns to predict properties of Group 7 elements
- describe displacement reactions.

**Foul Fact**

Five thousand soldiers died from chlorine poisoning in World War 1.

▲ Chlorine is pale green and bromine is dark red. In the solid state iodine crystals are grey-black. Iodine vapour is purple.

**Key Words**

Group 7, halogen, displace, displacement reaction

**Better bar charts**

Plot a bar chart for the Group 7 boiling-point data on the opposite page. Swap bar charts with a partner. Can you suggest improvements?

**Have you ever smelt chlorine in tap water? Chlorine and its compounds do a vital job. Tiny amounts destroy deadly bacteria, making water safe to drink and swim in.**

**A** State one use of chlorine.

### Are Group 7 elements like other non-metals?

Chlorine is in **Group 7** of the Periodic Table. The other elements of the group are fluorine, bromine, iodine, and astatine. The Group 7 elements are also called **halogens**.

▲ Group 7 is towards the right of the Periodic Table.

The halogens have low melting points, like most non-metals. They do not conduct electricity. Iodine is a brittle solid at room temperature.

**B** Name the elements in Group 7.

### Are there patterns in Group 7 properties?

**Physical properties**

The table shows melting- and boiling-point data.

| Element | Melting point (°C) | Boiling point (°C) | State at room temperature |
|---------|-------------------|-------------------|---------------------------|
| fluorine | −220 | −188 | gas |
| chlorine | −101 | −35 | gas |
| bromine | −7 | 59 | liquid |
| iodine | 114 | 184 | solid |

In Group 7, melting point increases from top to bottom. This is different to Group 1, where melting point decreases from top to bottom.

**C** Describe the pattern in boiling points for the Group 7 elements.

The colours of the elements get darker from top to bottom.

## Chemical properties

The Group 7 elements are reactive. All the Group 7 elements react with iron. The word equations summarise the reactions.

$$\text{iron} + \text{chlorine} \rightarrow \text{iron chloride}$$

$$\text{iron} + \text{bromine} \rightarrow \text{iron bromide}$$

$$\text{iron} + \text{iodine} \rightarrow \text{iron iodide}$$

The reaction of chlorine with iron is very vigorous. There is a bright flame. The reactions get less vigorous going down the group. This is different to Group 1, in which reactions get more vigorous from top to bottom.

▲ Iron reacts vigorously with chlorine.

**D** Describe how the reaction of the Group 7 elements with iron changes going down the group.

## What are displacement reactions?

Angus adds chlorine solution to potassium bromide solution. He records his observations.

| | Appearance |
|---|---|
| chlorine solution (before reaction) | pale green |
| potassium bromide solution (before reaction) | colourless |
| mixture after reaction | orange |

The orange substance is bromine. It is a product of the reaction. In the reaction, chlorine **displaces** bromine from potassium bromide. Elements nearer the top of Group 7 displace elements lower in the group from their compounds. Examples of **displacement reactions** are:

$$\text{chlorine} + \text{potassium bromide} \rightarrow \text{potassium chloride} + \text{bromine}$$

$$\text{bromine} + \text{potassium iodide} \rightarrow \text{potassium bromide} + \text{iodine}$$

◀ Chlorine solution reacting with potassium bromide solution.

## Summary Questions

**1** 🔥 Copy and complete the sentences below.

The Group 7 elements are also called the _____. The halogens are on the _____ of the stepped line. This means they are _____. The melting and boiling points _____ from top to bottom. The reactions get _____ vigorous from top to bottom.

*(5 marks)*

**2** 🔥🔥 Predict which of the reactions below will happen. Explain your choices.

a   fluorine + potassium chloride → potassium fluoride + chlorine

b   iodine + potassium chloride → potassium iodide + chlorine

c   bromine + sodium iodide → sodium bromide + iodine

d   chlorine + sodium bromide → sodium chloride + bromine

*(3 marks)*

**3** 🔥🔥🔥 Describe the patterns in the physical and chemical properties of the Group 7 elements.

*(6 marks)*

67

## Learning objectives

After this topic you will be able to:

- describe the physical and chemical properties of the Group 0 elements
- use patterns to predict properties of Group 0 elements.

▲ Eye surgeons use krypton lasers to repair tears in the retina at the back of the eye.

## What do double glazing, bar-code scanners, and helium balloons have in common?

They all make use of elements in the same group of the Periodic Table, **Group 0**. Group 0 includes helium, neon, argon, krypton, xenon, and radon. The elements of Group 0 are also called the **noble gases**.

**A** Name the six noble gases.

## Are there patterns in Group 0 properties?

### Physical properties

The noble gases have very low melting and boiling points, like many other non-metals. They are colourless gases at room temperature. The table shows their boiling points.

| Element | Boiling point (°C) |
|---------|--------------------|
| helium  | −269               |
| neon    | −246               |
| argon   | −186               |
| krypton | −152               |
| xenon   | −108               |

**B** Describe the pattern in boiling points for the Group 0 elements

Group 0 – the noble gases

| | | | | | | | | | | | | | | | | | He |
|---|---|---|---|---|---|---|---|---|---|---|---|---|---|---|---|---|---|
| Li | Be | | | | | | | | | | | B | C | N | O | F | Ne |
| Na | Mg | | | | | | | | | | | Al | Si | P | S | Cl | Ar |
| K | Ca | Sc | Ti | V | Cr | Mn | Fe | Co | Ni | Cu | Zn | Ga | Ge | As | Se | Br | Kr |
| Rb | Sr | Y | Zr | Nb | Mo | Tc | Ru | Rh | Pd | Ag | Cd | In | Sn | Sb | Te | I | Xe |
| Cs | Ba | La | Hf | Ta | W | Re | Os | Ir | Pt | Au | Hg | Tl | Pb | Bi | Po | At | Rn |
| Fr | Ra | Ac | Rf | Db | Sg | Bh | Hs | Mt | Ds | Rg | | | | | | | |

H

▲ Group 0 is on the right of the Periodic Table.

## Key Words

Group 0, noble gases, unreactive

The noble gases glow brightly when high-voltage electricity passes through them. This property explains why noble gases are used in advertising signs. The letters contain neon gas.

▲ This sign contains neon gas.

▲ Helium has a lower density than the air. This is why it is used in helium balloons.

▲ Argon is a better insulator than air, so it is used in the gap between the two panes of glass in double glazing.

## Chemical properties

The noble gases take part in very few reactions. Scientists say they are **unreactive**. From top to bottom of the group, the noble gases get slightly more reactive.

- As far as we know, helium and neon never take part in chemical reactions.
- By the year 2000, a group of Finnish scientists had made the compound argon fluorohydride, but it only existed at temperatures below −265 °C.
- Krypton reacts with the most reactive element there is, fluorine, to make krypton difluoride, $KrF_2$.
- Xenon, like the other Group 0 elements, is very unreactive. However, it does form compounds with fluorine and oxygen.

**C** State the meaning of the word unreactive.

## Where do noble gases come from?

All the noble gases exist in the atmosphere, mixed with other gases. Companies use distillation to separate them from the air. Helium is also found mixed with natural gas under the ground or under the sea. It is expensive to separate helium from the mixture.

### Using Group 0

Imagine you work for an advertising agency. You have been asked to make a magazine advert to explain why the noble gases are important.

First, discuss with a partner what the advert will include. Make notes to summarise your ideas. Then create your advert. Make sure it is eye-catching and persuasive.

## Summary Questions

1 🧪 Each sentence below has one mistake. Copy the sentences, correcting the mistakes.

The noble gases are all in Group 1 of the Periodic Table. The element at the top of the group is neon. The noble gases are metals. They have vigorous reactions. From bottom to top of the group, boiling point increases.

*(5 marks)*

2 🧪🧪 The table shows the melting points of the noble gases. Describe the pattern, and predict the melting point of argon.

| Element | Melting point (°C) |
|---------|--------------------|
| helium | −270 |
| neon | −249 |
| argon | |
| krypton | −157 |
| xenon | −112 |

*(2 marks)*

3 🧪🧪🧪 Write a song or rap to summarise the patterns in properties of the noble gases, and their uses.

*(6 marks)*

69

## Key Points

- In the Periodic Table, metals are on the left of the stepped line, and non-metals are on the right.
- Most metals have high melting points. They are good conductors of heat and electricity. They are shiny and have high densities. They are malleable, ductile, and sonorous.
- Most non-metals have low melting points. They are poor conductors of heat and electricity. In the solid state they are dull and brittle.
- Metal oxides are basic. Those that dissolve in water form alkaline solutions. Non-metal oxides are acidic.
- Physical properties describe things you can observe and measure.
- Chemical properties describe how substances take part in chemical reactions.
- You can use the arrangement of elements in the Periodic Table to explain and predict patterns in physical and chemical properties.
- In the Periodic Table, the horizontal rows are periods.
- In the Periodic Table, the vertical columns are groups.
- Going across periods and down groups, there are patterns in the elements' properties.
- Group 1 elements have low melting and boiling points, and low densities. They are reactive.
- Group 1 elements react vigorously with water to make hydroxides and hydrogen. The reactions get more vigorous from top to bottom of the group.
- Going down Group 7, melting and boiling points increase. The colours of the elements get darker. They are reactive.
- In a displacement reaction a more reactive element displaces a less reactive element from its compounds.
- Group 0 elements are called the noble gases. They are unreactive.

## Key Words

metal, non-metal, metalloid, physical property, chemical property, acid rain, group, density, period, Group 1, reactive, halogen, Group 7, Group 0, displacement reaction, displace, noble gas, unreactive

## Maths challenge

**The elements of Group 3**

The table opposite shows some properties of the Group 3 elements.

| Element | Density (g/cm³) | Boiling point (°C) |
|---|---|---|
| boron | 2.3 | 3930 |
| aluminium | 2.7 | 2470 |
| gallium | 5.9 | 2400 |
| indium | 7.3 | 2000 |
| thallium | 11.8 | 1460 |

**Task**

Display the data on two bar charts. Then write a few sentences to describe the patterns in properties.

**Tips**

- For both bar charts, write the names of the elements on the x-axis.
- Each bar chart needs a different label and a different scale for the y-axis.
- Make sure the y-axis scales are even.

# End-of-chapter questions

1  The bar chart shows the melting points of three elements in the same group of the Periodic Table.

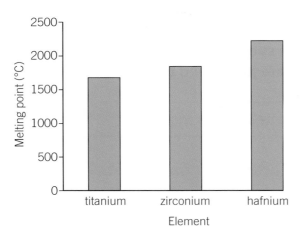

a  Describe the pattern shown on the bar chart. *(2 marks)*

b  Use the bar chart to estimate the melting point of zirconium. *(2 marks)*

*(4 marks)*

2  Read the text below. Then answer the questions.

Russian chemist Mendeleev created the Periodic Table in 1869. He arranged the 60 elements then known in order of the mass of their atoms. He grouped together elements with similar properties. He left gaps for elements he predicted would be discovered later. One gap was below aluminium. Mendeleev predicted some properties for this missing element. He predicted a low melting point, and a density of 6.0 g/cm³.

In 1875 French chemist Boisbaudran discovered the missing element. He called it gallium. In 1876 he measured the melting point of gallium as being between 29 °C and 30 °C. Later, he found the melting point of six samples of gallium. His results are in the table.

| Sample number | Melting point (°C) |
|---|---|
| 1 | 30.14 |
| 2 | 30.16 |
| 3 | 30.14 |
| 4 | 30.15 |
| 5 | 30.16 |
| 6 | 30.16 |

a  Explain why Mendeleev left gaps in his Periodic Table. *(1 mark)*

b  State whether or not Mendeleev was correct in his prediction for the melting point of the missing element. Explain your decision. *(2 marks)*

c  Suggest why Boisbaudran measured the melting point of six samples of gallium. *(1 mark)*

d  Use the data in the table to calculate the mean melting point of the samples of gallium. *(1 mark)*

e  Boisbaudran took a sample of gallium and worked out its density. He obtained a value of 4.7 g/cm³. Suggest why he decided to take a fresh sample of gallium and do the experiment again. *(2 marks)*

*(7 marks)*

3  Compare the patterns in properties of the Group 1 elements with the patterns in properties of the Group 7 elements. *(6 marks)*

# 2.1 Mixtures

## Learning objectives

After this topic you will be able to:

- describe particle arrangements in mixtures
- explain how to identify pure substances.

**Have you cleaned your teeth today? Toothpaste is a mixture. A mixture is made up of several different substances. The substances are not chemically joined together. They are just mixed up.**

**A** State what is meant by a mixture.

## How are mixtures and compounds different?

The photo on the left shows a mixture of two elements, iron and sulfur. The elements are not joined together. You can see yellow sulfur powder and shiny grey iron. You can use a magnet to separate the mixture. The iron sticks to the magnet, leaving sulfur powder behind.

The photo below shows one dark-grey substance. The substance is a compound, iron sulfide. In the compound, atoms of iron and sulfur are strongly joined together. You could not separate them using a magnet. You would need a chemical reaction to separate them.

The table shows how mixtures and compounds are different.

▲ A mixture of two elements, iron and sulfur.

|  | Mixture | Compound |
| --- | --- | --- |
| Are its substances joined together? | No. | Yes – atoms of its elements are chemically joined together. |
| What are its properties? | The substances in the mixture keep their own properties. | A compound has different properties to those of its elements. |
| Is it easy to separate? | Yes. | You need to do chemical reactions to split a compound into its elements. |
| How much of each substance does it contain? | You can change the amounts of substances. | The relative amounts of each element cannot change. |

▲ A compound, iron sulfide.

## Link

You can learn more about compounds in C1 2.3 Compounds

**B** State two differences between mixtures and compounds.

## How can you identify pure substances?

A pure substance has a sharp melting point. Shilpa has two samples of stearic acid, X and Y. One sample is **pure** – it has no other substances mixed with it. Shilpa's other sample is **impure**. Different substances are mixed with it.

Shilpa sets up the apparatus shown at the top of the next page to find out which sample is pure.

Shilpa heats Sample X. She records the temperature every minute. She plots a graph. She does the same for Sample Y.

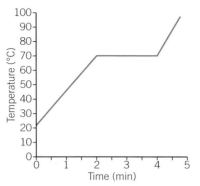

▲ Sample X graph.

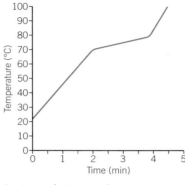

▲ Sample Y graph.

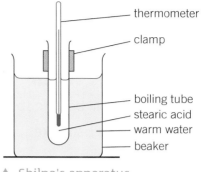

▲ Shilpa's apparatus.

labels: thermometer, clamp, boiling tube, stearic acid, warm water, beaker

Sample X has a sharp melting point. Its temperature stays at 70 °C until all the solid has melted. This shows that Sample X is pure. Sample Y melts between 70 °C and 80 °C. It does not have a sharp melting point. It is impure.

**C** Describe how to find out if a sample of a substance is pure.

## Are there other mixtures?

Most materials are mixtures. Some exist naturally:

● Most rocks are mixtures of compounds.
● Seawater is a mixture of water, sodium chloride, and other salts.

Chemists make mixtures that are suitable for their purpose. They work out the best amounts of each substance to add to the mixture. For example, toothpaste may include a chemical called hydrated silica to remove plaque, sodium fluoride to prevent cavities, sodium lauryl sulfate to make foam, carrageenan to thicken the toothpaste, and titanium oxide to make it white.

### Toothpaste tales

Write the text for a new toothpaste box. Include the ingredients and write down a reason why each one is included. Make sure the reasons are easy for people who use the toothpaste to understand.

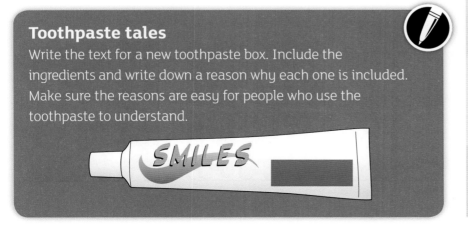
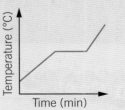

**Key Words**

mixture, pure, impure

## Summary Questions

1 Copy the sentences that are true. Write corrected versions of the sentences that are false.

   a A mixture is made up of different substances that are chemically joined together.

   b You cannot change the amounts of substances in a mixture.

   c A pure substance has no other substances mixed with it.

   *(3 marks)*

2 Tim heats a sample. He plots the temperature every minute. Use the graph to decide whether the sample is a pure substance or a mixture of substances. Explain your decision.

   *(2 marks)*

3 Write a paragraph to compare mixtures and compounds.

   *(6 marks)*

# 2.2 Solutions

## Learning objectives

After this topic you will be able to:

- describe solutions using key words
- use the particle model to explain dissolving.

**Do you like coffee? When you add water to coffee powder, you make a solution. A solution is a mixture of a liquid with a solid or gas. All parts of the mixture are the same. You cannot see the separate substances.**

Catherine adds sugar to water, and stirs. The sugar **dissolves** in the water. Water is the **solvent**. Sugar is the **solute**.

**A** State what a solution is.

### Does a solute disappear when it dissolves?

You cannot see sugar in a solution. But if you taste the solution, you know the sugar is there. You must never taste things in the laboratory – they might be poisonous.

Some solutions are coloured. Coffee solution is brown, and copper sulfate solution is blue. The colours show that the solute is there.

You can also use mass to find out whether something is a solution:

- The mass of one litre of pure water is 1000 g.
- The mass of a solution made by dissolving 20 g of sugar in 1000 g of water is (1000 g + 20 g) = 1020 g.

**B** Identify the solute in coffee solution.

### How can we explain dissolving?

When sugar dissolves, water particles surround each sugar particle. The sugar particles can mix with the liquid. They are arranged randomly, and move around.

▲ The mass of solution on the left is the same as the total mass of sugar and water on the right.

### Solution masses

Sarah dissolves 3 g of copper sulfate in 100 g of water. Calculate the mass of the solution.

### Foul Fact

Some solvents can kill. Sniffing butane from deodorant causes unconsciousness, an irregular heartbeat, and frostbite.

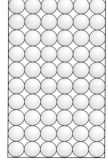

▲ Particles in solid sugar.

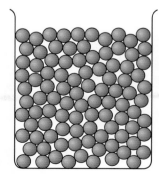

▲ Particles in liquid water.

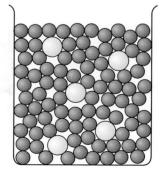

▲ Particles in sugar solution.

You can use rice and beans to model particles in a solution. In the photo, rice grains represent water particles. Beans represent sugar particles.

▲ Rice and beans can model particles in a solution.

**C** Describe the arrangement of particles in a solution.

## Is water the only solvent?

Nail varnish does not dissolve in water. That's why it does not come off in the shower. But nail varnish does dissolve in a chemical called propanone. That's why nail-varnish remover is mainly propanone.

Some glues are solutions. They contain a sticky substance dissolved in a solvent. As the solvent evaporates, the glue dries.

## Can gases dissolve?

Many gases dissolve in solvents. Carbon dioxide gas makes drinks fizzy. In the bottle, there is a solution. Carbon dioxide, sugar, and flavourings are dissolved in water. When you open the bottle, gas leaves the solution.

▲ Fizzy drinks contain dissolved carbon dioxide gas.

### Modelling dissolving

Plan how to use rice and beans, and other materials, to explain dissolving to primary-school children. Draw diagrams to show what you will do, and write notes to remind you what to say.

## Key Words

solution, dissolve, solvent, solute

## Link

You can learn more about solutes and solvents in C2 2.5 Evaporation and distillation

## Summary Questions

1. 🔬 Copy the sentences below, choosing the correct bold words.

   When salt dissolves in water, a **solvent/solute/solution** forms. Salt is the **solvent/solute/solution** and water is the **solvent/solute/solution**. In the solution, **water/salt** particles surround the **water/salt** particles.

   *(5 marks)*

2. 🔬🔬 Laura has three beakers. Each contains 200 cm³ of a colourless liquid. Describe how Laura could find out which beakers contain pure water, and which contain solutions. Explain your answer.

   *(3 marks)*

3. 🔬🔬🔬 Draw a visual summary of the information on this page. Include examples and pictures.

   *(6 marks)*

# 2.3 Solubility

## Learning objectives
After this topic you will be able to:
- explain what a saturated solution is
- explain the meaning of solubility.

**Imagine a glass of water. Could you dissolve more salt, or more sugar, in the water? How could you find out?**

At room temperature you can dissolve more than 200 g of sugar in 100 g of water. That's more than 40 teaspoons. But if you add even more sugar to the solution, it just falls to the bottom. It does not dissolve. You have made a **saturated solution**.

A saturated solution contains the maximum mass of a substance that will dissolve. There is always some undissolved substance in the container.

You can make a saturated solution of salt (sodium chloride) by adding more than 36 g of salt to 100 g of water.

**A** State the meaning of the term saturated solution.

## What is solubility?
The mass of solute that dissolves in 100 g of water to make a saturated solution is called the **solubility** of the solute. Every substance has its own solubility. The table gives solubility values for sugar and salt.

| Substance | Solubility at 20 °C (g/100 g of water) |
|---|---|
| sugar (sucrose) | 202 |
| salt (sodium chloride) | 36 |

The data shows that more sugar than salt can dissolve in 100 g of water. Sugar is more **soluble** than salt. The greater the mass of a substance you can dissolve in 100 g of water, the more soluble the substance.

The bar chart opposite shows the solubilities of four more substances.

**B** Name the most and least soluble substances shown on the bar chart.

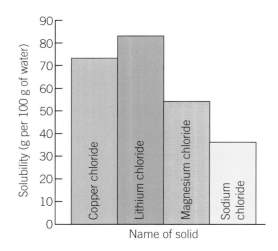

Some substances cannot dissolve in water. They are **insoluble**. Chalk (calcium carbonate) and sand (silicon dioxide) are insoluble in water.

## How does temperature affect solubility?

Think again about dissolving sugar. Can you dissolve more sugar in hot water, or in cold water?

| Temperature (°C) | Solubility of sugar (g/100 g of water) |
|---|---|
| 20 | 202 |
| 40 | 236 |
| 60 | 289 |
| 80 | 365 |
| 100 | 476 |

The data shows that the higher the temperature, the greater the mass of sugar that dissolves.

Most substances get more soluble as temperature increases. But the increase is greater for some substances than for others. Compare the solubility values of sugar at 20 °C and at 100 °C to those of salt.

| Temperature (°C) | Solubility of salt (g/100 g of water) |
|---|---|
| 20 | 36 |
| 100 | 39 |

▲ The solubility of potassium manganate (VII) is 6.3 g/100 g of water at 20 °C.

### Fantastic Fact

One of the most soluble salts is potassium nitrite. You can dissolve 306 g of this salt in 100 g of water at 20 °C.

## Summary Questions

1 ⚗ Write four sentences from the sentence starters and enders below.

| Sentence starters | Sentence enders |
|---|---|
| A saturated solution… | …does not dissolve. |
| An insoluble substance … | …is the mass of substance that dissolves in 100 g of water. |
| Solubility … | …is a solution that contains the greatest mass of solid that can dissolve. |
| | …contains undissolved solid. |

*(4 marks)*

2 ⚗⚗ Plot the values in the table on a graph, and draw the line or curve of best fit. Describe the relationship shown.

| Temperature (°C) | Solubility of zinc bromide (g/100 g of water) |
|---|---|
| 20 | 446 |
| 40 | 590 |
| 60 | 616 |
| 80 | 647 |
| 100 | 669 |

*(4 marks)*

3 ⚗⚗⚗ Design an experiment that you could do to compare the solubility of sugar and salt.

*(6 marks)*

### Grappling with graphs

The graph shows how the solubilities of six substances change with temperature. With a partner, take it in turns to choose a line on the graph and describe what it shows. Next, compare pairs of curves. Finally, choose two curves to compare in writing.

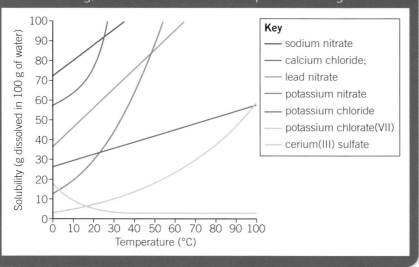

**Key**
— sodium nitrate
— calcium chloride;
— lead nitrate
— potassium nitrate
— potassium chloride
— potassium chlorate(VII)
— cerium(III) sulfate

# 2.4 Filtration

## Learning objectives

After this topic you will be able to:

- explain how filtration works
- describe how to filter a mixture.

### Link

You can learn more about separating a solution from an insoluble solid in C1 4.4 Making salts

▲ An oil filter.

### Solubility puzzle

Sandeep measures the solubility of zinc sulfate. Little by little, he adds zinc sulfate to water in a beaker. Eventually, no more dissolves. There is some solid at the bottom of the beaker. Discuss how Sandeep could use filtration, and measure masses, to find the solubility of zinc sulfate.

**Look at the pictures. What do they have in common?**

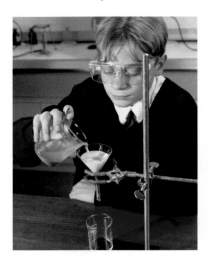

All the pictures show **filtration**. Filtration, or **filtering**, separates a liquid from an insoluble solid. Filtering also separates a solution from a solid that is mixed with it, but not dissolved.

**A** State two types of mixture that can be separated by filtration.

### How does filtering work?

You can separate sand from water by pouring the mixture into filter paper. Water passes through the filter paper. Sand does not.

Filter paper has tiny holes in it. Water particles are smaller than the tiny holes. In the liquid state, water passes through the holes. This is called the **filtrate**.

Grains of sand are bigger than the tiny holes, so they cannot pass through. The grains of sand stay in the filter paper. This is called the **residue**.

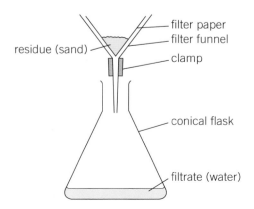

**B** Martha filters a mixture of glitter and water. Name the filtrate and the residue.

## How is filtration useful?

Filtration has many uses:

- It separates coffee solution from ground-up coffee beans.
- Oil filters in cars contain materials such as cotton, or wood fibre. These materials trap solid bits of dirt. Liquid oil passes through gaps between the fibres. The dirt would damage the engine if it stayed in the oil.
- Sand filters help make water safe to drink. One type works like this:
  - River water passes slowly through sand and gravel.
  - As the water moves downwards, bits of dirt get stuck in the sand. Tiny creatures living in the sand remove bacteria. Water leaving the filter is nearly ready to drink.

**C** List three uses of filtration.

▲ Sand filtration helps make water safe to drink.

▲ This is a LifeStraw. It contains hollow fibres. The fibres filter the water, removing bacteria and parasites.

## Separating a solution from an insoluble solid

If you have a mixture of sand and salt, you can separate the sand like this:

- Add water to the mixture.
- Stir. The salt dissolves. The sand does not.
- Pour the mixture into a filter paper funnel. Salt solution passes through the paper. The residue is sand.

## Key Words

filtration, filtering, filtrate, residue

## Summary Questions

1 ⚗ Use the words below to finish labelling the diagram.

residue   filtrate   insoluble
solid   liquid

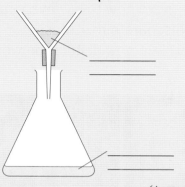

*(4 marks)*

2 ⚗⚗ Naomi adds 100 g of different compounds to separate beakers of water, and stirs to dissolve. Each beaker contains 100 g of water. She filters each mixture, and measures the mass of solid that remains. Use the data to work out the most and least soluble substances. Show your working.

| Name of substance | Mass of substance added to 100 g of water (g) | Mass of residue after filtering (g) |
|---|---|---|
| calcium chloride | 100 | 25 |
| calcium hydrogen carbonate | 100 | 84 |
| calcium bromide | 100 | 0 |
| calcium iodide | 100 | 33 |

*(4 marks)*

3 ⚗⚗⚗ Design a model you could make to explain filtering. Draw labelled diagrams to show your ideas. Identify the advantages and disadvantages of the model.

*(6 marks)*

## Learning objectives

After this topic you will be able to:

- explain how to use evaporation to separate mixtures
- explain how distillation works.

▲ These salt pans on the island of Gozo, Malta are formed when seawater evaporates, leaving behind salt.

**Link**

You can learn more about evaporation and condensation in C1 1.5 More changes of state

▲ Bolivia's salt desert.

## For many centuries, people have obtained salt from seawater. How do they do this?

Evaporation separates salt from seawater. The Sun transfers energy to the water molecules and they leave the surface of the solution. When all the water has evaporated, solid salt remains.

**A** Describe how salt can be separated from seawater.

## When else is evaporation useful?

Have you ever made copper sulfate crystals from copper oxide and sulfuric acid? First, you mix the reactants. They react to make copper sulfate solution. You filter the solution to remove extra copper oxide powder.

Then you heat the solution with a Bunsen burner. Some of the water quickly evaporates. You leave the remaining solution in a warm place. The rest of the water evaporates slowly. Solid copper sulfate crystals slowly form.

▲ Copper sulfate crystals. The more slowly the water evaporates, the bigger the crystals formed.

▲ Evaporation makes some glues dry. The solvent evaporates. A sticky substance remains, joining the surfaces.

Lithium is important for batteries. Huge amounts of lithium compounds are dissolved in water under a desert in Bolivia. The government plans to bring the solution to the surface. The water will evaporate. Solid lithium compounds will remain.

**B** State three uses of evaporation.

## Ancient filters

Jabir ibn Hayyan lived in Persia almost 2000 years ago. He developed some of the earliest distillation apparatus, called the alembic. Here is a diagram of his alembic. Discuss with a partner how the alembic might work. Then write a paragraph describing your ideas.

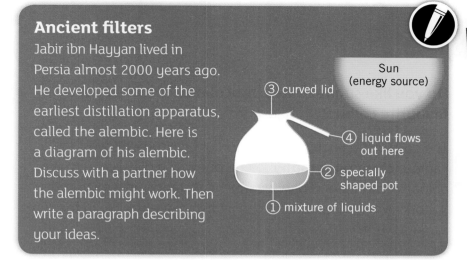

Sun (energy source)

③ curved lid

④ liquid flows out here

② specially shaped pot

① mixture of liquids

### Key Words

distillation

## What is distillation?

Imagine you are all alone on a desert island. There is nothing to drink. How could you get drinking water from the sea?

You could use **distillation**. Distillation is a process that uses evaporation and condensation to obtain a solvent from a solution. In the laboratory you can use the apparatus below.

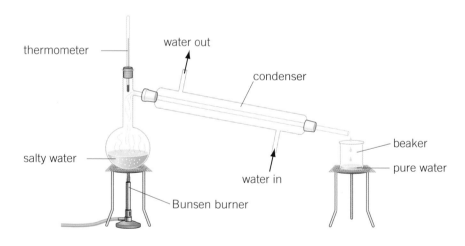

thermometer

water out

condenser

beaker

pure water

salty water

water in

Bunsen burner

It works like this:

- Water in the salt solution boils.
- Steam leaves the solution.
- Steam travels through the condenser, and cools down.
- The steam condenses to form liquid water.
- Liquid water drips into the beaker.

Saudi Arabia has little rain, and no permanent rivers. The country uses distillation to obtain drinking water from seawater.

You can also use distillation to separate water from inky water.

## Summary Questions

1  The sentences below describe how distillation works. Write the sentences in a sensible order. The first, middle, and last ones have been done for you.

**B  The solution is heated.**

E  The solvent condenses.

C  The solvent runs down the condenser.

**A  The solvent particles cool down.**

D  Solvent particles leave the solution.

F  Solvent particles enter the condenser.

**G  The solvent drips into a beaker.**

*(4 marks)*

2  State whether you would use evaporation or distillation to obtain the substances below from their mixtures. Give a reason for each decision.

a  copper chloride crystals from a solution of copper chloride

b  propanone, the solvent in nail varnish remover

c  ethanol, the solvent in some types of glue

d  solid potassium chloride from potassium chloride solution

*(4 marks)*

3  Compare how evaporation and distillation separate mixtures.

*(6 marks)*

# 2.6 Chromatography

## Learning objectives

After this topic you will be able to:

- explain how chromatography separates mixtures
- analyse chromatograms to identify substances in mixtures.

▲ The coatings of these chocolates contain mixtures of dyes.

**Key Words**

chromatography, chromatogram

**Link**

You can learn more about chromatography in C3 3.3 Message in a bottle

Detectives have used chromatography to look for explosives on the body hair of bomber suspects.

**Do you like sugar-coated chocolates? Which is your favourite colour?**

The coloured crunchy coatings contain mixtures of dyes. You can use **chromatography** to find out which dyes are in which colours. Chromatography separates substances in a mixture. It works when the substances in a mixture are soluble in the same solvent.

**A** State what chromatography does.

## How does chromatography work?

To find out which dyes are in a green felt-tip pen, sets up the apparatus below. Water moves up the paper. As it passes the green spot, the dyes in the ink dissolve. Water carries the dyes upwards. Some dyes move faster than others, so the dyes separate. This makes a **chromatogram**.

▲ Poppy's apparatus.

▲ Chromatogram of ink from a green felt-tip pen.

In this chromatogram, the blue dye has moved further than the yellow dye. This might be because the blue dye is more soluble. Or it might be because the yellow dye sticks more strongly to the paper.

**B** State what a chromatogram is.

## How is chromatography useful?

Aidan grinds up a spinach leaf in a pestle and mortar. He puts a spot of spinach juice near the bottom of some chromatography paper. He dips the paper in a solvent.

The solvent travels up the paper, taking spinach juice with it. This makes a chromatogram. The chromatogram shows the pigments (colours) in spinach. Each pigment is a different nutrient.

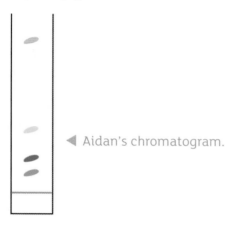

◀ Aidan's chromatogram.

Scientists have used a different sort of chromatography to identify food nutrients. Cassava is an important food in Nigeria. Scientists used chromatography to compare the amounts of vitamin A in different sorts of cassava. Children may go blind if they don't have enough vitamin A in their diet.

The scientists found that dark-green cassava leaves have more vitamin A than light-green leaves. Yellow cassava roots have more vitamin A than white roots. They advise people to eat dark-green leaves and yellow roots.

▲ Yellow cassava roots.

▲ Cassava leaves.

### Clever chromatography

Make notes about three uses of chromatography. Organise your notes in a logical order. Then write a few paragraphs describing how chromatography is useful. Ask a partner to check your writing to make sure you have used scientific words correctly.

### Link

You can learn more about nutrients in B2 1.1 Nutrients

## Summary Questions

**1** 🧪 Copy and complete the sentences below.

Chromatography separates substances in _____. It works if all the substances in the mixture are soluble in _____. The picture made by chromatography is called _____.

*(3 marks)*

**2** 🧪🧪 Explain why, in chromatography, some substances travel further up the paper than others.

*(3 marks)*

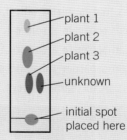

plant 1
plant 2
plant 3
unknown
initial spot placed here

**3** 🧪🧪 Look at the chromatogram above. It was obtained from the leaves of three plants. Write down which plant the unknown sample is from. Explain your choice.

*(2 marks)*

**4** 🧪🧪🧪 A teacher has found a rude note in his classroom. There are three students who might have written it. Write instructions for how he can use chromatography to find out which student wrote the note. Point out possible problems with the method, or in using the results.

*(6 marks)*

## Key Points

- A mixture is made up of substances that are not chemically joined together.
- In a mixture, the substances keep their own properties. You can change the amounts of the substances.
- A pure substance has a sharp melting point. An impure substance does not.
- A solution is a mixture of a liquid with a solid or gas. All parts of the solution are the same. You cannot see the separate substances.
- In a solution, the substance that dissolves is called the solute.
- In a solution, the liquid in which the solute dissolves is called the solvent. Solvents include water, propanone, and ethanol.
- When a substance dissolves, solvent particles surround the solute particles.
- A saturated solution is a solution in which no more solute can dissolve.
- The solubility of a substance is the mass that dissolves in 100 g of water. Every substance has its own solubility.
- The solubility of a substance varies with temperature.
- Substances that cannot dissolve in a certain solvent are insoluble in that solvent.
- Filtration separates a liquid from an insoluble solid. It also separates a solution from a solid that is mixed with it, but not dissolved.
- You can separate a solute from its solution by evaporation.
- You can separate a solvent from its solution by distillation.
- You can separate substances in a mixture by chromatography if all the substances are soluble in the same solvent.

## BIG Write

### Dissolving words

You work for a company that publishes revision guides. Your boss wants to you write the page on dissolving for Key Stage 3 science.

### Task:

Write the text for the revision page on dissolving. Include labelled diagrams to illustrate your page.

### Tips:

- Before you start, make a rough draft of the page to show what it will include.
- Highlight key words, and explain their meanings.

## Key Words

mixture, pure, impure, solution, dissolve, solvent, solute, saturated solution, solubility, soluble, insoluble, filtration, filtering, residue, filtrate, distillation, chromatography, chromatogram

# End-of-chapter questions

1 🔺 Describe how to obtain the substance in bold from each mixture below.

For each mixture, give the name of the process and state where the named substance would be at the end of the process.

a **sand** from a mixture of sand and water
*(2 marks)*

b **salt** from a solution of salt in water
*(2 marks)*

c a **dye of one colour** from the mixture of dyes in a felt-tip pen *(2 marks)*
*(6 marks)*

2 🔺🔺 Milly wants to make a golf ball float in water. She has the apparatus in the diagram below.

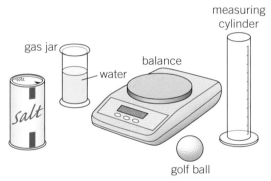

Milly dissolves different masses of salt in 100 g of water. She records whether or not the ball floats. Her results are in the table below.

| Mass of salt dissolved in 100 g of water (g) | Does the golf ball float? |
| --- | --- |
| 5 | no |
| 10 | no |
| 15 | no |
| 20 | yes |
| 25 | yes |
| 30 | yes |

a Name the independent variable in Milly's experiment. *(1 mark)*

b Name the dependent variable. *(1 mark)*

c Name **one** control variable. *(1 mark)*

d Calculate the total mass of solution made when Milly adds 10 g of salt to the water.
*(2 marks)*

e Use data in the table to state the smallest mass of salt that Milly adds to the water to make the ball float. *(1 mark)*

f Predict the mass of salt Milly would need to add to 200 g of water to make the ball float. Explain your prediction. *(2 marks)*
*(8 marks)*

3 🔺🔺 The table below shows the solubilities of two substances at different temperatures.

| Temperature (°C) | Maximum mass of cerium(III) sulfate that dissolves in 100 g of water (g) | Maximum mass of sodium nitrate that dissolves in 100 g of water (g) |
| --- | --- | --- |
| 0 | 21 | 74 |
| 20 | 9 | 88 |
| 30 | 7 | 95 |
| 40 | 6 | 101 |
| 60 | 4 | 123 |
| 80 | – | 148 |
| 100 | – | 180 |

a Plot the data on a line graph. *(5 marks)*

b Draw the line or curve of best fit for each set of data on your graph. *(2 marks)*

c Describe and compare the patterns shown on your graph. *(4 marks)*
*(11 marks)*

4 🔺🔺🔺 Describe and explain how you could extract pure water from inky water using the apparatus below.

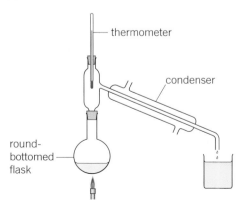

*(6 marks)*

# 3.1 Acids and metals

## Learning objectives

After this topic you will be able to:

● compare the reactions of different metals with dilute acids

● explain the test for hydrogen gas.

◀ Magnesium ribbon in dilute hydrochloric acid.

## Key Words

acid, metal

## Sulfuric similarities?

Plan an experiment to answer these questions: Do metals that react vigorously with hydrochloric acid also react vigorously with sulfuric acid? Is hydrogen formed as a product?

## Foul Fact

In the US, a person died from zinc poisoning after eating 461 pennies. American pennies are mainly zinc.

**Zookeepers were worried. A hyena was ill. Its foot was swollen. It refused to eat. What was wrong?**

Vets used X-rays to solve the mystery. The hyena had swallowed 20 zinc coins. In the stomach, zinc reacted with hydrochloric **acid**. The reaction made zinc chloride.

zinc + hydrochloric acid → zinc chloride + hydrogen

Zinc chloride dissolves in water. It mixes with blood and travels around the body. This causes zinc poisoning.

### How do other metals react with acids?

**Metals** all have similar physical properties. They are shiny. They conduct heat and electricity. Metals have patterns in their chemical properties too.

Anna pours dilute hydrochloric acid into a test tube. She adds magnesium ribbon.

The mixture bubbles vigorously. The magnesium ribbon appears to get smaller, and disappear. A colourless solution remains. There has been a chemical reaction:

magnesium + hydrochloric acid → magnesium chloride + hydrogen

Anna repeats the experiment with different metals. Zinc and iron bubble steadily in acid. Lead reacts more slowly.

magnesium          zinc          iron          lead

All the reactions make a solution of a salt, and hydrogen gas:

zinc + hydrochloric acid → zinc chloride + hydrogen

iron + hydrochloric acid → iron chloride + hydrogen

lead + hydrochloric acid → lead chloride + hydrogen

**A** Name the products in the reaction of a metal with an acid.

## How do you test for hydrogen?

A reaction in a test tube makes bubbles. How can you tell if the bubbles contain hydrogen gas?

1 Collect the gas by holding an empty test tube above the reaction test tube.

2 Light a splint.

3 Hold the splint in the test tube that now contains the gas.

4 Listen. If the splint goes out with a squeaky pop, the gas is hydrogen.

The squeaky pop happens because hydrogen and oxygen react explosively. The product is water.

hydrogen + oxygen → water

**B** Describe how you could test for hydrogen gas.

## Do all metals react with dilute acids?

Some metals do not react with dilute acids. Nothing happens if you add gold, silver, or copper to dilute hydrochloric acid.

Here is a list of how vigorously different metals react with dilute hydrochloric acid:

| magnesium | most reactive |
|---|---|
| zinc | |
| iron | |
| lead | |
| copper, silver and gold | do not react |

Gold does not react ▶ with dilute acids.

▲ If you hear a squeaky pop then hydrogen is present.

## Link

You can learn more about why gold does not react with acid in C2 3.3 The reactivity series

## Summary Questions

1 ⚗ Copy the sentences below, choosing the correct bold words.

Some metals react with hydrochloric acid. The products are **a salt/an alkali** and **oxygen/ hydrogen** gas. Iron reacts more vigorously than **magnesium/zinc/ lead** and less vigorously than **magnesium/lead/copper**. Some metals, for example, **zinc/silver/ magnesium**, do not react with dilute hydrochloric acid.

*(5 marks)*

2 ⚗⚗ Some breakfast cereals contain small amounts of iron. Iron is an important mineral.

a Predict the products of the reaction of iron when it reacts with hydrochloric acid in the stomach acid. Explain your prediction. *(3 marks)*

b Describe how you could test if your prediction was correct. *(2 marks)*

3 ⚗⚗⚗ Draw a visual summary of the reactions of metals and acids, making as many links as possible.

*(6 marks)*

# 3.2 Metals and oxygen

## Learning objectives

After this topic you will be able to:

- compare the reactions of different metals with oxygen
- use state symbols in balanced formula equations.

### State a case

When you write state symbols, use lower case letters – it's (g), not (G).

**Have you ever burned magnesium? What did you see? Magnesium burns vigorously. It reacts with oxygen from the air. The product is magnesium oxide.**

$$\text{magnesium} + \text{oxygen} \rightarrow \text{magnesium oxide}$$
$$2Mg(s) + O_2(g) \rightarrow 2MgO(s)$$

In the balanced equation above, (s) and (g) are **state symbols**:

- (s) means solid
- (g) means gas

Magnesium reacts with oxygen even when you do not heat it. If you leave magnesium in the air, its surface atoms react with oxygen. This forms a thin layer of magnesium oxide.

▲ The magnesium ribbon on the left has a layer of magnesium oxide on its surface.

**A** Write the state symbols for a substance in the gas state and in the solid state.

## How do other metals react with oxygen?

If you sprinkle zinc powder into a Bunsen flame, you see bright-white sparks. Zinc oxide forms:

$$\text{zinc} + \text{oxygen} \rightarrow \text{zinc oxide}$$
$$2Zn(s) + O_2(g) \rightarrow 2ZnO(s)$$

There is a similar reaction with iron filings. The product is iron oxide.

Copper does not burn in a Bunsen flame. Instead, it forms black copper oxide on its surface.

$$\text{copper} + \text{oxygen} \rightarrow \text{copper oxide}$$
$$2Cu(s) + O_2(g) \rightarrow 2CuO(s)$$

▲ Iron filings burn in air.

Gold is unreactive. It does not burn. Its surface atoms do not react with oxygen. This explains why gold stays shiny.

◄ Gold makes excellent connectors in audio equipment.

**B** Name two metals that react vigorously with oxygen from the air.

## How do reactions with acids and oxygen compare?

Magnesium reacts vigorously with dilute acids. It also burns in oxygen. Magnesium is a **reactive** metal. Gold does not react with dilute acids or with oxygen. It is unreactive.

There is a pattern. Metals that react vigorously with dilute acids also react vigorously with oxygen. Metals that do not react with dilute acids do not react with oxygen.

| Metal | Reaction with dilute acid | Reaction with oxygen |
|-------|---------------------------|----------------------|
| magnesium | reacts very vigorously | burns vigorously |
| zinc | reacts steadily | burns less vigorously |
| iron | reacts steadily | burns |
| lead | reacts slowly | do not burn; when heated, form layer of oxide on surface |
| copper | no reaction | |
| gold | | no reaction |

**C** List the metals in the table in order of how vigorously they react with oxygen, starting with the most reactive.

### Fair test?

Jamilla compares the burning reactions of metals. She wants to list four metals in order of how vigorously they react. She has magnesium ribbon, an iron nail, zinc filings, and a piece of copper pipe. She also has a Bunsen burner and tongs. With a partner, discuss how Jamilla can compare the burning reactions. How could she improve her investigation?

**Key Words**

state symbol, reactive

**Fantastic Fact**

Magnesium doesn't just react with oxygen from the air; it also reacts with nitrogen, making magnesium nitride.

## Summary Questions

1 ⚗ Copy and complete the sentences below.

Some metals burn vigorously in air, for example, _____ . The products are metal _____ . Some metals form an oxide layer on their surface when heated, for example, _____ . Some metals, for example _____ , do not react with oxygen.

*(4 marks)*

2 ⚗⚗ Write the balanced formula equation for the reaction of calcium with oxygen. Include state symbols.

*(3 marks)*

3 ⚗⚗ Potassium reacts explosively with dilute hydrochloric acid. Predict how vigorously it reacts with oxygen, and the products of the reaction. Explain your answers.

*(4 marks)*

4 ⚗⚗⚗ Create a song or rap to describe patterns in the reactions of metals with acids and oxygen.

*(6 marks)*

# 3.3 Metals and water

## Learning objectives

After this topic you will be able to:

- compare the reactions of metals with water
- use the reactivity series to predict reactions.

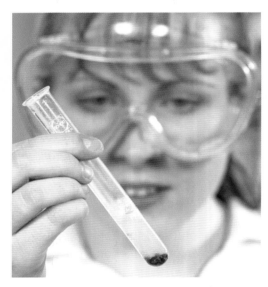

▲ Calcium reacts vigorously with water.

### Tim's tin

Tim wants to know the position of tin in the reactivity series. He does practical tests to collect the data in the table.

| Metal | Observations on adding to dilute hydrochloric acid |
|---|---|
| tin | bubbles slowly |
| magnesium | bubbles vigorously |
| copper | no change |

Talk about how Tim's data help answer his question. Discuss tests he could do to discover more about the position of tin.

**Look at the metals around you. Do they react with water? Stainless steel taps do not. Nor do copper water pipes, nor gold jewellery.**

◀ Copper water pipes do not react with water.

Some metals do react with water. Calcium bubbles vigorously, then seems to disappear. The bubbles are hydrogen gas.

$$\text{calcium} + \text{water} \rightarrow \text{calcium hydroxide} + \text{hydrogen}$$

**A** Name the products of the reaction of calcium with water.

### How do other metals react with water?

The Group 1 metals react vigorously with water. There is a flame when potassium reacts with water. Sodium and lithium react slightly less vigorously.

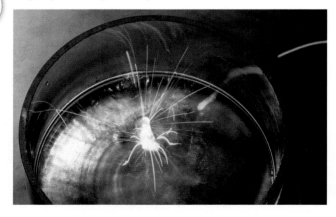

◀ Potassium reacts vigorously with water.

There is a pattern in the Group 1 metal reactions with water. They all make soluble hydroxides and hydrogen gas.

$$\text{potassium} + \text{water} \rightarrow \text{potassium hydroxide} + \text{hydrogen}$$
$$2K(s) + 2H_2O(l) \rightarrow 2KOH(aq) + H_2(g)$$

The state symbols include:

- (l) for the liquid state
- (aq) for a substance dissolved in water.

**B** Write the state symbols for a substance in the liquid state and dissolved in water.

## How do metals react with steam?
Magnesium reacts slowly with cold water. But it reacts quickly with steam.

$$\text{magnesium} + \text{water} \rightarrow \text{magnesium oxide} + \text{hydrogen}$$
$$Mg(s) + H_2O(g) \rightarrow MgO(s) + H_2(g)$$

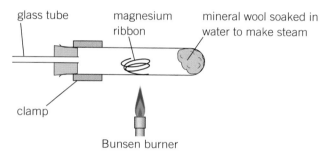

glass tube    magnesium ribbon    mineral wool soaked in water to make steam

clamp

Bunsen burner

▲ Magnesium reacts with steam in this apparatus.

Zinc and iron also react with steam. The products are hydrogen, and a metal oxide.

Copper and gold are unreactive. They do not react with cold water or steam, just as they do not react with dilute acids and oxygen.

**B** Name two metals that react with steam but not cold water.

## What is the reactivity series?
The patterns of metal reactions with acids, oxygen, and water are similar. The **reactivity series** describes these patterns. It lists the metals in order of how vigorously they react. The metals at the top have very vigorous reactions. Going down the list, the metals get less reactive.

The reactivity series. ▶

**reactive**
potassium
sodium
lithium
calcium
magnesium
aluminium
zinc
iron
lead
copper
silver
gold
**unreactive**

**Key Words**

reactivity series

## Summary Questions

1 Write six sentences from the sentence starters and enders below.

| Sentence starters | Sentence enders |
|---|---|
| Sodium… | …is less reactive than copper. |
| Gold… | …reacts very vigorously with water. |
| Iron… | …does not react with oxygen, water, or acid. |
| | …is unreactive. |
| | …is near the top of the reactivity series. |
| | …is more reactive than copper. |

*(6 marks)*

2 Write a balanced equation for the reaction of sodium (Na) with water. The products are sodium hydroxide (NaOH) and hydrogen.

*(3 marks)*

3 Use the evidence in the table below to predict the position of nickel in the reactivity series. Explain your prediction.

| Metal | Observations after leaving metal in water and air for one week | Observations on adding dilute sulfuric acid |
|---|---|---|
| nickel | no change | bubbles form slowly |
| iron | makes red-brown flaky substance | bubbles form, more vigorously than nickel |
| lead | no change | no change |

*(6 marks)*

## Learning objectives

After this topic you will be able to:

● predict pairs of substances that react in displacement reactions
● use the reactivity series to explain displacement reactions.

▲ This rock contains copper compounds.

**What is copper used for? Electric cables, water pipes, and computer parts all include the metal.**

Most copper comes from rock that contains copper compounds. Scientists get copper from rock by using chemical reactions. Here's how:

● Add sulfuric acid to the rock. Copper sulfate solution forms.
● Add waste iron to the copper sulfate solution.

There is a chemical reaction. One of the products is copper:

$$\text{iron} + \text{copper sulfate} \rightarrow \text{iron sulfate} + \text{copper}$$
$$\text{Fe(s)} + \text{CuSO}_4\text{(aq)} \rightarrow \text{FeSO}_4\text{(aq)} + \text{Cu(s)}$$

Iron is more reactive than copper. It **displaces** copper from its compound, copper sulfate. The reaction is a **displacement** reaction. In a displacement reaction, a more reactive element displaces, or pushes out, a less reactive element from its compound.

**A** State what a displacement reaction is.

## Other displacement reactions

Elliott adds magnesium to copper sulfate solution. Magnesium is more reactive than copper. So magnesium displaces copper from its compound.

$$\text{magnesium} + \text{copper sulfate} \rightarrow \text{magnesium sulfate} + \text{copper}$$
$$\text{Mg(s)} + \text{CuSO}_4\text{(aq)} \rightarrow \text{MgSO}_4\text{(aq)} + \text{Cu(s)}$$

### Key Words

displace, displacement, thermite reaction

### Link

You can learn more about the displacement reactions of halogens in C2 1.4 The elements of Group 7

▲ Magnesium displaces copper from copper sulfate.

If you add copper to magnesium sulfate solution, there is no reaction. Copper is less reactive than magnesium. So copper cannot displace magnesium from its compounds.

**B** State why copper cannot displace magnesium in magnesium sulfate solution.

## Do oxides take part in displacement reactions?

Aluminium is more reactive than iron. It displaces iron from its compounds. For example:

aluminium + iron oxide → aluminium oxide + iron

$$2Al(s) + Fe_2O_3(s) \rightarrow Al_2O_3(s) + 2Fe(l)$$

This is the **thermite reaction**. It involves mixing the two powders, and heating them strongly. The reaction is exothermic. The reaction mixture gets so hot that the iron melts.

◀ The dramatic thermite reaction.

Other metal–metal oxide pairs react. The metal on its own needs to be more reactive than the metal in the compound. For example:

iron + copper oxide → iron oxide + copper

$$2Fe(s) + 3CuO(s) \rightarrow Fe_2O_3(s) + 3Cu(s)$$

Iron has displaced copper from copper oxide.

Copper does not react with iron oxide. This is because copper is less reactive than iron.

### Planning paragraphs

Make notes for a piece of writing to explain displacement reactions. Decide how to divide the information into paragraphs. Plan what to include in each paragraph.

Then write your paragraphs. Swap with a friend. Can you suggest improvements?

magnesium
aluminium
zinc
iron
lead
copper
silver
gold

▲ Part of the reactivity series.

## Summary Questions

1 🔥 Copy the sentences below, correcting the five mistakes.

In a displacement reaction, a less reactive metal pushes out a more reactive metal from its compound. For example, iron displaces aluminium from aluminium oxide.

*(5 marks)*

2 🔥🔥 Predict which pairs of substances will react. Give reasons for your decisions.

a zinc and copper sulfate solution

b iron and zinc chloride solution

c aluminium powder and copper oxide powder

d iron filings and lead oxide powder

*(8 marks)*

3 🔥🔥🔥 Draw a cartoon that explains how displacement reactions occur.

*(6 marks)*

# 3.5 Extracting metals

## Learning objectives

After this topic you will be able to:

- use the reactivity series to decide which metals can be extracted from their ores by heating with carbon
- calculate the amounts of metals in ores.

### What links the pictures?

The items are made from steel. Steel is mainly iron. But where does iron come from? You cannot find the element on its own in the Earth's crust.

### What is an ore?

In the Earth's crust, iron is joined to other elements, in compounds. In many of these compounds iron is joined to oxygen. These are iron oxides.

Most iron oxide is mixed with other compounds in rock. A rock that you can extract a metal from is called an **ore**.

- Iron ore is a mixture of iron oxide and other compounds.
- Aluminium ore is a mixture of aluminium oxide and other compounds.

▲ Bauxite aluminium ore is the most commonly mined aluminium ore.

---

**A** State the meaning of the word ore.

---

### How are metals extracted from ores?

There are two main stages in extracting iron from its ore. These are:

1  Separate iron oxide from the compounds it is mixed with.
2  Use chemical reactions to extract iron from iron oxide.

The chemical reactions involve heating iron oxide with charcoal. Charcoal is a form of carbon. It is cheap, and easy to get hold of.

---

**B** Describe two stages in extracting a metal from its ore.

---

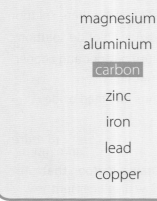

magnesium

aluminium

carbon

zinc

iron

lead

copper

▲ Part of the reactivity series, including carbon.

## Which metal oxides react with carbon?

Carbon is a non-metal. But we can place it in the reactivity series, between aluminium and zinc.

Any metal that is below carbon in the reactivity series can be displaced from its compounds by carbon. You can heat carbon powder with copper oxide powder. Carbon displaces copper from copper oxide:

$$\text{carbon} + \text{copper oxide} \rightarrow \text{copper} + \text{carbon dioxide}$$
$$C(s) + 2CuO(s) \rightarrow 2Cu(s) + CO_2(g)$$

You can also heat carbon with lead oxide.

$$\text{carbon} + \text{lead oxide} \rightarrow \text{lead} + \text{carbon dioxide}$$
$$C(s) + 2PbO(s) \rightarrow 2Pb(s) + CO_2(g)$$

**c** Carbon displaces copper from copper oxide. Write a word equation for this reaction.

## Can carbon extract any metal from its compounds?

You cannot use carbon to get aluminium from aluminium oxide. This is because aluminium is more reactive than carbon. It is above carbon in the reactivity series.

Gold always exists as the element itself. It does not form compounds because it is very unreactive. The gold just needs separating from the substances it is mixed with.

## Fantastic Fact

We use awesome amounts of ore. In 2010 world iron ore production was 2 400 million tonnes. China dug out 900 million tonnes of this.

### Ore waste

Iron ore from different places contains different amounts of iron. Companies extract iron from ores containing between 16% and 70% iron. Calculate the masses of waste from 1 tonne (1000 kg) of each of these ores: an ore that is 50% iron, an ore that is 16% iron, and an ore that is 70% iron.

**Key Words**

ore

## Summary Questions

**1** Copy the sentences below, choosing the correct bold words.

An ore is a **substance/rock** that you can extract metal from. Most metals exist in the Earth's crust as **compounds/elements**. These are **joined to/mixed with** other substances in ores.

*(3 marks)*

**2** An ore contains 6% copper. Calculate the mass of copper in 100 kg of this ore. Show your working.

*(2 marks)*

**3** Use the reactivity series to write the balanced symbol equation for the reaction of carbon with zinc oxide. Include state symbols.

*(2 marks)*

**4** Explain why some metals can be extracted from compounds by heating with carbon, and why some cannot. Include examples to illustrate your answer.

*(6 marks)*

# 3.6 Ceramics

## Learning objectives

After this topic you will be able to:

- describe ceramic properties
- explain why the properties of ceramics make them suitable for their uses.

## Have you ever wondered what a toilet is made from?

Toilets are made from pottery. Pottery is an example of a **ceramic** material. A brick is a block of a ceramic material. Ceramic materials are compounds. They include metal silicates, metal oxides, metal carbides, and metal nitrides.

▲ Ceramics are brittle.

▲ Toilets are made from pottery, which is a ceramic.

▲ Bricks are made by heating clay. This hardens the clay. A brick is a block of ceramic material.

**A** State what a ceramic material is.

## What are the properties of ceramics?

All ceramic materials have similar physical properties. They are:

- hard – you can only scratch them with harder materials
- brittle – they break easily
- stiff – they are difficult to bend
- solid at room temperature, with very high melting points
- strong when forces press on them
- break easily when stretched
- electrical insulators.

Ceramics also have similar chemical properties to each other. They do not react with water, acids, or alkalis.

**B** List four physical properties and one chemical property of ceramics.

### Splendid ceramics

You work for a ceramics company. Your boss wants you to write an article for a newspaper, explaining why ceramics are useful. Start by making notes on what to include. Then decide how to organise your ideas into paragraphs. Next, work out how to get readers interested. Finally, write your article.

## Why are ceramics useful?

Ceramics have many uses. Their uses depend on their properties.

Bricks are strong when forces press on them. They are also durable and attractive. This makes them suitable for buildings.

Ceramics do not conduct electricity. They are not damaged by water. This makes them useful for electrical power-line insulators.

Ceramics have high melting points. This makes them suitable for jet-engine turbine blades, which get very hot.

Ceramics do not react with water, acids, or alkalis. You can decorate them. This makes them useful for plates, bowls, mugs, and jugs.

▲ Ceramics are used as a building material.

▲ Ceramics are good insulators.

▲ Ceramics have high melting points.

▲ Ceramics do not react with water, acids, or alkalis.

**C** List three uses of ceramics.

## Why do ceramics have these properties?

In ceramic materials, a huge number of atoms join together in one big structure. There are strong forces between the atoms.

This structure explains the properties of ceramic materials.

- You need a great amount of energy to break forces between atoms. This explains why ceramics have high melting points.
- The bonds between atoms are very strong. This is why they are hard. You break some bonds when you scratch ceramic materials.

### Key Words

ceramic

### Fantastic Fact

The ceramic hafnium carbide has the highest melting point of all known ceramics, at about 3900 °C.

### Summary Questions

1. Copy and complete the following sentences using the words below.

   **insulators silicates compounds high brittle oxides hard**

   Ceramics are _____. They include metal _____ and metal _____.
   Ceramics are _____ and _____.
   They have _____ melting points.
   They are electrical _____.

   *(7 marks)*

2. Look at the data in the table. Decide which materials could be ceramics. Explain your choices.

   | Material | Relative hardness | Melting point (°C) |
   |---|---|---|
   | A | 2.0 | 321 |
   | B | 9.0 | 3532 |
   | C | 3.0 | 825 |
   | D | 9.0 | 2930 |
   | E | 5.8 | 2800 |

   *(4 marks)*

3. Summarise the information about ceramics in a table, including how and why they are useful.

   *(6 marks)*

# 3.7 Polymers

## Learning objectives

After this topic you will be able to:

- describe polymer properties
- explain how polymer properties make them suitable for their uses.

▲ Wool is a natural polymer used in clothing.

▲ Cotton is another natural polymer used in clothing.

▲ Rubber is a natural polymer used to make tyres.

**Foul Fact**

Lobsters, cockroaches, and ants make a polymer – chitin – to form their exoskeletons.

## Do you know what umbrellas, beach balls, and carrier bags have in common?

They are made from **polymers**. A polymer is a substance with very long molecules. A polymer molecule has identical groups of atoms, repeated many times.

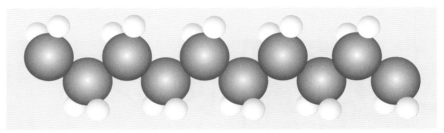

▲ This is part of a molecule of a polymer called poly(ethene). One molecule has hundreds of $-C_2H_4-$ units, joined in a long chain. The black spheres represent carbon atoms. The white spheres represent hydrogen atoms.

There are many polymers. Different polymers have different properties. Their properties make them suitable for their uses.

**A** State what a polymer is.

## Why are natural polymers useful?

Plants and animals make **natural polymers**, including wool, cotton, and rubber.

Sheep make wool. Wool fibres trap air between them. This means that wool traps heat, making it useful for jumpers and socks.

Cotton plants make cotton fibres. Cotton fabric is strong, durable, and absorbs sweat. It is useful for summer clothing like t-shirts.

Rubber trees produce rubber. Rubber is flexible, waterproof, and durable. These properties make it suitable for tyres.

**B** Give an example of a polymer, and one of its uses.

## Why are synthetic polymers useful?

**Synthetic polymers** do not occur naturally. They are made in chemical reactions. There are hundreds of synthetic polymers. Scientists work hard to develop new polymers. Each polymer has its own properties.

## Poly(ethene)

Poly(ethene) is the scientific name for polythene. There are two types of poly(ethene).

- The molecules in low-density poly(ethene) (LDPE) slide over each other. This makes it flexible. LDPE is also strong. LDPE is used for carrier bags.
- High-density poly(ethene) (HDPE) is also strong and flexible. It is harder than LDPE. Its surfaces can be very smooth. HDPE is used in artificial knee joints. Artificial joints also include metal, such as titanium.

Both types of poly(ethene) do not wear away or break down (decay) naturally. This property is very important for artificial knee joints. But the same property makes it hard to get rid of carrier bags.

◀ Poly(ethene) bags can be dangerous to wildlife.

## Poly(vinyl chloride)

Poly(vinyl chloride) (PVC) is waterproof, flexible, and does not conduct electricity. These properties make PVC suitable for waterproof clothes and insulating electric cables.

**C** State why low-density poly(ethene) makes good carrier bags.

### Plotting polymers

Every polymer has its own properties. Plot the density data in the table below on a bar chart. Show your chart to a partner. Ask them to check your scale, labels, and accuracy.

| Polymer | Density (g/cm³) |
|---|---|
| low-density poly(ethene) | 0.92 |
| high-density poly(ethene) | 0.96 |
| poly(propene) | 0.90 |
| poly(vinyl chloride) | 1.30 |
| soft rubber | 1.10 |

### Key Words

polymer, natural polymer, synthetic polymer

## Summary Questions

**1** 🔺 Copy and complete the sentences below.

A polymer has _____ molecules. Each molecule has identical groups of _____, repeated many times. There are two types of polymer: _____ polymers and _____ polymers. Synthetic polymers include PVC and _____. Poly(ethene) is _____ because its molecules slide over one another.

*(6 marks)*

**2** 🔺🔺 The list gives some properties of poly(styrene).

Choose properties from the list that explain why polystyrene is suitable for:

**a** packaging

**b** disposable cups.

**Properties:** low density; does not conduct electricity; poor conductor of heat; white colour.

*(4 marks)*

**3** 🔺🔺🔺 The table gives data about three synthetic polymers. Use the data to compare the polymers.

| Polymer | Strength when pulled (N/mm²) | Relative hardness | Density (g/cm³) |
|---|---|---|---|
| poly(vinyl chloride) | 48 | 20 | 1.30 |
| nylon | 60 | 10 | 1.16 |
| acrylic | 74 | 34 | 1.19 |

*(6 marks)*

## Learning objectives

After this topic you will be able to:
- describe composite properties
- explain why composite properties make them suitable for their uses.

▲ The builder pours concrete into the gaps between the steel rods. The concrete sets hard.

▲ Part of a carbon-fibre-reinforced plastic bicycle frame.

**In constructing a new building, builders use reinforced concrete. What makes this material so strong?**

Reinforced concrete consists of steel bars with concrete around it. Concrete is not damaged when forces press on it. But it breaks easily when stretched. Steel is not damaged by stretching forces. Together, steel and concrete put up with strong squashing and stretching forces.

Reinforced concrete is a **composite** material. A composite is a mixture of materials. Each material has different properties. The composite has properties that are a combination of the properties of the materials it is made up of. Scientists experiment with different mixtures. They develop composites with the best properties for particular uses.

**A** State what a composite material is.

## Other composites
### Carbon-fibre-reinforced plastic

This bicycle frame is made from **carbon-fibre**-reinforced plastic (CFRP). The composite consists of two materials:
- carbon fibres, which are thin tubes of carbon. The fibres are woven into a fabric.
- a gluelike polymer, which is moulded into different shapes when soft.

Some cyclists prefer CFRP bicycles to steel ones. Reasons for this are:
- CFRP has a lower density, making bicycles lighter
- CFRP does not rust
- CFRP is very strong
- you can mould CFRP into any shape.

CFRP has some disadvantages. Bicycles made from CFRP are expensive. If crashed, they are badly damaged.

**B** Name two materials in carbon-fibre-reinforced plastic.

## Glass-fibre-reinforced aluminium

▲ The world's largest passenger aeroplane, the Airbus A380, is made from composite materials.

The aeroplane Airbus A380 contains around 20% composite materials. One of these composites is glass-fibre-reinforced aluminium. The materials in this composite include:

- thin layers of aluminium
- layers of glass fibre
- a gluelike polymer to join the layers.

**C** Name two materials in glass-fibre-reinforced aluminium.

### Comparing composites

Callum makes three blocks of a composite material from mud and straw. He puts different amounts of straw in each block. The mud dries. Discuss how Callum could use the apparatus in the diagram to compare the strengths of the blocks. Write down the variables, and suggest how to make the investigation fair.

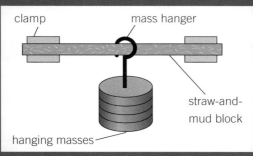

clamp
mass hanger
straw-and-mud block
hanging masses

## Key Words

composite, carbon fibre

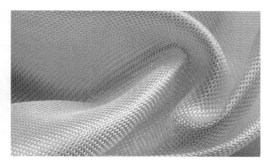

▲ Woven glass fibre.

## Summary Questions

**1** 🔬 Copy the sentences below, choosing the correct bold word.

A composite material is a **mixture/compound** of two or more materials. Each of these materials has **different/the same** properties. The composite material has properties that are **a combination of/exactly the same as** these properties.

*(3 marks)*

**2** 🔬🔬 Fibreglass is a composite material. It is made from a polymer called polyester resin, and glass fibres. Use the data in the table to explain why fibreglass is a better material for canoes than polyester resin alone.

| Material | Density (g/cm³) | Strength when pulled (MPa) | Strength when squashed (MPa) |
|---|---|---|---|
| polyester resin | 1.3 | 55 | 140 |
| fibreglass | 1.6 | 250 | 150 |

*(3 marks)*

**3** 🔬🔬🔬 Draw a visual summary of the information on composites.

*(6 marks)*

101

## Key Points

- The reactivity series lists metals in order of how vigorously they react. The most reactive metals are at the top. The table summarises some reactions.

| Metal | Reaction with dilute acid | Reaction on heating in air | Reaction with water |
|---|---|---|---|
| potassium | Explode. Products are metal salts and hydrogen. | Burn vigorously. Products are metal oxides. | React vigorously. Products are a metal hydroxide solution and hydrogen. |
| sodium | | | |
| lithium | | | |
| calcium | React, making bubbles. | | |
| magnesium | | | React with steam. Products are hydrogen and a metal oxide. |
| zinc | Products are metal salts and hydrogen. | | |
| iron | | | |
| lead | | Do not burn. Form oxide layer on surface. | |
| copper | Do not react. | | Do not react. |
| silver | | Do not react. | |
| gold | | | |

- More reactive metals displace less reactive metals from compounds.
- Zinc, and metals below it in the reactivity series, are extracted by heating their oxides with carbon.
- Ceramic materials include pottery and brick. They are hard and brittle, with high melting points.
- Polymers have long molecules. There are hundreds of polymers. Each has unique properties that make it suitable for particular purposes.
- A composite material is a mixture of materials. It has properties that are a combination of the properties of the materials in the mixture.

# Case study

### Ranking reactivity
You have three metals, but you don't know what they are. With a partner, discuss what tests to do, to rank them in order of reactivity. How would the results show this? Decide how to make the tests fair.

### Task
With your partner, write instructions for the investigation.

### Tips
- Include a results table.
- Remember to include all the variables.
- Swap instructions with a partner and suggest improvements.

## Key Words

state symbol, reactive, reactivity series, displace, displacement, thermite reaction, ore, ceramic, polymer, natural polymer, synthetic polymer, reinforced concrete, composite, carbon fibre

# End-of-chapter questions

1 🧪 Anne adds metals to water. Draw lines to match each metal to an observation.

| Metal | Observation |
|---|---|
| copper | moves on surface of water |
| | lilac flame |
| potassium | bubbles vigorously |
| calcium | no change |

*(3 marks)*

2 🧪 Lamek compares the reactivity of iron, lead, and zinc with hydrochloric acid.
 a Write down **two** things Lamek must do to compare the reactions fairly. *(2 marks)*
 b Write down **one** safety precaution Lamek must take. Give a reason for this. *(2 marks)*
 c Predict which metal will react most vigorously. Give a reason for your choice. *(1 mark)*
 d Name the gas formed when a metal reacts with a dilute acid. *(1 mark)*
 *(6 marks)*

3 🧪🧪 Write down the properties of ceramics, choosing from the list.

hard
soft
brittle
low melting point
electrical insulator
high melting point

*(4 marks)*

4 🧪🧪 Copy and complete the word equations.
 a lithium + water → _____ + _____
 b _____ + _____ → magnesium oxide
 c zinc + hydrochloric acid → _____ + _____
 d magnesium + _____
    → magnesium sulfate + _____
 *(8 marks)*

5 🧪🧪🧪 Katya is investigating displacement reactions. She heats the pairs of substances in the list.

| Pair W | iron and aluminium oxide |
|---|---|
| Pair X | iron and copper oxide |
| Pair Y | copper and magnesium oxide |
| Pair Z | iron and lead oxide |

 a Write down the letters of **two** pairs of substances that react. Explain your choices. *(4 marks)*
 b Choose **one** pair of substances that react. Write a word equation for the reaction. *(2 marks)*

6 🧪🧪🧪 Bob has the salt solutions in the list below. He does not know which is which.
 ● magnesium chloride
 ● zinc chloride
 ● copper chloride

Bob also has pieces of magnesium, iron, zinc, and copper.

Explain how Bob could use his materials to work out which solution is which.
*(6 marks)*

# The Earth and its atmosphere

## Learning objectives

After this topic you will be able to:

- compare the layers of the Earth
- describe the composition of the atmosphere.

▲ Everything needed to make this packet of crisps comes from the Earth.

## What goes into a packet of crisps?

The potatoes come from plants. The plants use water, carbon dioxide from the air, and nutrients from the soil to grow. The salt comes from the sea, or from a mine. Aluminium for the bags comes from bauxite rock. The crisps are packed in nitrogen, which was separated from the air.

Everything for the packet of crisps – and everything we use – comes from the Earth, the air, or the oceans.

## What is the structure of the Earth?

The Earth is made up of four layers.

- The outer layer is the rocky **crust**. It is between 8 km and 40 km thick.
- Beneath the crust is the **mantle**. This is made mostly of solid rock, but it can flow. Very slowly, hotter rock rises and cooler rock sinks.
- About halfway to the centre of the Earth is the **core**. This is mainly iron and nickel. The **outer core** is liquid. The **inner core** is solid.

Of course, no-one has dug to the centre of the Earth. Scientists learn about its structure by studying shock waves from earthquakes. They also examine rocks on the surface and under oceans, and materials that volcanoes bring to the surface.

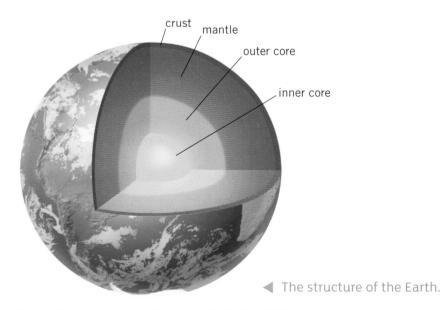

◀ The structure of the Earth.

## Fantastic Fact

For each mile that you drill down into the Earth, the temperature increases by 40 °C.

**A** Name the four layers of the Earth.

## What's in the crust?

Most rocks are mixtures of compounds. The pie chart shows the elements that make up these compounds.

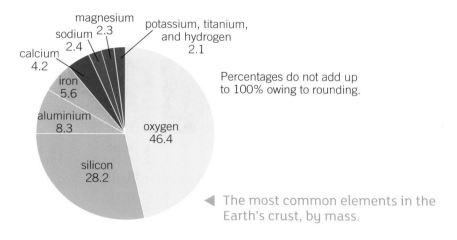

Percentages do not add up to 100% owing to rounding.

◀ The most common elements in the Earth's crust, by mass.

**B** List the six most common elements in the Earth's crust.

## What is the atmosphere?

The **atmosphere** is a mixture of gases that surrounds the Earth. The part of the atmosphere nearest the Earth is the **troposphere**. This layer goes up to about 10 km above the surface of the Earth. The troposphere is mainly a mixture of two elements, oxygen and nitrogen. There are smaller amounts of other substances, including argon and carbon dioxide.

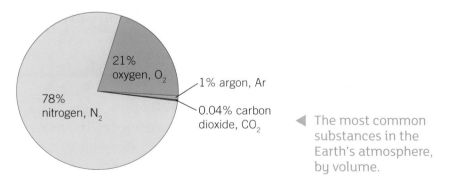

◀ The most common substances in the Earth's atmosphere, by volume.

**C** State what the atmosphere is.

### Questioning the crust

Use the pie charts above to write questions about the composition of the Earth's crust and the atmosphere. Swap with a partner, and answer each other's questions.

## Key Words

crust, mantle, core, outer core, inner core, atmosphere, troposphere

## Fantastic Fact

The world's deepest hole is in Kola, Russia. It is more than 12 km deep.

## Summary Questions

**1** Copy and complete the sentences below.

Surrounding the Earth is a mixture of gases called the _____. The Earth itself is made up of four layers. On the outside is the _____. Next is the mantle. The substances of the mantle are mostly in the _____ state. The core consists mainly of two elements – iron and _____. The substances of the outer core are in the _____ state.

*(5 marks)*

**2** The list below gives the names of the four most common substances in the atmosphere. Draw a ring around the name of the most abundant element. Underline the name of the most abundant compound.

argon     nitrogen

oxygen     carbon dioxide

*(2 marks)*

**3** Write a paragraph to compare the properties and composition of the Earth's crust, mantle, and core.

*(6 marks)*

## Learning objectives

After this topic you will be able to:

- explain two properties of sedimentary rocks
- explain how sedimentary rocks are made.

▲ Water soaks into this rock. It is porous.

▲ As they grow, tree roots break up this rock.

▲ Water transports sediments down this stream.

**The pictures show three different types of rock. How are they similar and how are they different?**

  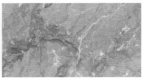

▲ Limestone.    ▲ Granite.    ▲ Marble.

There are hundreds of rock types. Scientists classify them into three groups:

- **sedimentary** rocks
- **igneous** rocks
- **metamorphic** rocks

**A** Name the three groups of rock.

## What are the properties of sedimentary rocks?

Sedimentary rocks are made up of separate grains. You can see these with a hand lens.

Sedimentary rocks are **porous**. They have gaps between their grains. Air or water can get into these gaps.

Most sedimentary rocks are soft. You can scratch them easily.

**B** Describe three properties of sedimentary rocks.

## How are sedimentary rocks made?

Sedimentary rocks are made up of pieces of older rocks. The process has several stages.

### Weathering

**Weathering** breaks up all types of rock into smaller pieces called **sediments**. There are different types of weathering:

- **Physical weathering** happens because of temperature changes. In **freeze–thaw** weathering, water gets into a crack in a rock. When the temperature is very cold, the water freezes. This forms ice. Ice takes up more space than liquid water. It pushes against the sides of the crack. This happens many times. Eventually, the rock breaks.

- **Chemical weathering** happens when rain falls on rocks. Acids in the rain react with substances in the rock.
- **Biological weathering** happens when plants and animals break up rocks.

Weathering makes sediments but does not move them away from the original rock.

## Erosion and transport

Next, sediments move away from their rock. Together, the breaking of rock into sediments and their movement away, is called **erosion**.

**Transport** processes move sediments far from the original rock. Water, ice, wind, and gravity can all move sediments.

## Deposition

Eventually, sediments stop moving. They settle in one place. This is **deposition**. Layers of different types of sediment may settle on top of each other.

## Compaction and cementation

Over many years deposited sediments join together to make new rocks. This happens by:

- **compaction** – the weight of sediments above squashes together the sediments below *or*
- **cementation** – another substance sticks the sediments together.

**C** List four stages in making sedimentary rocks.

## How are sedimentary rocks useful?

There are many types of sedimentary rock. They have different properties and uses.

▲ Sandstone is a good building material.

▲ Limestone is made from shells and skeletons that sank to the bottom of the sea. It is an attractive building material.

### Sedimentary sequence

With a partner, plan an exciting talk to explain how sedimentary rocks are formed. Present your talk to another pair. Then listen to their talk. How did they make it interesting?

## Key Words

sedimentary, igneous, metamorphic, porous, weathering, sediment, physical weathering, freeze–thaw, chemical weathering, biological weathering, erosion, transport, deposition, compaction, cementation

## Summary Questions

**1** Write five correct sentences from the sentence starters and enders.

| Sentence starters | Sentence enders |
|---|---|
| Weathering… | …involves the weight of sediment above making sediments below stick together. |
| Erosion… | …moves sediments far away from the original rock. |
| Transport… | …breaks rock into smaller pieces. |
| Deposition… | …breaks rock into smaller pieces and moves them away from the original rock. |
| Compaction… | …is the settling of sediments. |

*(5 marks)*

**2** Describe two properties of sedimentary rocks, and explain why they have these properties.

*(4 marks)*

**3** Create a flow diagram to explain how sedimentary rocks are formed.

*(6 marks)*

## Learning objectives

After this topic you will be able to:

- compare the ways that igneous and metamorphic rocks form
- explain how igneous and metamorphic rocks form.

▲ You can easily see the crystals in this granite. Each crystal is made of one compound. Granite is a mixture of compounds.

▲ A granite pavement.

▲ Basalt railway ballast.

### What type of rock does the picture on the right show?

The rock is basalt. Basalt is an example of an **igneous** rock. Igneous rock forms when liquid rock cools and freezes.

Igneous rock consists of crystals. There are no gaps between the crystals. This explains why igneous rocks are not porous.

▲ Svartifoss, Iceland.

### How are igneous rocks useful?

Igneous rocks are hard. They are also **durable**, which means they are difficult to damage. These properties mean that igneous rocks are useful for pavements and underneath railway tracks.

**A** State three properties of igneous rocks.

### Different sized crystals

Underground, liquid rock is called **magma**. Granite forms from magma. Underground, the magma cools and freezes slowly. The particles have time to arrange themselves into big crystals.

Basalt forms when liquid rock cools and freezes quickly. This happens under the sea, or on the surface of the Earth when volcanoes erupt, for example. On the surface, liquid rock is called **lava**. There isn't enough time for large crystals to grow so basalt crystals are smaller than granite crystals. You need a hand lens to see them.

▲ This lava will cool and freeze to form basalt.

## What are metamorphic rocks?

The pictures show **metamorphic** rocks.

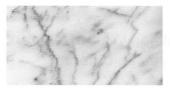  

▲ Marble.　　　　　▲ Gneiss.　　　　　▲ Slate.

Metamorphic rocks form when heat, high pressure, or both change existing rock. For example:

- Marble starts out as limestone. Marble forms when limestone below the Earth's surface heats up. The limestone does not melt, but its particles are rearranged.
- Slate starts out as a type of sedimentary rock called mudstone. Slate forms when high pressure underground squashes the mudstone. This squeezes out water, and makes layers of new crystals.

**B** Describe how marble and slate are formed.

## How are metamorphic rocks useful?

Metamorphic rocks are made up of crystals. They are not porous.

▲ Marble is not porous. Many people like how it looks. This explains why it is suitable for kitchen worktops.

▲ Slate is not porous. It is made up of layers, so it can be split into thin sheets. This is why it makes good roofing tiles.

**C** Describe the properties of slate that make it suitable for roofing tiles.

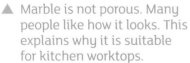

### Granite quarry

Rubislaw Quarry, near Aberdeen, is probably the biggest hole in Europe. Between 1740 and 1971 quarry workers dug 6 million tonnes of granite from the quarry. Calculate the mean mass of granite dug out of the quarry each week during this time period.

---

### Link

You can learn more about rocks in C2 4.4 The rock cycle

### Key Words

durable, magma, lava

### Fantastic Fact

Basalt doesn't only exist on Earth. There is basalt on Mars, Venus, the Moon, and Jupiter's largest moon, Io.

### Summary Questions

**1** Copy and complete the sentences below, choosing the correct bold words.

High pressure underground may change any rock type into **igneous/ metamorphic** rock. When liquid rock cools and freezes, **igneous/ metamorphic** rock forms. Granite and basalt are examples of **igneous/ metamorphic** rocks. Slate and marble are examples of **igneous/ metamorphic** rocks. Igneous and metamorphic rocks are **porous/ non-porous** because they are made up of **grains/crystals**. Igneous rocks are **hard/soft**.

*(7 marks)*

**2** Explain why some igneous rocks have small crystals, and others have bigger crystals.

*(3 marks)*

**3** Compare the ways in which igneous and metamorphic rocks form. Include examples in your answer.

*(6 marks)*

### Learning objectives

After this topic you will be able to:

- use the rock cycle to explain how the material in rocks is recycled.

▲ An Icelandic volcano.

**Imagine you came back to Earth a million years after your death. How would the rocks around you be different?**

All the time, rocks are changing. Weathering breaks down rock. Sediments make new rock. Volcanoes erupt, and their lava freezes. And, deep within the crust, heating and high pressure change rocks of all types.

**A** Describe one way that rocks change over time.

### What is the rock cycle?

Different rock types, and the processes that change one rock type into another, are linked in the **rock cycle**. The rock cycle shows how rocks change, and how their materials are recycled over millions of years.

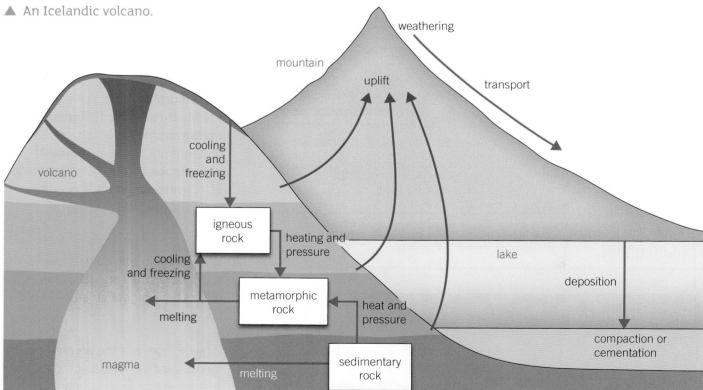

▲ The rock cycle.

## How does the rock cycle recycle materials?

There are many routes around the rock cycle. Here is one example:

- On the side of a mountain, water pours into a crack. Every night, the water freezes. The ice pushes against the sides of the crack. Sediments break free. Gravity transports them down the mountain.
- A stream flows over the sediments. It transports them to a lake. Sediments settle on the lake bed. Over many years, sediments join together. This makes sedimentary rock.
- Layers of rock build up. The lower layers heat up. Particles in these layers move, forming crystals. Metamorphic rock forms.
- Near the metamorphic rock, hot magma pushes upwards. The magma heats the rock. The rock melts, and becomes part of the magma.
- Magma moves upwards. It forces its way to the surface, and erupts from a volcano. The liquid rock cools and freezes. Igneous rock forms.

## What is uplift?

The Earth's crust moves constantly. When continents collide, huge forces from inside the Earth push rocks upwards, and mountains can form. This is called **uplift**. Taiwan, near China, is moving upwards by 1 cm every year. Earthquakes often happen at the same time as uplift.

Uplift provides evidence for the rock cycle. It brings up rocks that were once buried. Mount Everest contains fossils of sea animals because it is made from limestone that formed on the seafloor.

▲ Fossils from Mount Everest.

**B** State what is meant by uplift.

---

**Rock route**

With a partner, talk about different routes around the rock cycle. Make notes about one of these routes. Then write about this route in detail. Organise your writing in paragraphs, and use key words correctly.

## Key Words

rock cycle, uplift

---

## Summary Questions

1 🥼 Copy and complete the sentences below.

The _____ _____ shows how the materials in rocks are _____, and how different rock types are linked. When forces from inside the Earth push rocks upwards, _____ occurs. This is how _____ are formed. Mount Everest is made from _____ that formed on the seafloor.

*(5 marks)*

2 🥼🥼 Name the processes that changes...

   a ...metamorphic rock into magma. *(1 mark)*

   b ...magma into igneous rock. *(2 marks)*

   c ...layers of sediment into sedimentary rock. *(1 mark)*

3 🥼🥼🥼 Write the script for a drama to describe a route around the rock cycle.

*(6 marks)*

# 4.5 The carbon cycle

## Learning objectives

After this topic you will be able to:

- explain why the concentration of carbon dioxide in the atmosphere did not change for many years
- use the carbon cycle to identify stores of carbon.

## Link

You can learn more about how plants use carbon dioxide in B2 2.1 Photosynthesis

▲ Burning fossil fuels adds carbon dioxide to the atmosphere.

## A question of balance

With a partner, identify four ways that you could reduce the amount of carbon dioxide that you add to the atmosphere in your everyday life. Explain how each method reduces the concentration of carbon dioxide in the atmosphere.

**Imagine you took 10 000 particles from the air. How many of them would be carbon dioxide molecules?**

Fewer than four in 10 000 particles of air are carbon dioxide molecules. But carbon dioxide is vital. Without it, plants cannot make their food. Without carbon dioxide, Earth would be too cold for life as we know it.

**A** Give two reasons to explain why carbon dioxide is a vital part of the atmosphere.

## Carbon dioxide: into and out of the atmosphere

Carbon dioxide is constantly entering and leaving the atmosphere.

These processes *add* carbon dioxide to the atmosphere:

- **Respiration** transfers energy from food in plants and animals. Carbon dioxide is a waste product of respiration.

    glucose + oxygen → carbon dioxide + water

- **Combustion** Fuels such as wood, petrol, and methane produce carbon dioxide on burning.

    methane + oxygen → carbon dioxide + water

Burning fossil fuels adds carbon dioxide to the atmosphere.

**B** Name two processes that add carbon dioxide to the atmosphere.

These processes *remove* carbon dioxide from the atmosphere:

- **Photosynthesis** Plants use carbon dioxide and water to make glucose.

$$\text{carbon dioxide + water} \xrightarrow{\text{light}} \text{glucose + oxygen}$$

- **Dissolving** in the oceans.

**C** Name two processes that remove carbon dioxide from the atmosphere.

If carbon dioxide is added to the atmosphere and removed from it at the same rate, its concentration does not change.

## What is the carbon cycle?

The **carbon cycle** shows how carbon dioxide enters and leaves the atmosphere. It also shows how carbon and its compounds enter and leave **carbon stores**. Carbon stores include:

- the atmosphere
- oceans, containing dissolved carbon dioxide
- sedimentary rocks, such as calcium carbonate
- fossil fuels, such as coal, oil, and natural gas
- plants and animals
- soil.

**D** Name six carbon stores.

◀ This yew tree in Wales has stored carbon compounds in its trunk for over 4000 years.

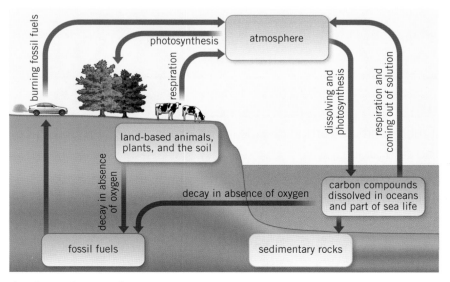

▲ The carbon cycle.

## Key Words

respiration, combustion, photosynthesis, dissolving, carbon cycle, carbon store

## Fantastic Fact

Some of the oldest living carbon stores are a group of olive trees in Lebanon, called The Sisters. They are between 6000 and 8000 years old.

## Summary Questions

**1** 🧪 Copy and complete the sentences below, choosing the correct bold words.

Carbon dioxide enters the atmosphere by **photosynthesis/ respiration** and **dissolving/ combustion**. It leaves the atmosphere by **photosynthesis/ respiration** and **dissolving/ combustion**. The atmosphere is a store of carbon. Other stores of carbon include **igneous/ sedimentary** rocks and fossil fuels such as **oil/sunlight**.

*(6 marks)*

**2** 🧪🧪 Describe a route that a carbon atom might take around the carbon cycle. Name four carbon stores the atom passes through and how it moves from one store to another.

*(5 marks)*

**3** 🧪🧪🧪 Create a carbon-cycle board game, in which players throw a dice to follow different routes around the carbon cycle.

*(6 marks)*

# 4.6 Climate change

## Learning objectives

After this topic you will be able to:

- explain why global warming happens
- explain some impacts of global warming

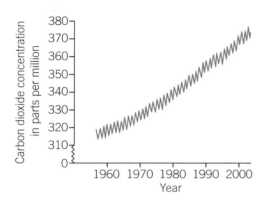

The changing concentration of carbon dioxide in the atmosphere.

## What links the pictures?

The pictures show impacts of climate change. **Climate change** is a long-term change in weather patterns. Increasing amounts of carbon dioxide in the atmosphere cause climate change.

### Why more carbon dioxide?

For many years, the concentration of carbon dioxide in the atmosphere stayed the same.

But since 1800 things have changed. Every year, more carbon dioxide enters the atmosphere. The extra carbon dioxide is removed at a slower rate than it enters. The concentration of carbon dioxide increases.

Humans add extra carbon dioxide to the atmosphere by:

- burning fossil fuels to generate electricity, heat homes, and fuel vehicles
- cutting down forests, or burning them, to make space for crops or cattle; this is called **deforestation**. As a result of deforestation there are fewer trees to remove carbon dioxide from the atmosphere.

**A** Describe two ways that humans add more carbon dioxide to the atmosphere than is removed.

## Link

You can learn more about radiation in P2 2.4: Energy transfer: particles

## Foul Fact

Carbon dioxide is not the only greenhouse gas. Methane is a greenhouse gas too. One cow burps 280 kg of methane into the air every year.

### What is the greenhouse effect?

If there were no carbon dioxide in the atmosphere, Earth would be too cold for life.

The Sun heats the Earth's surface. The warm Earth produces radiation. Some of this radiation goes back into space.

Carbon dioxide in the atmosphere absorbs some of the **radiation** produced by the Earth so it does not go back into space. This keeps the Earth warmer than it would be if the radiation went back into space. This is the **greenhouse effect**. Carbon dioxide is a **greenhouse gas**.

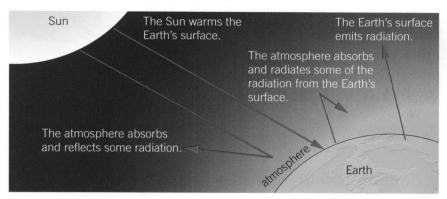

▲ The greenhouse effect. Not to scale.

Extra carbon dioxide has caused an increase in the global average air temperature. This is **global warming**.

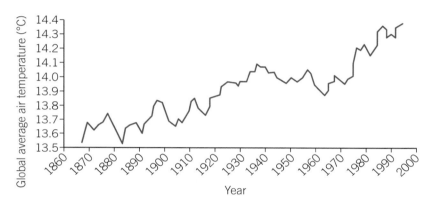

▲ The changing global average air temperature since 1800.

**B**. Describe the meaning of global warming.

## What are the impacts of climate change?

By 2100 scientists predict that the global average air temperature could increase by up to 5 °C. This increase is already causing problems. For example:

- melting polar ice is making sea levels rise, causing flooding on low-lying coasts
- more droughts, heavier rainfall, and heatwaves.

These changes may cause some species to become extinct. More frequent droughts will make it harder to grow enough food.

### Key Words

climate change, deforestation, radiation, greenhouse effect, greenhouse gas, global warming

### Global graphs

With a partner, discuss the two graphs on this spread. What do they show? How do their shapes compare? Then think about the data. What apparatus might scientists use to collect temperature data? How might they collect carbon dioxide concentration data that is fair to compare? Now write up your findings.

### Link

You can learn more about extinction in B2 3.7 Extinction

### Summary Questions

1 Choose one bold phrase to write next to each definition.

**global warming   climate change
greenhouse effect   deforestation**

Definitions
- gases in the atmosphere increasing the global average air temperature
- the increase in the global average air temperature
- cutting down or burning forests
- changes to long-term weather patterns

*(4 marks)*

2 Draw a labelled diagram to explain the greenhouse effect and global warming.

*(4 marks)*

3 Explain in detail the causes and effects of climate change.

*(6 marks)*

# 4.7 Recycling

## Learning objectives

After this topic you will be able to:

- explain how aluminium is recycled
- analyse the advantages and disadvantages of recycling.

▲ Lots of different materials can be recycled.

## What do you recycle?

You can recycle many types of material, including paper, metals, and plastics. But is it worth the effort?

## Where do resources come from?

The materials that make everything we use come originally from the Earth's crust, atmosphere, or oceans. These resources will not last forever.

The table shows an estimate of when the materials we get four elements from might run out.

| Element | Uses of element | When the source of the element will run out (estimated year) |
|---|---|---|
| phosphorus | making fertilisers | between 2060 and 2110 |
| gold | jewellery, electrical connections | 2040 |
| tin | food containers, solder | 2030 |
| aluminium | aeroplanes, overhead power cables, kitchen foil | 2500 |

**A** State where all the materials we use originally come from.

## What is recycling?

**Recycling** means collecting and processing materials that have been used so that the materials can be used again. Examples of recycling include:

- recycling paper to make new paper
- recycling plastic bottles to make fleeces
- recycling aluminium cans to make aluminium sheets to make more cans.

## How is aluminium recycled?

Alex puts out an aluminium can for recycling. A lorry takes it to a factory. At the factory, machines shred the can and remove its decoration.

A furnace melts the aluminium shreds. The liquid cools and freezes in a mould. This is an aluminium ingot.

▲ An aluminium ingot.

▲ If we continue to use tin as we do now, tin ore might run out by 2030.

The ingot is heated to 600 °C to soften it. Huge rollers roll it into thin sheets. The sheets are made into new cans.

**B** Describe what recycling is.

## Advantages and disadvantages

There are many advantages of recycling. For example:

- Recycling means resources will last longer.
- Recycling uses less energy than using new materials. Around 255 MJ of energy is needed to extract 1 kg of aluminium from its ore. Only 15 MJ is needed to make 1 kg of recycled aluminium.
- Recycling reduces waste and pollution. Extracting aluminium from its ore creates huge amounts of dangerous 'red mud' waste.

**C** List three advantages of recycling.

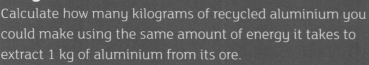

### Recycle and remake
Calculate how many kilograms of recycled aluminium you could make using the same amount of energy it takes to extract 1 kg of aluminium from its ore.

There are some disadvantages to recycling. Some people think that separating rubbish is a nuisance. The lorries that collect recycling use fuel and create pollution.

**D** State two disadvantages of recycling.

### Can you recycle everything?
Some materials are easier to recycle than others. Companies that recycle plastic waste need to separate different sorts of plastic from each other. This is often done by hand, and takes a long time.

◀ This girl is wearing a fleece made from recycled bottles.

### Bottled fleeces
A company states that it needs 25 two-litre plastic bottles to make one fleece. Estimate the number of bottles needed to make a fleece for everyone in your school.

## Link

You can learn more about metal ores in C2 3.5 Extracting metals

## Key Words

recycling

## Summary Questions

1 ⚗ Write down the two statements below that are examples of recycling.

- collecting old glass bottles, melting the glass, and making new bottles
- using a plastic bag from the supermarket to wrap your packed lunch in
- collecting and melting poly(propene) bottle tops, and using them to make poly(propene) rope

*(2 marks)*

2 ⚗⚗ Describe how aluminium is recycled.

*(4 marks)*

3 ⚗⚗⚗ Evaluate the advantages and disadvantages of recycling.

*(6 marks)*

## Key Points

- Everything we use comes from the Earth's crust, atmosphere, or oceans.
- The Earth consists of the crust, mantle, outer core, and inner core.
- The atmosphere is the mixture of gases around the Earth. It is mainly nitrogen and oxygen, with smaller amounts of argon and carbon dioxide.
- Sedimentary rocks form as a result of weathering, erosion, transport, deposition, and compaction or cementation.
- Sedimentary rocks have separate grains. They are porous. Most are soft.
- Igneous rocks forms when liquid rock freezes. They consist of crystals. They are non-porous, hard, and durable.
- Metamorphic rocks form when heating, high pressure, or both change existing rock. They consist of crystals. They are non-porous.
- The rock cycle shows how materials in rock are recycled over millions of years.
- Huge forces inside the Earth push rocks upwards to form mountains. This is called uplift.
- Carbon stores include the atmosphere, oceans, sedimentary rocks, fossil fuels, and organisms.
- The carbon cycle shows how carbon compounds enter and leave carbon stores.
- The concentration of carbon dioxide in the atmosphere is increasing because of deforestation and burning fossil fuels.
- Extra carbon dioxide in the atmosphere causes climate change.
- Recycling involves collecting and processing materials that have been used to make new objects.

## Maths challenge

**Ranking recycling**

Imagine that you work for a recycling company and that your job is to design the website. Your boss has given you the data below.

**Task**

Design the homepage of the website. Include a chart or graph of the information in the table. In your chart, show the changes in the percentages of waste recycled in each country between 2001 and 2010.

**Tips**

Provide information about where our resources come from and how we can recycle them.

| Country | % of waste recycled in 2001 | % of waste recycled in 2010 |
|---|---|---|
| Austria | 57.3 | 62.8 |
| Portugal | 15.5 | 18.8 |
| Iceland | 17.3 | 23.4 |
| Ireland | 11.3 | 35.7 |
| Norway | 44.3 | 42.1 |
| UK | 12.4 | 38.8 |

Data: European Environment Agency

## Key Words

crust, mantle, core, outer core, inner core, atmosphere, troposphere, sedimentary, igneous, metamorphic, porous, weathering, sediment, physical weathering, freeze-thaw, chemical weathering, biological weathering, erosion, transport, deposition, compaction, cementation, durable, magma, lava, rock cycle, uplift, respiration, combustion, photosynthesis, dissolving, carbon cycle, carbon store, climate change, deforestation, radiation, greenhouse effect, greenhouse gas, global warming, recycling.

# End-of-chapter questions

**1** Write the missing labels on the diagrams.

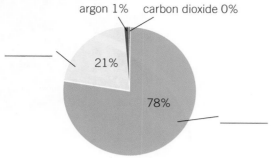

gases in the atmosphere of the Earth

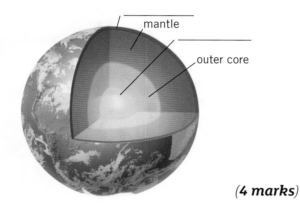

*(4 marks)*

**2** The diagram shows the carbon cycle.

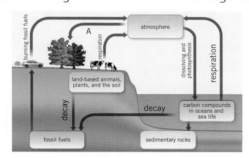

a Name **three** stores of carbon shown on the carbon cycle. *(3 marks)*

b Name the process represented by arrow A. *(1 mark)*

c Name **two** processes that add carbon dioxide to the atmosphere. *(2 marks)*

d Give **two** reasons to explain why the amount of carbon dioxide in the atmosphere has increased since the year 1800. *(2 marks)*

*(8 marks)*

**3** The diagram shows the rocks on a cliff face.

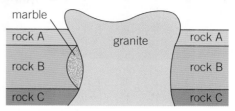

a Rocks A, B, and C are sedimentary rocks. Write the letter of the layer of sedimentary rock that formed first. *(1 mark)*

b Write the letter of the youngest sedimentary rock. *(1 mark)*

c Granite is an igneous rock. Explain how the granite in the diagram was formed. *(3 marks)*

d Suggest why the granite sticks up above rock A. *(2 marks)*

e Marble is a metamorphic rock. Suggest **two** reasons why it formed only in the position shown on the diagram. *(2 marks)*

*(9 marks)*

**4** Harry investigates the speed of cooling on crystal size. He places drops of liquid salol onto microscope slides. Once the salol freezes he observes the crystals.

Harry lists the variables in his investigation:

X temperature of microscope slide

Y number of drops of salol

Z size of crystals

a Name the independent variable. *(1 mark)*

b Name the dependent variable. *(1 mark)*

c Explain why Harry must control the other variable. *(1 mark)*

d Describe what Harry would observe if the crystals formed quickly and if they formed slowly. *(2 marks)*

*(5 marks)*

**5** Explain how the materials that rocks are made from are recycled in the rock cycle.

*(6 marks)*

# Physics ②

It's hard to imagine a world without electricity. In this unit you will discover how circuits work and how the electricity in your house is generated. You will learn why it is important to insulate a house and what you pay for when you pay your electricity bill. You will also find out how to use graphs to tell a story, and how forces explain gas and air pressure.

## You already know

- Lots of appliances run on electricity.
- You need a complete loop for an electric circuit to work.
- Some materials, like metals, are good conductors of electricity.
- You can change the volume of a buzzer or the brightness of a lamp by changing the number of cells.
- Switches can control lamps and buzzers.
- Forces can be transferred using gears, pulleys, levers, and springs.
- Light travels as a wave and can be reflected, refracted, or absorbed.
- Unbalanced forces can change the speed of an object.
- Magnets have two poles and attract or repel, depending which poles are facing each other.
- Some metals are magnetic. The Earth is a giant magnet.

**Q**

What happens to the brightness of a lamp if you use more cells?

# BIG Questions

- What happens in an electric circuit?
- What happens in a power station?
- Why are aircraft cabins pressurised?

Can you solve this Picture Puzzler?

The first letter of each of these images spells out a science word that you will come across in this unit.

## Picture Puzzler
# Close Up

*Can you tell what this zoomed-in picture is?*

***Clue:*** *You will need one to make an electromagnet.*

## Making connections

In **P2** you will learn about energy and motion.

In **C1** you will learn about the Earth and the properties of elements.

In **B2** you will learn about energy in food chains.

# 1.1 Charging up

## Learning objectives

After this topic you will be able to:

- explain how objects can become charged
- describe how charged objects interact
- describe what is meant by an electric field.

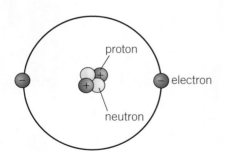

▲ You can bend a stream of water with static electricity.

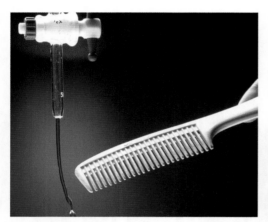

▲ An atom contains three types of particle.

## Link

You can learn more about atoms in C1 2.2 Atoms

Because of static electricity you can stick a balloon to a wall or bend a stream of water. Static electricity produces lightning. What is static electricity, and where does it come from?

## Attracting and repelling

There are two types of **electric charge**: **positive** charge (+) and **negative** charge (–). Charges **attract** or **repel** each other, like magnets do.

- **Positive** charges *repel* **positive** charges.
- **Negative** charges *repel* **negative** charges.
- **Positive** charges *attract* **negative** charges.

▲ Repelling.     ▲ Attracting.

> **Memory jogger**
> Remember it like this: 'Like charges repel, unlike charges attract.'

**A** State the two types of electric charge.

## Where does the charge come from?

Everything is made of particles called **atoms**.

Atoms in turn are made of three types of smaller particle:

- **protons**, which have a positive charge
- **electrons**, which have a negative charge
- **neutrons**, which have no charge.

Charge is a property of a particle or object, just like mass.

Atoms contain equal numbers of protons and electrons. Overall an atom has no charge: it is **neutral**.

When you rub a balloon on your jumper some electrons are transferred from the jumper to the balloon. The balloon now has an overall negative charge. Your jumper has an overall positive charge. They will attract.

before · after

▲ Rubbing a balloon transfers electrons from your jumper to the balloon.

The balloon is made of rubber. The electrons stay on the balloon.

**B** State the charge on an electron, a proton, and a neutron.

## Lightning

In a thundercloud air moves around, producing regions that have a positive or a negative charge. Electrons jump from one charged area to another and this produces a big **current**, which quickly heats the air. You see **lightning** and hear thunder.

## What is an electric field?

There is an **electric field** around a charge, just as there is a gravitational field around a mass. If you put a charged object in an electric field, a force will act on it.

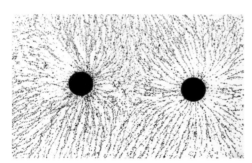

◄ Pepper grains line up in an electric field. This shows the electric field between two charges that are repelling.

### Atomic puzzle

Unscramble the words below and pair them up. Explain why you have chosen to pair them that way.

notpro   oneturn   iviespot   gianteve   laterun   centrelo

## Key Words

electric charge, positive, negative, attract, repel, atom, proton, electron, neutron, neutral, current, lightning, electric field

▲ Lightning can strike a plane.

## Fantastic Fact

Since you took your last breath lightning has struck the Earth 100 times. On average, airliners will get struck by lightning once a year.

## Summary Questions

**1** 🧪 Copy and complete the sentences below.

There are two types of electric charge: _____ charge and _____ charge. When you rub a polythene rod with a cloth you transfer _____ from the cloth to the rod. Two polythene rods would _____ if you brought them close together. A polythene rod would _____ a rod that had a positive charge.

*(5 marks)*

**2** 🧪🧪 A student rubs a balloon on his jumper and sticks it to the wall. Explain in terms of electrons why the balloon sticks to the wall.

*(3 marks)*

**3** 🧪🧪🧪 Compare a gravitational field and an electric field.

*(6 marks)*

# 1.2 Circuits and current

## Learning objectives

After this topic you will be able to:

- describe what is meant by current
- describe how to measure current.

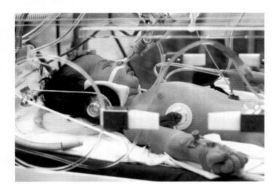

▲ A baby is kept warm using electric circuits.

▲ Divers need a torch to explore underwater caves.

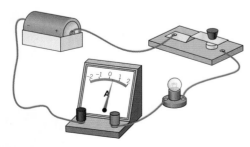

▲ You connect an ammeter in a circuit to measure current.

**Doctors use an incubator to help keep a premature baby alive. An electric current flows through a heater that keeps the baby warm.**

## What is current?

- When you complete a circuit, charged particles or charges move in the metal wires.
- The **current** is the amount of charge flowing per second.

When you press the **switch** on a torch the light comes on. The switch opens and closes a gap in the circuit. You need to close the gap and make a complete circuit for a current to flow.

When people talk about 'electricity' they usually mean 'electric current'.

**A** Describe what a current is.

You can measure the current with an **ammeter**.

- Current is measured in amperes or **amps**.
- The symbol for amps is A. For example, the current in the circuit opposite is 0.4 A.

**B** Name the meter that you use to measure current.

## Where do the charges come from?

The **cell** or **battery** pushes charges around the circuit. The battery does not produce the charges that move. They were already there in the wires. In a metal the charged particles that move are electrons.

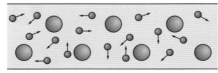

▲ The electrons are already in the wire.

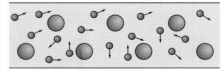

▲ The electrons move when you connect the battery.

## Using circuit symbols

You can build circuits using components such as batteries, bulbs, and **motors**. It would take a long time to draw a picture of each circuit so you can use circuit symbols instead.

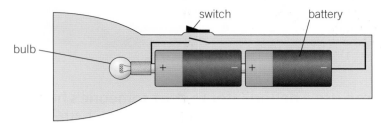

▲ This is a picture of a torch...

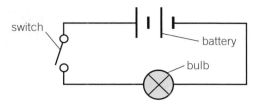

▲ ...and this is the circuit diagram.

In the torch diagram there are two cells. Cells used together like this are called a battery. People often use the word 'battery' for a single cell, but in physics we call it a cell.

You must make sure that you connect cells the right way round or they will not work.

## Modelling electric circuits – part 1

You cannot see what happens in the wires when a current flows. Scientists use models such as the rope model to show what is happening. One person pulls the rope, and another person grips the rope lightly. The rope moves around. In this model:

- The rope represents the charges in the circuit.
- The amount of rope moving past a point per second is the current.

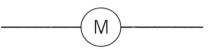

▲ Circuit symbols make it simpler to draw circuits.

## Key Words

current, switch, ammeter, amps, cell, battery, motor

## Summary Questions

**1** 🧪 Copy and complete the sentences below.

Current is the amount of _____ flowing per _____. In a metal wire charged particles called _____ move when you connect a battery. You can use a meter called an _____ to measure current. Current is measured in _____, which has the symbol _____.

*(6 marks)*

**2** 🧪🧪

**a** Draw a circuit diagram to show how you could use a switch to turn a battery-powered motor on and off. *(2 marks)*

**b** Describe what happens in the wires when you close the switch. *(1 mark)*

**3** 🧪🧪🧪 Explain how you would use equipment and models to teach a primary-school student that the charges do not originate in the battery.

*(6 marks)*

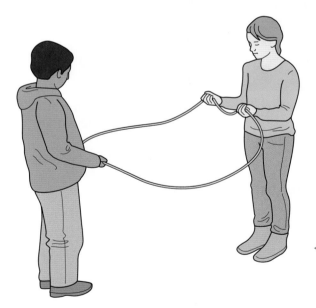

◀ A rope model can help you to understand circuits.

## Confusing words?

For each of these words write one sentence using the word with its correct scientific meaning. Write a second sentence where it has a different, everyday meaning.

- charge
- current
- cell

## Learning objectives

After this topic you will be able to:

● describe what is meant by potential difference

● describe how to measure potential difference

● describe what is meant by the rating of a battery or bulb.

A doctor can use a defibrillator to start someone's heart if it stops. Defibrillators produce a large potential difference (sometimes called a voltage), much bigger than a battery can produce.

### What is potential difference?

The cell or battery provides the push to make charges move. The push is called a **potential difference**, or p.d. for short.

● The potential difference across a cell tells you about the size of the force on the charges.

● The potential difference also tells you how much energy can be transferred to the components in the circuit by the charges.

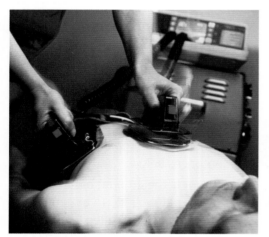

▲ You can save someone's life with a big potential difference.

▲ Batteries come in different shapes and sizes.

▲ In a potato cell a chemical reaction between the metals and the potato produces a potential difference.

### Measuring potential difference

You measure potential difference using a **voltmeter**.

● Potential difference is measured in **volts**.

● The symbol for volts is V. For example, the potential difference across the cell opposite is 6 V.

You can measure the potential difference of a cell by connecting a voltmeter across it. This is also called the **rating**.

---

**A** Name the meter that you use to measure potential difference.

---

▲ You connect a voltmeter either side of the component.

You can measure the potential difference across a component in a circuit using a voltmeter.

**B** State the unit of potential difference.

Circuit components such as bulbs also have a rating. The bulb in the circuit on the opposite page has a rating of 6 V. It is designed to work at a potential difference of 6 V, and no higher.

### 'Potential difference' or 'voltage'?

Sometimes people talk about the '**voltage**' of a cell or battery. It is better to talk about potential difference. You can think of a circuit as being a bit like this:

**Foul Fact**

Mary Shelley wrote *Frankenstein* after finding out that Louis Galvani made dead frogs' legs move using a battery in 1818.

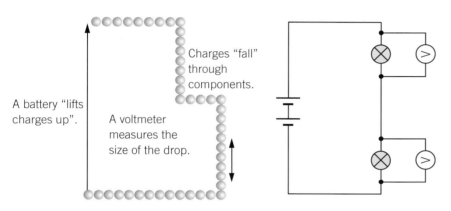

Charges "fall" through components.

A battery "lifts charges up".

A voltmeter measures the size of the drop.

▲ You can think of the battery 'lifting' up the charges. In the circuit above the voltmeters would read the same.

### Modelling electric circuits – part 2

You can use the rope model when you are thinking about potential difference. In the rope model:

- The person pulling the rope is like the battery.
- A bigger potential difference across the cell would come from the 'battery' person pulling harder.

**Are bigger batteries better?**

A student wants to collect some data about the size of batteries and the potential difference across each one. Write a plan that they could use to collect the data.

## Key Words

potential difference, voltmeter, volts, rating, voltage

## Summary Questions

1 Copy and complete the sentences below.

The potential difference of a cell or battery tells you the size of the _____, and how much _____ can be transferred by the charges. You measure potential difference or p.d. with a _____. The _____ of a battery tells you the p.d across it, and the _____ on a bulb tells you the p.d. at which it is designed to work.

*(5 marks)*

2 A student connects a circuit with a cell, an ammeter, and a buzzer and listens to the buzzer. She adds another cell.

a Describe and explain what happens to the current. *(2 marks)*

b Describe and explain what happens if she turns one of the cells around. *(2 marks)*

3 A lot of people get current and potential difference (or voltage) mixed up. Use a model to explain the difference in detail.

*(6 marks)*

# 1.4 Series and parallel

## Learning objectives

After this topic you will be able to:

- describe the difference between series and parallel circuits
- describe how current and potential difference vary in series and parallel circuits.

▲ Modern Christmas lights stay on if one bulb blows.

**Christmas lights make a great display. In old sets of lights, if one of the bulbs broke they would all go out.**

## Two types of circuit

The old type of Christmas lights were connected in **series**. All the bulbs formed one loop, including the battery and the switch.

There is another type of circuit called a **parallel** circuit. In a parallel circuit there is more than one loop or branch. Parallel circuits are sometimes called 'branching circuits'.

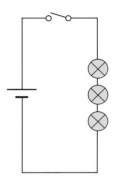

▲ In a series circuit there is only one loop.

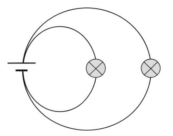

▲ This is a parallel circuit because there is more than one loop...

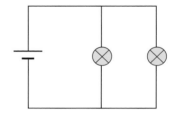

▲ ...which you can also draw like this.

Parallel circuits are very useful because if one bulb breaks, the other lights stay on. You can control each lamp separately in a parallel circuit by adding a switch to each branch. Each bulb is independent of the others.

**A** State two differences between series and parallel circuits.

## What happens to the current?

### Series circuits

In the circuit opposite, the ammeters $A_1$, $A_2$, and $A_3$ all show the same reading. In a series circuit the current is the same everywhere.

If you add components to a series circuit the current will get smaller.

### Parallel circuits

A parallel circuit has more than one loop. In the circuit at the top of the next page, the current in each branch is the same. The ammeters $A_2$ and $A_3$ show the same reading.

▲ In a series circuit, the reading on all the ammeters is the same.

The ammeters $A_1$ and $A_4$ measure the total current. The currents in all the branches of a parallel circuit add together to make the total current. Here the total current is double the current in each branch.

If you add another branch to a parallel circuit the current in the other branches stays the same but the total current increases.

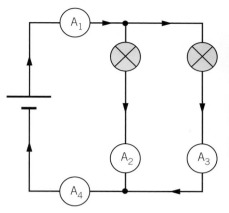

▲ In a parallel circuit, the current in all the branches adds to the total current.

**B** State what happens to the total current as you add more branches in a parallel circuit.

## Modelling circuits – part 3

You can use the rope model when you are thinking about different types of circuit. In the rope model:

### Series circuits
- The rope moves at the same speed everywhere.
- As more people hold the rope, the rope moves more slowly.

### Parallel circuits
- There are more loops of rope.
- All the loops are driven by the same 'battery' person.

## What happens to the potential difference?

### Series circuits
The potential difference across each component *adds up to the* potential difference across the battery.

### Parallel circuits
The potential difference across each component *is the same as* the potential difference across the battery.

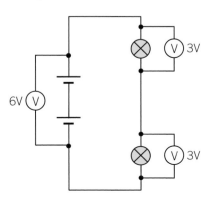

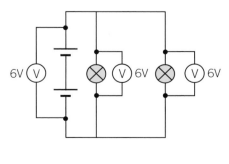

### Current issues
In a circuit with a single cell and a single bulb, the current is 0.2 A. Calculate the current if you add another bulb in series with the first bulb. Explain your answer.

**Key Words**

series, parallel

### Fantastic Fact
A family in Australia holds the world record for Christmas tree lights. Their display contained over 330 000 separate lights.

## Summary Questions

**1** Copy the sentences below, choosing the correct **bold** words.

A series circuit has **more than one/one** loop. A parallel circuit has **more than one/one** loop. If a bulb in a **parallel/series** circuit breaks the rest of the bulbs stay on. If a bulb in a **parallel/series** circuit breaks the rest of the bulbs go out.

*(4 marks)*

**2** State what happens to the total current as you add more bulbs in a parallel circuit.

*(1 mark)*

**3** Compare the readings on ammeters and voltmeters when you connect them in series and parallel circuits.

*(6 marks)*

# 1.5 Resistance

## Learning objectives

After this topic you will be able to:

- describe what is meant by resistance
- calculate the resistance of a component and of a circuit
- describe the difference between conductors and insulators in terms of resistance.

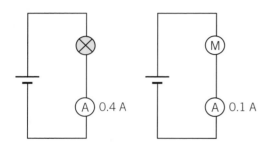

▲ The currents in these circuits are different, even though the cells are the same.

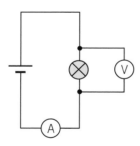

▲ You can use an ammeter and a voltmeter to find the resistance of a lamp.

### What's the resistance?

A bulb in a circuit has a current of 0.6 A through it and a potential difference of 12 V across it. Calculate the resistance of the bulb.

**The current in the wires connected to a television is much smaller than the current in the wires to a microwave. The reason for this is to do with resistance.**

◀ Electrical devices have different currents through them.

## Different components, different current

Components do different jobs in an electric circuit.

Each circuit component has a different **resistance**. This tells you how easy or difficult it is for the charges to pass through the component. Resistance is measured in **ohms**, which has the symbol $\Omega$. $\Omega$ is a letter from the Greek alphabet.

The current depends on the push of the battery and also the resistance of the component. You can calculate the current using this equation:

$$\text{current (A)} = \frac{\text{potential difference (V)}}{\text{resistance } (\Omega)}$$

You can use the idea of resistance to explain why the current decreases as you add more bulbs in a series circuit. Adding more bulbs increases the resistance, so the current is less.

**A** State what is meant by resistance.

## Measuring resistance

You can use an equation to calculate the resistance of a component.

Here is the equation to calculate resistance:

$$\text{resistance } (\Omega) = \frac{\text{potential difference (V)}}{\text{current (A)}}$$

**B** State the unit of resistance.

For example, if you found that the current through a bulb was 0.2 A when the voltage across it was 6 V, you could work out the resistance:

$$\text{resistance} = \frac{\text{potential difference}}{\text{current}}$$
$$= \frac{6\text{ V}}{0.2\text{ A}}$$
$$= 30\ \Omega$$

## What happens inside a wire?

You can use a model with marbles to show what happens inside a wire when a current flows. The charges that move in a wire are electrons.

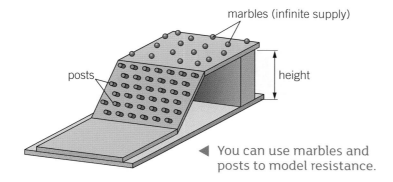

marbles (infinite supply)

posts

height

◀ You can use marbles and posts to model resistance.

The marbles behave like electrons. As they fall down the slope they collide with the posts. Inside a wire the moving electrons collide with the atoms of the wire. They transfer energy, and the wire gets hot.

## Conductors and insulators

Metals are good **conductors**. They have a very low resistance because they contain lots of electrons that can move. The resistance of a 10-m piece of copper wire is about 0.2 $\Omega$.

Other materials such as plastics do not have many electrons that are free to move. The resistance of plastic objects is very high, over a thousand million million ohms. The air is usually an **insulator** but it can conduct if the potential difference is big enough. Insulators have a high resistance.

◀ A spark happens when the air conducts electricity.

### Fantastic Fact

Many people think that Thomas Edison invented the lightbulb. What he invented was the first lightbulb with a filament that didn't burn out when a current flowed in it.

## Key Words

resistance, ohms, conductor, insulator

## Summary Questions

1  Copy and complete the sentences below.

The current in a circuit depends on the _____ and the _____ . The current will be bigger if the _____ is smaller. Inside a metal wire _____ collide with atoms and transfer _____ to them. _____ are materials that contain lots of charges that are free to move. _____ contain fewer charges that can move.

*(7 marks)*

2  In the circuit diagrams on the opposite page the cell has a potential difference of 3 V. Calculate the resistance of the motor and the lamp.

*(4 marks)*

3  Compare the resistance of conductors and insulators.

*(6 marks)*

## Learning objectives

After this topic you will be able to:

● describe how magnets interact
● describe how to represent magnetic fields
● describe the Earth's magnetic field.

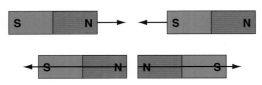

▲ Magnets can attract or repel other magnets.

### Memory jogger
Remember it like this: 'Like poles repel, unlike poles attract.'

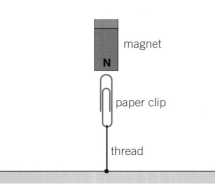

magnet

N

paper clip

thread

▲ There is a force on a steel paper clip in a magnetic field.

## Fantastic Fact

The Earth's magnetic field keeps flipping. About 500 000 years ago the magnetic north pole was actually the south pole.

**With a magnet you can make something move without even touching it.**

◀ Ferrofluid is a special liquid that is magnetic.

## Attracting and repelling

A **magnet** has a **north pole** and a **south pole**.

● **North poles** *repel* **north poles**.
● **South poles** *repel* **south poles**.
● **North poles** *attract* **south poles**.

**A** Name the two poles of a magnet.

Only certain materials are attracted to a magnet. They are called **magnetic materials**. Iron is a magnetic material, and so is steel because steel contains iron. Cobalt and nickel are also magnetic.

◀ Information on a credit card is stored in a magnetic strip.

## What is a magnetic field?

In an electric field there is a force on a charge. In a **magnetic field** there is a force on a magnet or a magnetic material.

You can find out the shape of a magnetic field in two ways:

- using plotting compasses
- using iron filings

small compasses

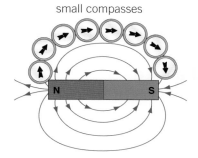

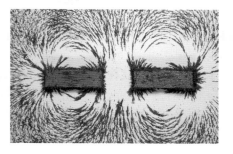

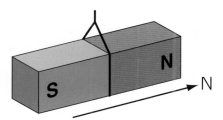

▲ A magnet lines up with the Earth's magnetic field.

The needle of a compass lines up with the magnetic field. So do the iron filings. You can draw lines called **magnetic field lines** to represent the field. The lines go from the north pole to the south pole of the magnet, with arrows pointing from the north to the south pole.

- If the magnetic field lines are closer together this shows that the magnetic field is stronger.
- A permanent magnet is a magnet that has its own magnetic field.

**B** State two ways that you can find out the shape of a magnetic field.

## The Earth's magnetic field

If you hang a magnet up it will line up in a direction pointing north to south. This is because it is in the magnetic field of the Earth.

The Earth behaves as if there is a huge bar magnet inside it. There is not really a bar magnet, and physicists are not sure what produces the Earth's magnetic field.

◄ The Earth's magnetic field is the same as that of a big bar magnet with the south pole at the top of the planet.

### How strong?

A student wants to measure the strength of different types of magnet by holding up a paperclip as shown in the diagram on the opposite page. Draw a table for their results.

## Summary Questions

**1** 🧪 Copy and complete the sentences below.

Magnets have a _____ pole and a _____ pole. Two poles that are the same will _____ and two poles that are different will _____ . The needle of a _____ lines up in the _____ _____ of a magnet.

*(6 marks)*

**2** 🧪🧪 Explain why the needle of a compass always points in the same direction wherever you point it in a room.

*(2 marks)*

**3** 🧪🧪🧪 Design a game of skill that uses magnets. Write a list of instructions for how to play the game using the key words on this page, and describe the scoring system.

*(6 marks)*

### Key Words

magnet, north pole, south pole, magnetic material, magnetic field, magnetic field line

## Learning objectives

After this topic you will be able to:

- describe how to make an electromagnet
- describe how to change the strength of an electromagnet.

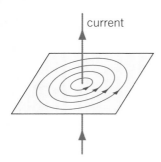

▲ The magnetic field around a wire.

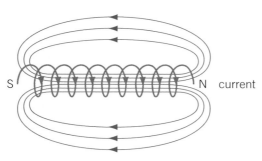

▲ The magnetic field around a coil of wire.

Doctors in hospitals have used electromagnets to remove steel splinters from a patient's eye.

**Permanent magnets are fun, but you can't turn them off.**

## The magnetic field around a wire

A wire with an electric current flowing through it has a magnetic field around it. You can investigate the field with a plotting compass. The field lines are circles.

## Making an electromagnet

You can make a circular loop of wire and pass a current through it. The magnetic field lines at the centre of the loop are straight.

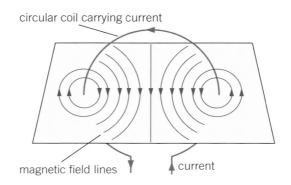

◄ The magnetic field around a loop of wire.

The magnetic field around a single loop isn't very strong. If you put lots of loops together to make a coil the field is much stronger. This is an **electromagnet**. The shape of the magnetic field is just like the shape of the magnetic field around a bar magnet.

You can turn an electromagnet on and off by turning the current on and off. The magnetic field is only produced when the current is flowing in the wire.

## Using a core

Electromagnets usually have a magnetic material in the centre of the coil, called a **core.** This makes the electromagnet much stronger. Most cores are made of iron. Iron is easy to **magnetise** but loses its magnetism easily.

Steel is hard to magnetise but keeps its magnetism. If you had a steel core in an electromagnet you could not turn the electromagnet off, because the steel would still be magnetic.

**A** State the type of material you can use for the core of an electromagnet.

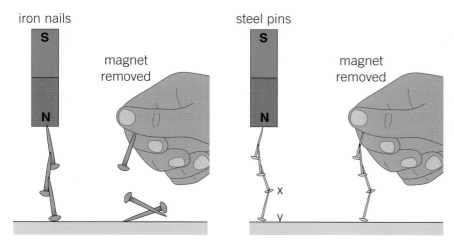

iron nails

steel pins

magnet removed

magnet removed

▲ Steel stays magnetic when you remove the magnet.

## How do I make an electromagnet stronger?

The strength of an electromagnet depends on:

- the number of turns, or loops, on the coil. More turns of wire will make a stronger electromagnet.
- the current flowing in the wire. More current flowing in the wire will make a stronger electromagnet.
- the type of core. Using a magnetic material in the core will make a stronger electromagnet.

**B** State three things that affect the strength of an electromagnet.

## Permanent magnet or electromagnet?

Permanent magnets and electromagnets both have their uses. There are two main differences between permanent magnets and electromagnets.

- You can turn an electromagnet on and off.
- You can make electromagnets that are much stronger than permanent magnets.

## Fantastic Fact

The strongest magnet is an electromagnet that produces a magnetic field 10 million times stronger than the Earth's magnetic field.

## Key Words

electromagnet, core, magnetise

▲ The strength of an electromagnet depends on the number of turns on the coil, the current, and the core.

## Summary Questions

**1** Copy and complete the sentences below.

When a _____ flows in a wire it produces a _____ _____ around it. You can make an electromagnet using a _____ of wire with a _____ flowing in it. The shape of the _____ _____ around an electromagnet is the same as that around a bar magnet.

*(5 marks)*

**2** Describe how to use a nail, a piece of wire, crocodile clips, leads, and a battery to make an electromagnet.

*(2 marks)*

**3** Use the ideas on these pages to explain in detail why the number of coils, the current, and the type of core affect the strength of an electromagnet.

*(6 marks)*

135

# 1.8 Using electromagnets

## Learning objectives

After this topic you will be able to:

- describe some uses of electromagnets
- describe how a simple motor works.

▲ You can travel at over 200 mph on a maglev train.

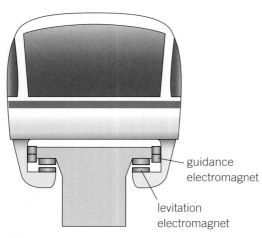

▲ Electromagnets lift a maglev train and push it forward.

**Have you ever travelled on a high-speed train? Trains that use electromagnets can go faster than a Formula 1 car. They don't have an engine. How do they work?**

## Lifting off

You have learned that magnets can repel each other. Engineers use this fact to build trains that use magnetic levitation. This means the train is lifted up using magnets.

Very powerful electromagnets on the track repel magnets on the train. There is no friction between the train and the track. This means the train can travel much faster than normal trains.

That's not all. The train is pushed forward by other electromagnets called guidance electromagnets. It does not need an engine.

**A** State the type of magnet used to levitate a train.

## Switching on

An X-ray machine can be very dangerous. It uses a very high potential difference. The radiographer using the machine uses a **relay** to turn the machine on, instead of a normal on/off switch.

### What is a relay?

A relay uses a small current in one circuit to operate a switch in another circuit. When the switch is closed the coil becomes an electromagnet. The two pieces of iron inside are magnetised. They attract each other and turn on the X-ray machine.

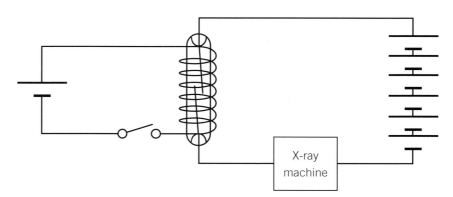

▲ A small current can turn on a much bigger current in a separate circuit.

## How do you start a car?

A car battery produces a large current that can be very dangerous. The driver switches on the circuit in the battery to start the car. They can do this safely using an electromagnet switch.

## How do you lift a car?

You can use an electromagnet to move large pieces of iron or steel in a factory, or to move cars in a scrap yard.

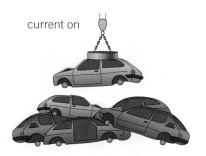

current on    current off

▲ Electromagnets can lift cars.

## How do you sort metal?

You can use an electromagnet to sort out scrap metal. Iron and steel will be attracted to the electromagnet. Other metals, such as aluminium, will not.

**B,** State one use of an electromagnet in a scrap yard.

## Moving and spinning

The turntable in a microwave needs to turn so that your food cooks evenly. The **motor** that makes it move is just one of many motors in your home. You can make a simple motor using two magnets and a coil of wire.

When you connect the coil to a battery a current flows in the coil. The coil becomes an electromagnet. The forces between the coil and the permanent magnet make the coil spin.

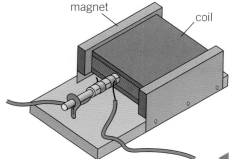

magnet    coil

◄ A simple motor.

## Fantastic Fact

There are more than 50 electric motors in the average family home.

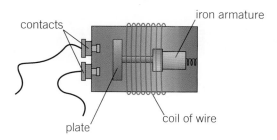

contacts    iron armature

plate    coil of wire

▲ A starter motor uses an electromagnetic switch.

### Recycle those cans!

Write a letter to the manager of your school's kitchen explaining how they could use electromagnets to sort the soft drinks cans for recycling.

## Summary Questions

**1** Copy and complete the sentences below.

Electromagnets can be used to levitate _____ and push them forward. A _____ acts like a switch to turn on circuits that can be dangerous. When a _____ flows in a coil of wire between two magnets then the coil _____. This is how an electric _____ works.

*(5 marks)*

**2** State the parts of an electric motor and how a motor works.

*(4 marks)*

**3** Design a system that uses electromagnets to hold open fire doors. The fire doors should close automatically when the fire alarm button is pressed. Explain in detail how your system works.

*(6 marks)*

## Key Points

- Objects can be charged positively or negatively by transferring electrons.
- Like charges repel and unlike charges attract.
- An electric field is a region where there is a force on charged particles or materials.
- Electric current is the amount of charge flowing per second. You measure current in amps (A) using an ammeter.
- The potential difference of a cell tells you the size of the push on the charges and how much energy can be transferred by them.
- You measure potential difference in volts (V) using a voltmeter. The rating of a cell or battery tells you the potential difference at which it operates.
- Series circuits contain only one loop, and the current is the same everywhere. Parallel circuits have branches and the currents in all the branches add up to make the total current.
- A component with a high resistance has a small current through it. Resistance is measured in ohms (Ω). You calculate the resistance using the potential difference across a component and the current through it. Insulators have a very high resistance and conductors have a very low resistance.
- Magnets have a north pole and a south pole. Like poles repel and unlike poles attract.
- Magnetic materials feel a force in the region around a magnet called a magnetic field. Magnetic field lines show the pattern of the magnetic field.
- A current flowing in a coil of wire wrapped around a magnetic material is an electromagnet. It behaves like a bar magnet but you can turn it on and off.
- Electromagnets are used in maglev trains, hospitals, and cars.

## Maths challenge

**Mixed-up electromagnets**

A student investigated the strength of electromagnets by seeing how many paperclips they will pick up. Here is his results table:

| Number of coils | Potential difference | Type of core | Type of wire | Number of paperclips |
|---|---|---|---|---|
| 10 | 1.5 V | iron | copper | 4 |
| 10 | 3.0 V | iron | copper | 8 |
| 10 | 4.5 V | iron | copper | 12 |
| 10 | 6.0 V | iron | copper | 16 |
| 40 | 3.0 V | iron | copper | 20 |
| 30 | 3.0 V | iron | copper | 16 |
| 20 | 3.0 V | iron | copper | 12 |
| 10 | 3.0 V | steel | copper | 10 |
| 10 | 3.0 V | aluminium | copper | 0 |

Use the data to:
- make separate tables for each of the variables that he changed
- plot an appropriate graph for each variable.

## Key Words

electric charge, positive, negative, attract, repel, atom, proton, electron, neutron, neutral, current, lightning, electric field, switch, ammeter, amps, cell, battery, motor, potential difference, voltmeter, volts, rating, voltage, series, parallel, resistance, ohms, conductor, insulator, magnet, north pole, south pole, magnetic material, magnetic field, magnetic field lines, electromagnet, core, magnetise, relay, motor

# End-of-chapter questions

**1** 🧪 Look at circuits A, B, and C.

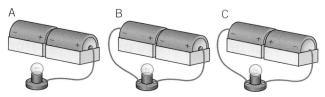

**a** State the letter of the circuit or circuits in which the bulb is lit. *(1 mark)*

**b** Describe what you could do to make the bulb light in the other circuit or circuits. *(2 marks)*

*(3 marks)*

**2** 🧪

**a** Draw a diagram to show the magnetic field around a bar magnet. *(2 marks)*

**b** Describe what would happen to the magnets in the diagrams A and B below. *(2 marks)*

**c** State one difference between a permanent magnet and an electromagnet. *(1 marks)*

*(5 marks)*

**3** 🧪🧪 Describe how a simple motor works.

*(2 marks)*

**4** 🧪🧪

**a** Draw a circuit diagram for the circuit below. *(2 marks)*

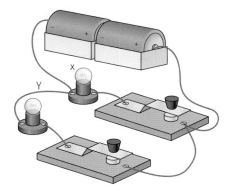

**b** State whether this is a series or a parallel circuit. *(1 mark)*

**c** Copy and complete the table to show what would happen when you press the switches. *(3 marks)*

| Switches closed | Bulbs lit |
|---|---|
| X | |
| Y | |
| X and Y | |

**d** Describe how you could measure the current flowing in each bulb. *(2 marks)*

*(8 marks)*

**5** 🧪🧪 A student connects one bulb, an ammeter, and a cell in series. He connects a voltmeter across the bulb.

**a** Draw a circuit diagram for this circuit. *(2 marks)*

The current through the bulb is 0.4 A. The potential difference across the bulb is 3 V.

**b** Explain what is meant by potential difference. *(1 mark)*

The bulb has a rating of 6 V.

**c** State what is meant by the rating of a lamp. *(1 mark)*

**d** Calculate the resistance of the lamp. *(2 marks)*

*(6 marks)*

**6** 🧪🧪 The student adds another lamp in series to the circuit above.

**a** Describe and explain what happens to the reading on the ammeter. *(2 marks)*

**b** Describe and explain what happens to the reading on the voltmeter. *(2 marks)*

*(4 marks)*

**7** 🧪🧪🧪 A student rubs a rod with a cloth and uses the rod to pick up small pieces of paper. Explain in detail how this happens.

*(6 marks)*

# 2.1 Food and fuels

## Learning objectives

After this topic you will be able to:

- compare the energy values of foods and fuels
- compare the energy in foods and fuels with the energy needed for different activities.

▲ You need the energy stored in food.

| Typical values | 100g contains | 45g serving contains |
|---|---|---|
| | | ...handful of fruit will |
| **Energy** | 1570kJ | 710kJ |
| | 375kcal | 170kcal |
| Protein | 10.3g | 4.6g |
| Carbohydrate | 73.8g | 33.2g |
| of which sugars | 15.0g | 6.8g |
| Fat | 2.0g | 0.9g |
| of which saturates | 0.3g | 0.1g |
| Fibre‡‡ | 8.2g | 3.7g |
| Sodium | 0.2g | 0.1g |
| Salt equivalent | 0.6g | 0.3g |
| ‡‡Fibre has been determined by AOAC | | |
| For guideline daily | | |

▲ You can see the energy associated with food on the food label.

### Link

You can learn more about nutrition in B2 1.3 Unhealthy diet

### Key Words

energy, joule, kilojoule

**What did you have for breakfast? You need energy from food to do many things, including walking, breathing, and even reading this! Your brain needs energy to work.**

### How much energy?

Different foods are stores of different amounts of **energy**. Energy is measured in **joules** (J). One joule is a very small amount of energy, so we often use **kilojoules** (kJ). 1 kJ = 1000 J.

**A** State the unit of energy.

### How much energy in food?

Food labels tell you how much energy is in the store associated with food.

The amount of energy stored in different foods varies greatly.

| Food | Energy (kJ) per 100 g |
|---|---|
| apple | 200 |
| banana | 340 |
| peas | 250 |
| chips | 1000 |
| cooked beef | 1000 |
| chocolate | 1500 |

When you choose which foods to eat you need to consider the nutritional value of the food as well as the energy that is in the store.

### How much energy in fuels?

▲ The energy associated with this lump of coal is about 3000 kJ...

▲ ... which is the same amount as two bars of chocolate.

Coal and chocolate are both stores of energy. Oil, wood, and other fuels are stores too. You need oxygen to burn both food and fuels. People use the energy in fuels to heat their house or cook their food. Electrical appliances need an electric current to work. When you burn fuel in a power station it produces a current that makes your microwave or hair straighteners work.

**B** Name three fuels.

## How much energy do you need each day?

You need different amounts of energy depending on what you do each day.

▲ Sleeping: 300 kJ per hour.

▲ Working: 600 kJ per hour.

▲ Playing: 3600 kJ per hour.

▲ Relaxing: 360 kJ per hour.

There is an energy cost to everything that you do. You need energy to keep your body warm, to breathe, move, and talk. While you are growing you need energy for your bones, muscles, and brain to grow.

| Activity | Energy (kJ) for each minute of activity |
|---|---|
| sitting | 6 |
| standing | 7 |
| washing, dressing | 15 |
| walking slowly | 13 |
| cycling | 25 |
| running | 60 |
| swimming | 73 |

Sportsmen need a lot more energy than the average person. People who walk to the North or South Pole need even more energy because they need extra energy to keep warm.

## Energy balance

An adult should just take in the energy they need for the activities that they do. If you take in more energy than you need your body stores it as fat to use in the future.

### How far?

On average people can walk about 90 metres per minute, and run about 150 metres per minute.

Calculate how far you would need to run to burn off the energy in 50 g of chocolate.

### Fantastic Fact

An adult man needs about 12 000 kJ per day. The same man walking to the North Pole would need about 27 000 kJ per day.

### Summary Questions

**1** ⚗ Copy and complete the sentences below.

Energy is stored in _____ and _____. The amount of energy stored is measured in _____. When you are asleep your body needs energy for keeping warm and _____. Children need more energy than adults to grow bigger _____ and _____.

*(6 marks)*

**2** ⚗⚗ Calculate the number of minutes you would need to cycle for to work off 200 g of chips.

*(2 marks)*

**3** ⚗⚗⚗ Use the information above to calculate the approximate energy cost of the activities that you do in one day. Compare the amount of fruit and vegetables with the amount of chips and chocolate that you would need to eat to give you this energy.

*(6 marks)*

# 2.2 Energy adds up

## Learning objectives

After this topic you will be able to:

- describe energy before and after a change
- explain what brings about changes in energy.

◀ Energy is a bit like money.

Do you have some money in your pocket? If you know how much you left home with, and you didn't spend any on the way, then you know how much you have now.

## Conservation of energy

Energy cannot just disappear, and you cannot end up with more than you had at the start. Energy cannot be created or destroyed, only transferred. This is the **law of conservation of energy**.

**A** State the law of conservation of energy.

## Energy stores

There is energy associated with food and fuels (and oxygen). You can think of that energy as being in a **chemical store**. Energy is transferred from the store when you burn the fuel or respire. There are other types of **energy store**:

| Energy to do with... | Type of store |
|---|---|
| food, fuels, batteries | chemical |
| hot objects | **thermal** |
| moving objects | **kinetic** |
| position in a gravitational field | **gravitational potential** |
| changing shape, stretching, or squashing | **elastic** |

## Before and after

A camping stove burns gas, which is a fuel.

| | Before: | After: |
|---|---|---|
| What we have | unburnt fuel, more oxygen cold soup | less fuel, more carbon dioxide and water hot soup (and slightly hotter air) |
| Thinking about energy | more energy in the chemical store less energy in the thermal store | less energy in the chemical store more energy in the thermal store |

If you could measure the energy in the chemical and thermal stores you would see that:

total energy before = total energy after

## Fantastic Fact

If all the energy in the food that you eat was converted to energy in a thermal store you would glow like a light bulb.

▲ Camping gas is a chemical store.

## Transferring energy

Electric current, light, and sound are ways of transferring energy between stores. After you use your phone, there is less energy in the chemical store and more energy in the thermal store of the surroundings.

**B** State three ways that energy is transferred between stores.

## Wasting energy, saving energy

In a car you want the burning fuel to transfer energy to the store that you want (the kinetic store of the car), not to other stores that you don't want (such as a thermal store). You want the car to move, not heat up.

In many situations energy is transferred to the thermal store of the surroundings. Scientists say that the energy is **dissipated**.

▲ The energy in the thermal store is dissipated.

When we talk about 'saving energy', what we really mean is saving fuel. Energy is always conserved, but if we can transfer more of it to the useful store, we save fuel.

## *Why* do things happen?

It is tempting to say that things happen *because* they have energy. Energy tells you what changes are possible, but it does not explain *why* things happen. Forces, not energy, explain why things move. For example, you can put fuel in a car but that does not make the car move. The force provided by the engine makes the car move.

### Remember those stores!
Use the first letter of each of the stores in the table above to write a mnemonic to help you to remember them.

▲ The ski-lift increases the energy in the gravitational potential store.

### Key Words

law of conservation of energy, chemical store, energy store, thermal, kinetic, gravitational potential, elastic, dissipated

### Summary Questions

**1** Copy and complete the sentences below, choosing the correct bold words.

The law of conservation of energy says that energy cannot be **created/ dissipated** or **destroyed/ transferred**. When you burn coal you transfer energy from a **chemical/ thermal** store to a **chemical/thermal** store. You **can/cannot** explain why things happen using energy.

*(5 marks)*

**2**

**a** Describe where and how energy is stored in a torch. *(2 marks)*

**b** Explain what happens to the energy stored in the torch when it is switched on. *(2 marks)*

**3** Use the ideas on these two pages to explain in detail what energy transfers happen when you cook sausages on a camp fire burning wood.

*(6 marks)*

## Learning objectives

After this topic you will be able to:

- state the difference between energy and temperature
- describe what happens when you heat up solids, liquids, and gases
- explain what is meant by equilibrium.

◀ Formula 1 teams heat up their tyres.

◀ Some thermometers use sensors to measure temperature.

▲ Sparks are hot, but they do not have much energy in the thermal store.

**Hot tyres grip the road much better than cold tyres. Formula 1 drivers heat up their tyres.**

### What is temperature?

Something that is hotter than your skin will feel hot, and something that is colder than your skin will feel cold. You cannot measure **temperature** with your skin.

You use a **thermometer** to measure temperature. Some thermometers have a liquid inside a very thin glass tube that expands when it is heated. Other thermometers are digital.

We measure temperature in degrees Celsius (°C).

**A** State the unit of temperature and the unit of energy.

### What's the difference?

There is a difference between energy and temperature. You can have a swimming pool and a beaker of water at exactly the same temperature.

Even though they are at the same temperature the swimming pool represents a much bigger thermal store of energy than the beaker of water.

▲ There is a lot of energy in the thermal store of a heated swimming pool.

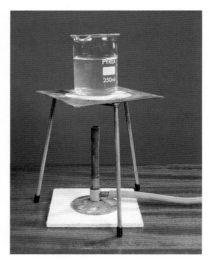

▲ There is less energy in the thermal store of a beaker of water at the same temperature than in the swimming pool's thermal store.

## What happens when you heat things up?

Heating changes the movement of particles. If you heat a solid the particles vibrate more. If you heat a liquid or a gas the particles move faster and vibrate more.

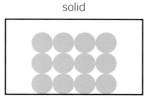 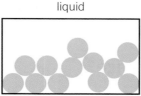 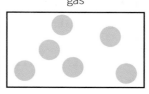

solid      liquid      gas

▲ Particles in solids, liquids, and gases.

Individual particles in a solid, liquid, or gas get don't get hotter. They move or vibrate faster. The energy that you need to increase the temperature of a material depends on:

- the mass of material
- what the material is made of
- the temperature rise that you want.

**B** State what happens to the particles in a liquid when you heat it up.

## Which way?

Hot objects cool down. Energy is never transferred from a cold object to a hot object, only from a hot object to a cooler object. The temperature difference is reduced and eventually both objects will end up at the same temperature. They will be in **equilibrium**. No more energy is transferred between their thermal stores.

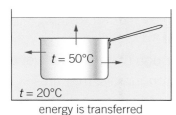 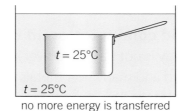

energy is transferred      no more energy is transferred

**C** State what is meant by equilibrium.

### Hot and cold

You might hear someone say "Shut the door, you'll let the cold in!"

Rewrite the statement so that it is scientifically correct and explain why it is now correct.

---

### Link

You can learn more about particles in C1 1.1 The particle model

### Key Words

temperature, thermometer, equilibrium

### Summary Questions

**1** 🔺 Copy and complete the sentences below.

You measure _____ in degrees Celsius using a _____. _____ does not depend on the amount of material that you have, but the _____ stored does. The particles in a _____ vibrate more when you heat the solid. Energy moves from hotter objects to colder objects until they are in _____.

*(6 marks)*

**2** 🔺🔺 Sort these things in order from least energy stored to most energy stored: a saucepan full of water at 50 °C, a cup of water at 30 °C, a saucepan full of water at 30 °C.

*(1 mark)*

**3** 🔺🔺🔺 You are cooking a pizza. You place your pizza on a metal tray at room temperature and put it in the oven. When the pizza is cooked you remove the tray from the oven. Eventually it reaches room temperature again. Describe and explain in detail what happens to the motion of the particles in the metal tray.

*(6 marks)*

## Learning objectives

After this topic you will be able to:

- describe how energy is transferred by particles in conduction and convection
- describe how an insulator can reduce energy transfer.

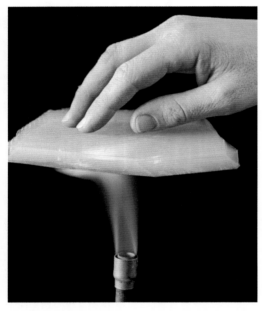

▲ This special material is called aerogel. Energy is transferred very slowly through it.

▲ The capsule that brought these astronauts back is insulated so that they do not burn up in the atmosphere.

**Have you ever lit a wooden splint in a Bunsen burner flame? The end of the splint is at a temperature of about 1000 °C but you can still hold the other end.**

### What's the difference?

When you put the saucepan of soup on the stove, the soup heats up.

The bottom of the saucepan is made of metal. A metal is a good **conductor** of energy. Energy is transferred through it very quickly. This is **conduction.**

Energy can be transferred by conduction, **convection**, or **radiation**.

**A** Write a definition for the word 'conductor'.

### Particles and conduction

In conduction particles transfer energy by colliding with other particles when they vibrate.

Energy transfer happens until the two surfaces are at the same temperature. If you keep one surface warm by heating it then you will maintain the temperature difference. The solid will continue to conduct.

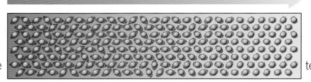

thermal store at a high temperature

thermal store at a low temperature

### Solid conductor, solid insulator?

Energy is not transferred very easily through materials like wood. Wood and many non-metals are poor conductors. They are **insulators**. This does not mean that they do not conduct at all but that energy is transferred very slowly through them.

### Insulating liquids and gases

Liquids are poor conductors. Divers wear wetsuits, which use a thin layer of water against the skin as an insulator to keep them warm.

## Fantastic Fact

Engineers at NASA claim to have made the loudest noise ever. This is so loud that it can make holes in solid materials.

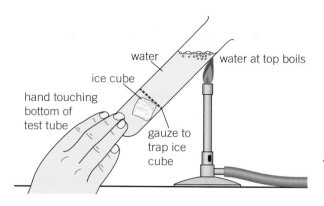

water    water at top boils

ice cube

hand touching bottom of test tube

gauze to trap ice cube

◀ A liquid is a very poor conductor of heat.

Gases do not conduct well at all because their particles are much further apart than the particles in a solid. Duvets and warm clothing are designed to trap small pockets of air, which is a good insulator.

**B** State what an insulator is.

## Particles and convection

When you heat soup in a pan it all heats up, not just the layer in contact with the bottom of the saucepan. This is what happens:

- The soup that is in contact with the bottom of the pan gets hotter so the particles there move faster.
- The particles in the hotter soup move further apart, so the soup becomes less dense.
- The hotter soup rises (floats up) and cooler, denser soup takes its place.

This is called a **convection current**. Convection also happens in gases.

▲ A convection current in a saucepan of water heats all of the water up.

▲ Hurricanes are produced by convection currents in the atmosphere, and the spin of the Earth.

## Particles and sound

When you play music, energy is transferred to the surroundings. The air and walls get a bit warmer. The particles in the air move a bit faster, and the particles in the walls vibrate more.

### Key Words

conductor, conduction, convection, radiation, insulator, convection current

### How fast?

A student wants to investigate how the temperature of a liquid affects how long it takes to cool down. Write a plan for the investigation, including a risk assessment.

### Summary Questions

**1** Copy and complete the sentences below.

Energy is transferred through a solid by _____ if there is a _____ _____ between the ends of it. Liquids and solids transfer energy by _____ because the particles can _____. Energy is transferred much more _____ through an insulator than it is through a conductor.

*(6 marks)*

**2**

**a** Explain in terms of particles why conduction happens in solids but not in liquids and gases.

*(2 marks)*

**b** Explain in terms of particles why convection happens in liquids and gases but not in solids.

*(2 marks)*

**3** An electric kettle contains an element at the bottom that gets hot when you switch it on. Use the ideas on these pages to explain in detail how all the water in a kettle boils.

*(6 marks)*

## Learning objectives

After this topic you will be able to:

- describe some sources of infrared radiation
- explain how energy is transferred by radiation.

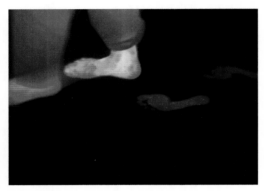

▲ A special camera detects these footprints.

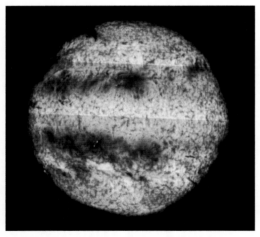

▲ This is what the Sun looks like if you can only see infrared.

## Link

You can learn more about the properties of light in P1 3.1 Light

You leave footprints on the floor when you walk across it in bare feet. You can't see them because your eyes detect visible light.

## What is radiation?

Very hot things such as burning coal give out light as well as **infrared radiation**. Some people call infrared 'thermal radiation' or 'heat'. The Sun emits lots of different types of radiation, including light and infrared. Both light and infrared radiation travel as waves.

## Transferring energy by radiation

You need particles to transfer energy by conduction and convection. You don't need particles to transfer energy by radiation. Light and infrared reach the Earth from the Sun by travelling through space. Space is a vacuum. There are no particles in a vacuum.

## Emitting infrared

All objects (including you) give out, or emit, radiation.

- The type of radiation that they emit depends on their temperature.
- How much radiation they emit per second depends on the type of surface.
- Infrared can be transmitted, absorbed, or reflected, just like light.

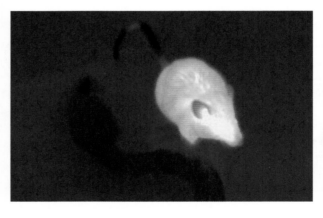

◄ The mouse is warmer and emits a lot more infrared than the snake.

**A** Name two sources of infrared radiation.

## Absorbing infrared

When the Sun is shining your skin feels hotter. Your skin detects the infrared when it absorbs it. Your skin is just one thing that detects infrared.

- A **thermal imaging camera** absorbs infrared and produces an image. The colours in the image are 'false'. The camera works out which areas are hotter and shows them redder in the image.
- A remote thermometer contains a sensor that detects infrared. It uses the radiation to work out the temperature.

You might feel hotter when you wear dark clothing. Dark colours absorb infrared, and light-coloured and shiny surfaces reflect infrared. If you hang clothes on a washing line the dark-coloured clothes will dry more quickly than the light-coloured ones.

### Reflecting infrared

At the end of a marathon, a runner's body temperature drops dramatically. Runners use foil to reflect the infrared back towards their bodies. This prevents their body temperature from falling too quickly.

◀ You can keep warm with a foil blanket.

**B** State what happens when infrared hits a shiny surface.

▲ A thermal imaging camera produces a coloured image of the fire.

---

**Cooling down**

A student investigated the effect of the colour of a can on the time it takes hot water inside to cool down.

| Colour of can | Temperature drop (°C) | | | Mean |
|---|---|---|---|---|
| | 1st measurement | 2nd measurement | 3rd measurement | |
| shiny metal | 12 | 15 | 16 | |
| shiny white | 5 | 18 | 14 | |
| matt black | 11 | 16 | 13 | |
| shiny black | 23 | 15 | 10 | |

a Identify the outlier or outliers.
b Calculate the mean temperature drop.
c Explain why it is not possible to make a conclusion from this experiment.

## Key Words

infrared radiation, thermal imaging camera

## Summary Questions

**1** 🧪 Copy and complete the sentences below.

The Sun and fire are examples of _____ of infrared. All objects emit _____ but the type of radiation depends on the _____. Infrared can be _____ from shiny surfaces, just like light. Dark-coloured surfaces _____ infrared better than light-coloured surfaces. Infrared does not need _____ to travel through. It can travel through empty space, or a _____.

*(7 marks)*

**2** 🧪🧪 Explain why:

a houses are painted white in hot countries *(1 mark)*

b you can't find people in burning buildings with a thermal imaging camera. *(2 marks)*

**3** 🧪🧪🧪 Draw a detailed visual summary about infrared radiation.

*(6 marks)*

# 2.6 Energy resources

## Learning objectives

After this topic you will be able to:

- describe the difference between a renewable and a non-renewable energy resource
- describe how electricity is generated in a power station.

**Have you ever thought about where the fuels and electric current that you use in your house come from? The energy resources of the planet are used to heat homes, make electric appliances work, and move people around.**

## Fossil fuels

Coal, oil, and gas are **energy resources** that were formed millions of years ago. That is why they are called **fossil fuels**. Oil and gas are made from the fossilised remains of sea creatures. Coal is the fossilised remains of trees. The trees and sea creatures were compressed and heated over millions of years, and that produced coal, oil, and gas.

Coal, oil, and gas are **non-renewable**. That doesn't mean that you can't use them again. It means that you cannot easily get more of them when they run out.

**A** Name three fossil fuels.

▲ Coal is one of many energy resources.

## What's in a power station?

**Thermal power stations** burn coal and gas. Oil is mainly used to produce petrol, plastics, and other useful materials.

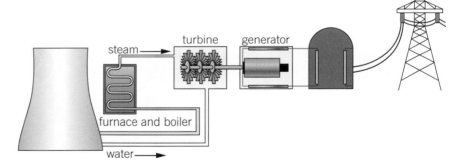

▲ A power station burns fossil fuels to drive a generator.

A fuel burns to heat water and produce steam. The steam drives a turbine, which is a bit like a big fan. The turbine drives a generator. This provides the push that means a current flows in a kettle in your home. The current transfers energy from the chemical store of the fuel to the thermal store of the water in the kettle.

One problem with burning fossil fuels is that they produce a lot of carbon dioxide. Carbon dioxide is a greenhouse gas, so it can contribute to climate change.

## Link

You can learn more about energy sources in P3 1.6 Your planet

## Key Words

energy resource, fossil fuel, non-renewable, thermal power station, renewable, nuclear

Burning fossil fuels also produce pollutants such as sulfur dioxide, nitrogen oxides, and particulates.

**B** Name the greenhouse gas that is produced when fossil fuels burn.

## What's the alternative?

Scientists agree that it would be better if we did not burn so many fossil fuels. They have found some alternative methods to produce a current. These resources are **renewable** because they will not run out. Many renewable resources come from the **nuclear** store of energy of the Sun.

### Renewable energy resources

▲ A wind turbine spins a generator directly.

▲ Tidal: water flows through turbines as the tide goes in and out.

▲ Waves turn a turbine.

▲ Biomass: you can burn plants instead of coal in a power station. The plants use carbon dioxide when they grow.

▲ Solar (photovoltaic) cells generate a potential difference from light.

▲ Hydroelectric: water falls down through turbines in the dam.

▲ Geothermal: hot rocks in the Earth heat water to form steam, which turns turbines.

**C** Name three renewable resources.

Renewable resources do not produce much carbon dioxide when they produce a current. They do produce carbon dioxide when they are being built.

**Link**

You can learn more about greenhouse gases in C2 4.6 Climate change

### Chris the carbon atom

Write a children's story that follows the journey of Chris the carbon atom. Chris starts out in the trunk of a tree that is turned into coal and then used to generate electricity. At the end of the journey he is in a molecule of carbon dioxide.

## Summary Questions

**1** Copy and complete the sentences below.

Coal is a _____ resource because it will run out. It is called a _____ _____ because it took millions of years to form. Wind is a _____ resource because it won't run out.

*(4 marks)*

**2** Explain how electricity is generated from coal.

*(4 marks)*

**3** Design a board game that teaches the players about the advantages and disadvantages of using renewable and non-renewable energy resources.

*(6 marks)*

# 2.7 Energy and power

## Learning objectives

After this topic you will be able to:

- explain the difference between energy and power
- describe the link between power, fuel use, and the cost of using domestic appliances.

## Fantastic Fact

When you make popcorn you are boiling water. The water inside the popcorn kernel turns to steam and it explodes.

▲ The power rating of this heater is 2000 W.

▲ Some houses transfer more energy to the surroundings than others.

**Some microwaves cook popcorn faster than others. Why is there a difference?**

## Powerful appliances

Microwave ovens have a **power rating** in **watts** (W). The power rating tells you how much energy is transferred *per second*, or the rate of transfer of energy.

You can calculate power using this equation:

$$\text{power (W)} = \frac{\text{energy (J)}}{\text{time (s)}}$$

The power of a microwave oven is about 800 W. A traditional oven has a power of about 12 000 W, or 12 **kilowatts**.

### Kilowatts and kilojoules

12 000 W is the same as 12 kilowatts, or 12 kW. There are 1000 W in 1 kW. You divide by 1000 to convert watts to kilowatts.

An oven with a rating of 12 kW transfers energy at a rate of 12 000 J per second. This is the same as 12 kilojoules per second. There are 1000 J in 1 kJ.

**A** State the unit of power.

## Keeping the temperature the same

All hot objects cool down. To keep a house at the *same* temperature you need to transfer energy to it at the *same* rate as energy is being transferred from it.

## What are you paying for?

When you pay an electricity bill you are paying for a fuel such as coal to be burnt in a power station. The power station generates the potential difference that we call 'mains electricity'. You are charged for the number of hours that you use each appliance, and for the power of the appliance.

You can calculate energy use in **kilowatt hours** (kWh), or joules. This is the unit that electricity companies use to calculate your bill.

A kilowatt hour is calculated like this:. Suppose you use a 12 kW (12 000 W) oven for 1 hour (3600 seconds):

energy used in kWh = 12 kW × 1 hour
= 12 kWh

energy used in J = 12 000 J/s × 3600 s
= 43 200 000 J

**B** State the unit of energy that electricity companies use.

To reduce your energy bills you could use fewer appliances, or appliances that require less power to produce the same output. You can also use appliances for fewer hours. Insulation reduces the rate at which energy is transferred to the surroundings, so it reduces the rate at which you need to supply energy to heat the house.

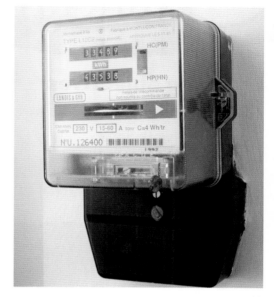

▲ The electricity meter shows how much energy you have used in kWh.

▲ The bulbs are the same brightness but the one on the right has a much lower power.

---

### What's the cost?

A shower has a power of 10 kW. A family uses the shower for 1 hour per day.

**a** Calculate how much energy, in kilowatt hours, they would have to pay for each week for using the shower.

**b** An electricity company charges 10p for each kWh. Calculate the cost in pounds.

---

## Key Words

power rating, watt, kilowatt, kilowatt hour

---

## Summary Questions

**1** 🧪 Copy and complete the sentences below.

Energy is measured in _____ and power is measured in _____. Power is the energy transferred per _____. You pay for the number of _____ that are transferred to your house by electricity. You could save money by using appliances with a _____ power rating, or by using them for _____ time.

*(6 marks)*

**2** 🧪🧪 The potential difference across a bulb is 3 V and the current through it is 0.2 A.

**a** Calculate the power. *(2 marks)*

**b** Calculate the energy transferred by the bulb in 10 seconds. *(2 marks)*

**3** 🧪🧪🧪 Compare the cost of using a kettle with a power rating of 2 kW and a kettle rated 1.2 kW.

*(6 marks)*

# 2.8 Work, energy, and machines

After this topic you will be able to:

● calculate work done
● apply the conservation of energy to simple machines.

▲ Riding downhill is much easier than riding uphill.

**Have you ever tried to ride your bike uphill in the same gear that you use to ride downhill? Choosing a lower gear makes it easier to go up hills.**

## Working out work

Not all energy transfers are to do with heating and cooling. You can transfer energy by doing **work**.

In physics the word 'work' has a special meaning.

● When you lift a book you do work against gravity.
● When you slide the book you do work against friction.

$$\text{work done} = \text{force} \times \text{distance}$$
$$\text{(J)} \qquad \text{(N)} \qquad \text{(m)}$$

▲ Lifting a book.

work done = force × distance
= 2 N × 1 m
= 2 J

▲ Sliding a book.

work done = force ×distance
= 1 N × 0.2 m
= 0.2 J

**A** State the equation for calculating work.

## Fantastic Fact

Using different size cogs on the front and back wheels of a bicycle can give you up to 34 gears.

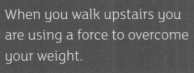

**Climb a mountain!**
When you walk upstairs you are using a force to overcome your weight.

## Making life easier

A **simple machine** makes it easier to lift things, move things, or turn things. It reduces the force that you need to do a job, or increases the distance that something moves when you apply a force.

### Levers

Most people use a **lever** to open a tin of paint. If you put a screwdriver between the lid and the rim of the tin, you can open the tin with a much smaller force.

The force applied to the lid by the lever is bigger than the force that you apply with just your hand. A lever is a force multiplier.

Your hand moves down and the other end of the lever moves up. Your hand moves much further than the other end of the lever.

▲ A screwdriver applies a bigger force than you could apply with just your hand.

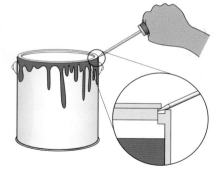

▲ The force may be bigger but the distance is smaller.

## Gears

The **gear** system on a bicycle is a simple machine. Gears are a bit like levers that are rotating. You can use a gear system to increase the force, change direction, or go faster.

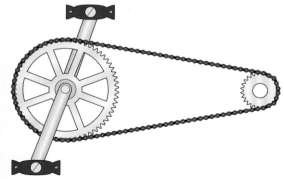

▲ You can select big or small cogs in bicycle gears.

▲ When the cog at the back is smaller, it takes less force to turn it. It is a speed multiplier.

**B** Name two types of simple machine.

## Getting something for nothing?

A small force acting over a big distance produces a big force. The big force can only move a small distance. You cannot get something for nothing.

The reason is the law of conservation of energy. If you increased the distance *as well* as the force then you would get more energy out than you put in. You cannot get out more than you put in.

**Key Words**

work, simple machine, lever, gear

## Summary Questions

**1** 🝪 Copy and complete the sentences below.

You need to know the _____ and the _____ to calculate work done. A simple _____ like a _____ can be used to open a paint tin because it is a _____ multiplier. A _____ on a bicycle can make it easier to cycle uphill. All simple machines obey the law of _____ of energy. You cannot get more _____ out than you put in.

*(8 marks)*

**2** 🝪🝪 You can use a stone under a plank of wood to lift a heavy rock.

**a** State the type of machine that you can make with this equipment. *(1 mark)*

**b** Calculate the work done by lifting a rock of weight 200 N a distance of 0.25 m. *(2 marks)*

**3** 🝪🝪 A person with a weight of 600 N climbs Mount Everest, a vertical height of 10 km. Compare the work done climbing Mount Everest and climbing 2.5 m upstairs to bed.

*(4 marks)*

**4** 🝪🝪🝪 Look at the diagram of the bicycle chain and cogs above. Explain in detail why you exert a force on the pedals, but you still obey the law of conservation of energy.

*(6 marks)*

# P2 Chapter 2 Summary

## Key Points

- There is energy in the chemical stores associated with food and fuel. Energy is measured in joules. You need different amounts of energy for different activities.
- Energy cannot be created or destroyed; it can only be transferred between stores. This is the law of conservation of energy. Light, sound, and electricity are ways of transferring energy between stores.
- Temperature is measured using a thermometer. The temperature doesn't depend on the amount of material, but the amount of energy in the thermal store does.
- When a hot object is in contact with a colder one energy is transferred from the hot object to the colder one. Energy will be transferred, and the temperature difference will decrease, until the objects are in equilibrium.
- Energy is transferred by conduction in solids and by convection in liquids and gases.
- Energy is transferred by radiation, which does not need a medium to travel through. All objects emit radiation. Infrared radiation can be detected by your skin or a thermal imaging camera. If the energy transferred to an object is less than the energy transferred from it the object will cool down.
- Fossil fuels such as coal, oil, and gas were formed over millions of years and are non-renewable. They can be used to drive a generator in a thermal power station. Wind, wave, and solar sources are examples of renewable energy resources.
- Power = energy/time, and electrical power = potential difference × current. You can work out the energy transferred by appliances in your home using the unit of kilowatt hours.
- You calculate work by multiplying a force by a distance. Simple machines like levers and gears can make it easier to do work but you do not get more energy out than you put in.

## Key Words

energy, joule, kilojoule, law of conservation of energy, chemical store, energy store, thermal, kinetic, gravitational potential, elastic, dissipated, temperature, thermometer, equilibrium, conductor, conduction, convection, radiation, insulator, convection current, infrared radiation, thermal imaging camera, energy resource, fossil fuel, non-renewable, thermal power station, renewable, power rating, watt, kilowatt, kilowatt hour, work, simple machine, lever, gear

## BIG Write

### Energy campaign

You are a local councillor who wants to raise awareness of the energy content of food and how that links to the energy needed for activities that people do.

### Task

Design an energy diary that students could use to take a snapshot of their own energy use over a day or a week.

### Tips

- Remember that you need energy for everything you do, even sleeping.
- Remind students that if they take in more energy than they need the body will store it as fat to use in the future.

# End-of-chapter questions

**1** ⚗ Here are some energy resources. List the renewable energy resources.

wind   solar   oil   coal   geothermal   gas

*(1 mark)*

**2** ⚗

**a** State which definition of power below is correct. *(1 mark)*

    **A** the energy transferred per hour

    **B** the energy transferred

    **C** the energy transferred per second

    **D** the force over a distance

**b** Select all the units of power from this list:

kW   J   watts   kilojoules   kilowatts   W   joules   kJ

*(1 mark)*

*(2 marks)*

**3** ⚗⚗ Here is an experiment to demonstrate convection.

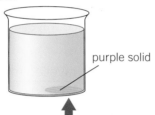

purple solid

Bunsen burner heats here

**a** Describe what will happen to the purple colour during heating. *(3 marks)*

**b** Explain why the purple colour forms a convection current. *(3 marks)*

*(6 marks)*

**4** ⚗⚗

**a** Name a fossil fuel that can be burned in a power station. *(1 mark)*

**b** Explain why it is called a 'fossil' fuel. *(1 mark)*

**c** Use your answer to part b to explain why fossil fuels are non-renewable. *(2 marks)*

*(4 marks)*

**5** ⚗⚗ A tennis ball has 10 J of energy when it is 1 m above the floor.

**a** Name the store associated with this energy. *(1 mark)*

**b** A student states that there will be 10 J of energy in the kinetic store just before it hits the ground.

    **i** Explain why the student has made that statement. *(1 mark)*

    **ii** Explain why the student might not be correct. *(1 mark)*

**c** Explain why the ball moves. *(2 marks)*

*(5 marks)*

**6** ⚗⚗ Calculate the work done in each of the situations below:

**a** a car engine that uses a force of 500 N to move a car 200 m *(2 marks)*

**b** a shopkeeper who uses a force of 50 N to lift a box 1.5 m. *(2 marks)*

*(4 marks)*

**7** ⚗⚗ You want to reduce your energy bills.

**a** Calculate the power of a lightbulb that transfers 6000 J every minute. *(2 marks)*

**b** Calculate the power of a different lightbulb that has a current of 0.05 A through it when there is a potential difference of 240 V across it. *(2 marks)*

**c** Both bulbs are equally bright. State and explain which lightbulb you should use. *(2 marks)*

*(6 marks)*

**8** ⚗⚗⚗ Some double-glazing systems trap air between two panes of glass.

**a** Explain how energy is transferred through a double-glazed window from a hot room to the cold air outside. *(3 marks)*

**b** State and explain how the rate of energy transfer would change if you removed the air from the gap. *(3 marks)*

*(6 marks)*

**9** ⚗⚗⚗ Explain in detail why insulating your house will reduce your energy bills.

*(6 marks)*

## Learning objectives

After this topic you will be able to:

- calculate speed
- describe relative motion.

▲ A cheetah can travel faster than a car.

▲ A speed camera measures how long it takes a car to travel a certain distance by taking a photo at the start of the distance and another at the end. It can then calculate the car's speed.

**It feels fast going downhill on a bike. Even going downhill you could not travel as fast as a cheetah.**

### How fast?

**Speed** is a measure of how far something travels in a particular time. In science you measure speed in **metres per second** (m/s). Car speed and speed limits are measured in miles per hour (m.p.h.) or kilometres per hour (km/h). A very fast car can move at over 300 km/h, but when you walk to school you are probably walking at 5 km/h or about 1 m/s.

**A** Write a definition of the word speed.

### How do you calculate speed?

To find the speed of an object moving at a steady speed you need to measure the time it takes to travel between two points.

You work out the speed from the distance travelled divided by the time taken:

$$\text{speed (m/s)} = \frac{\text{distance travelled (m)}}{\text{time taken (s)}}$$

A long-distance runner runs part of his race at a steady speed. It takes him 20 seconds to run 100 m.

$$\text{speed} = \frac{100 \text{ m}}{20 \text{ s}}$$
$$= 5 \text{ m/s}$$

When you are using an equation to calculate speed it is helpful to write it out like this. If you write the units of distance and time in the equation then you will have the correct units for the speed.

| | Speed (m/s) | Speed (km/h) | Speed (m.p.h.) |
|---|---|---|---|
| walking quickly | 1.7 | 6.1 | 3.7 |
| sprinting | 10 | 36 | 22 |
| typical speed limit | 14 | 50 | 31 |
| cheetah | 33 | 119 | 75 |
| aeroplane cruising speed | 255 | 918 | 570 |
| sound in air | 330 | 1180 | 738 |
| light in air | 300 000 000 | 10 000 000 000 | 670 000 000 |

**B** State the unit of speed that you use in science.

## Speed or average speed?

A marathon runner will take several hours to run the 26.2 miles (42.2 km) of a marathon. She does not run at exactly the same speed throughout the race.

▲ A marathon runner's speed changes during a race.

The speed that the runner is travelling at any time during the race is the **instantaneous speed**. This is the speed that you see on the speedometer in a car.

You can work out the **average speed** by dividing the *total* distance by the *total* time that it took to run the race. This average speed makes it easier to compare how fast different people, or boats, or cars, travel.

### Marathon times

A marathon runner runs the marathon in 2 hours 30 minutes, or 2.5 hours. Calculate the average speed of the runner in km/h.

## Relative motion

Have you ever looked out of the window of a stationary train in a station at a moving train and felt that your train is moving? This is an example of **relative motion**. Relative motion means how fast one thing is travelling compared to another. Being on a moving train looking at a stationary one feels the same as being on a stationary train looking at a moving one.

Speed is relative. If two cars are moving at the same speed in the same direction their relative speed is zero. If the cars are moving at 30 m.p.h. towards each other their relative speed is 60 m.p.h. The speed of 30 m.p.h. is relative to a stationary point.

**C** State what is meant by relative motion.

## Foul Fact

You cough at 60 m.p.h. but your sneeze would break the motorway speed limit. You sneeze at over 100 m.p.h.

## Key Words

speed, metres per second, instantaneous speed, average speed, relative motion

## Summary Questions

**1** 🧪 Copy and complete the sentences below.

To calculate speed you need to know the _____ and the _____. To calculate average speed you divide the _____ _____ by the _____ _____. You measure speed _____ to a stationary object.

*(5 marks)*

**2** 🧪🧪 A runner runs 100 m in 12.5 seconds. Calculate her average speed.

*(2 marks)*

**3** 🧪🧪 A car is travelling east at 50 km/h. On the same road another car is travelling west at 20 km/h. The cars are moving away from each other. Describe their relative motion.

*(2 marks)*

**4** 🧪🧪🧪 Use the speed equation to explain how a speed camera calculates a car's speed.

*(6 marks)*

## Learning objectives

After this topic you will be able to:

- interpret distance–time graphs
- calculate speed using a distance–time graph.

**Key Words**

distance–time graph, acceleration

▲ The car and motorbike are travelling at different speeds.

### Fantastic Fact

You might hear people talk about the time it takes a car to accelerate from 0 to 60 m.p.h. A very fast car can accelerate from 0 to 60 m.p.h. in 2.3 seconds.

### Working it out

Look at the distance–time graph opposite for a constant speed. Calculate the speed using information on the graph.

**How long does it take you to get to school? You can tell the story of a journey with a graph.**

### What is a distance–time graph?

A **distance–time graph** is a useful way of showing how something moves. It shows the distance that something travels over a certain time.

Here is a graph that shows Lucy's journey to school. The line shows how far she travelled each minute of the journey.

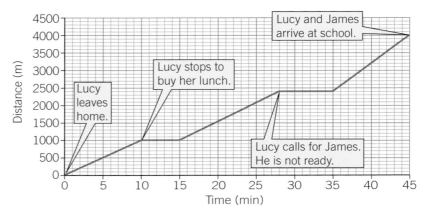

▲ A distance–time graph for Lucy's journey to school.

**A** State what a distance–time graph shows.

### What does the graph tell us?

This is a very simple distance–time graph. The object moves the same distance each second.

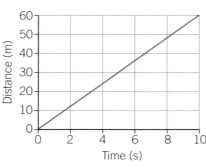

▲ A distance–time graph for a constant speed.

What happens if you stay still? The line on the distance–time graph is horizontal.

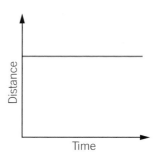

▲ A distance–time graph for a stationary object.

The slope of a distance–time graph tells you the speed. If the line is steep the object is moving fast. If it is not very steep then the object is moving more slowly.

***

**B** State what the slope of a distance–time graph shows you.

***

In the graph opposite, both the car and the motorbike are moving at a steady speed. The line for the motorbike shows a faster speed and the line for the car shows a slower speed.

## A more realistic graph

When you are travelling in a car your speed does not stay the same for the whole journey. The speed changes through the journey.

The changing speed is shown by the slope of the graph. The slope changes gradually, not suddenly.

If your speed is changing you are accelerating. **Acceleration** tells you how quickly your speed is changing.

When you drop a ball it gets faster and faster. It accelerates towards Earth. The distance–time graph is curved. The distance–time graph is also curved if an object is slowing down.

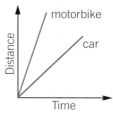

▲ A distance–time graph for two different speeds.

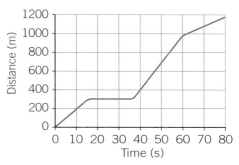

▲ A more realistic distance–time graph.

▲ The distance a ball falls in one second increases as it accelerates.

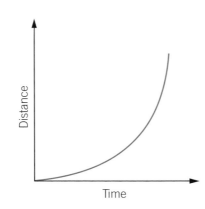

▲ A distance–time graph for an accelerating object.

## Working out speed from a distance–time graph

You can calculate speed from a distance–time graph. For example, in the first section of Lucy's graph she walks 1000 m in 10 minutes or 600 seconds.

$$\text{average speed} = \frac{\text{total distance}}{\text{total time}}$$

$$= \frac{1000 \text{ m}}{600 \text{ s}}$$

$$= 1.7 \text{ m/s}$$

## Summary Questions

**1** 🧪 Copy and complete the sentences below.

A distance–time graph shows the _____ that an object travels in a certain _____. The _____ of the line tells you the speed. If the line is horizontal the object is _____. If the line is a curve the speed of the object is _____.

*(5 marks)*

**2** 🧪🧪 Look at the graph for Lucy's journey to school.

   **a** Calculate Lucy's speed for the final 10 minutes of the graph. *(4 marks)*

   **b** State the value of the speed in the horizontal sections of the graph. *(1 mark)*

**3** 🧪🧪🧪 Imagine two students travelling 3 km to school. One walks and the other travels by car. Sketch a graph for each journey and compare the graphs that you have drawn.

*(6 marks)*

## Learning objectives

After this topic you will be able to:

- describe the factors that affect gas pressure
- describe how atmospheric pressure changes with height.

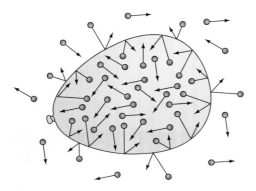

▲ If there are more collisions on the inside than the outside the balloon gets bigger.

▲ In a smaller volume gas molecules will collide more often with the walls of the container.

### Balloon pressure

A student wants to investigate how the volume of a fixed amount of air in a balloon changes with temperature. Write a plan for the investigation.

## Have you ever blown a balloon up until it bursts?

◄ The moment when a balloon bursts.

### What is gas pressure?

When you blow up a balloon there are millions of air molecules hitting the inside of the balloon.

The collisions between the air molecules and the balloon produce **gas pressure** (air pressure). Lots of collisions make a high gas pressure because there is a big force over a small area. Gas pressure is exerted in all directions.

### Changing volume

If you squash a gas into a smaller volume there will be more collisions between the gas molecules and the walls of the container. The pressure increases.

### Changing temperature

When a gas cools down its molecules move more slowly. If the container doesn't change shape, then the pressure goes down. There are fewer collisions with the sides of the container.

**A** State what happens to the speed of gas molecules when the temperature goes down.

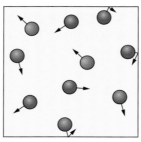

▲ Cool gas: fewer and less energetic collisions.

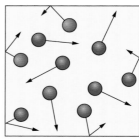

▲ Hot gas: more collisions that are more energetic.

## Compressed gas

When you pump up a bicycle tyre you increase the gas pressure. As you pump more gas into a container the gas becomes **compressed**. There are more molecules in the same space, so there are more collisions. The pressure is bigger, so the force exerted by the gas over the area of the container is big. You need a strong container to hold a compressed gas.

## Atmospheric pressure

There is air all around you. The air exerts a pressure on your body all the time called **atmospheric pressure**. You do not feel the pressure. It is cancelled out by the pressure of the gases and liquids in your body pushing out.

◄ Marshmallows contain pockets of air that expand when you pump out the air around them.

## Changing atmospheric pressure

The atmospheric pressure at sea level is bigger than the atmospheric pressure high up a mountain. Gravity pulls the air particles towards the Earth. Where the particles are closer there are more collisions. The pressure is higher.

The gas has a higher **density** at sea level. There is more mass of gas in a certain volume.

The smaller atmospheric pressure makes it hard for mountain climbers to breathe in enough oxygen. Mountaineers often take oxygen tanks when they climb high mountains such as Everest. The tanks contain oxygen gas that has been compressed into a small volume.

**B** State what happens to the atmospheric pressure as you go up a mountain.

## Key Words

gas pressure, compressed, atmospheric pressure, density

Think of your favourite famous person. When you breathe in you are breathing in at least 10 air molecules that they have breathed out.

## Link

You can learn more about gas pressure in C1 1.7 Gas pressure

## Summary Questions

**1** Copy the sentences below, choosing the correct bold words.

A gas exerts a pressure on the walls of its container because the particles **collide with/stick to** the walls. If the gas gets hotter the pressure will be **bigger/smaller**. If the volume gets bigger the pressure will be **bigger/smaller**. As you go up a mountain the air pressure is **bigger/smaller** because there are **fewer/more** gas particles.

*(5 marks)*

**2** A climber climbs a mountain.

**a** Explain why he might take a cylinder of oxygen with him. *(2 marks)*

**b** Explain why the oxygen needs to be compressed. *(2 marks)*

**3** A teacher heats some water in a drinks can until it is boiling and steam comes out of the can. She quickly turns the can over and puts it into some water. Explain in detail why the can collapses.

*(6 marks)*

## Learning objectives

After this topic you will be able to:

● describe how liquid pressure changes with depth

● explain why some things float and some things sink.

▲ The cup on the left was taken down to a depth of 3000 m.

▲ The water comes out in all directions.

### Why does it float?

A primary-school student says that 'heavy things sink and light things float'.

Use the example of a ferry to explain to them why that is not the case.

**How do you squash a polystyrene cup without touching it? Take it deep beneath the sea and the pressure in the water will do it for you.**

### Liquid pressure

When you swim underwater the water exerts a pressure on you. The water molecules are pushing on each other and on surfaces, and this **liquid pressure** acts in all directions.

When you squeeze a bag with holes in it the water is pushed out of all the holes because of liquid pressure. The water comes straight out of each hole and then falls because of gravity.

▲ The water behind a dam exerts a pressure on the concrete.

If you put water in a syringe, cover the end, and try to compress the liquid you will find it impossible. Liquids are **incompressible**. This is because the particles in a liquid are touching each other and there is very little space between them. In a gas there is lots of space between the particles so gases can be compressed. Liquids pass on any pressure applied to them.

**A** Write down what incompressible means.

### Pressure and depth

The wall of a dam is not straight. It curves outwards at the bottom.

The pressure at the bottom of the lake is bigger than the pressure at the top. The pressure at a particular depth in a liquid depends on the weight of water above it.

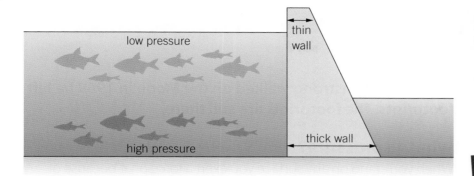

▲ A dam is thicker at the bottom.

**B** State what happens to liquid pressure as you go deeper in a lake.

## Floating and sinking

It is liquid pressure that produces upthrust, the force that keeps things afloat. If you push a balloon into a bucket of water you can feel the water pushing back. Upthrust acts on any object that is floating, or is submerged in a liquid.

It is easy to work out why a rubber duck floats. There are lots more water molecules hitting the bottom of the rubber duck than there are air molecules hitting the top. This produces the upthrust. The duck sinks until there is enough upthrust to balance the weight.

If the area in contact with the water is too small, there is not enough upthrust to make the object float.

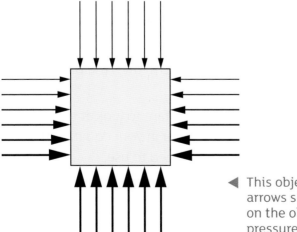

◄ This object is submerged. The arrows show the forces acting on the object because of the pressure in the water.

When a submarine is underwater there is a difference in pressure between the top and bottom of the submarine. That produces a force that pushes the submarine up. This force is upthrust.

### Fantastic Fact

The water pressure at the bottom of the Atlantic Ocean is equivalent to the weight of eight cars pushing on an area the size of your thumb.

### Key Words

liquid pressure, incompressible

### Link

You can learn more about upthrust in P1 1.1 Introduction to forces

### Summary Questions

1 🧪 Copy and complete the sentences below.

The pressure in a liquid acts in _____ directions. The pressure _____ as you go deeper because the _____ of the water above you gets _____. The difference in pressure explains why there is a force called _____ on a floating object.

*(5 marks)*

2 🧪🧪

a Explain in terms of pressure why a boat made of modelling clay floats. *(2 marks)*

b Explain why the same mass of modelling clay shaped into a ball sinks. *(2 marks)*

3 🧪🧪🧪 You push a ping pong ball to the bottom of a bucket of water. Explain in detail what happens to the ball when you let it go.

*(6 marks)*

## Learning objectives

After this topic you will be able to:

- calculate pressure
- apply ideas of pressure to different situations.

▲ There is no wind on the Moon to blow Neil Armstrong's footprints away.

▲ The tracks on the earthmover stop it sinking into the mud.

## Key Words

pressure, newtons per metre squared

**When Neil Armstrong walked on the Moon in 1969 he left footprints. The footprints are still there.**

## What is pressure?

When you stand on any surface you exert a force on it because of your weight. Your weight is spread out over the area of your foot. You are exerting a **pressure** on the ground. If you are standing on a soft surface such as mud the pressure might be big enough for you to sink.

An earthmover is very heavy. It has a weight of about a million newtons, the same as about 15 000 people! A single person standing on the same muddy ground might sink. The earthmover does not sink because its weight is spread out over a bigger area.

Pressure is a measure of how much force is applied over a certain area. The pressure acts in a direction that is at 90°, or normal, to the surface.

**A** State the direction that pressure acts.

## How do you calculate pressure?

You calculate pressure using this equation:

$$\text{pressure (N/m}^2) = \frac{\text{force (N)}}{\text{area (m}^2)}$$

You measure force in newtons (N) and area in metres squared ($m^2$). Pressure is measured in **newtons per metre squared** (N/m²).

Sometimes it is easier to measure smaller areas in centimetres squared ($cm^2$). If you measure the area in $cm^2$ then the pressure is measured in N/cm².

When you do calculations it is very important to look at the units of area. If you write them next to the number in your equation then you will see which unit of pressure you need to use.

**B** State the units of pressure.

## Fantastic Fact

To produce the same pressure on the floor that you exert when you push in a drawing pin, you would need over 5000 people standing on your shoulders.

# Big and small pressure

The studs on the bottom of a hockey or football boot have a small area compared with the area of the foot. This produces a bigger pressure. The studs sink into the ground and help the player to move quickly.

The weight of a hockey player is 600 N.

The area of her two feet is 200 cm².

$$\text{pressure} = \frac{\text{force}}{\text{area}}$$
$$= \frac{600\ \text{N}}{200\ \text{cm}^2}$$
$$= 3\ \text{N/cm}^2$$

The total area of the studs is 20 cm².

$$\text{pressure} = \frac{\text{force}}{\text{area}}$$
$$= \frac{600\ \text{N}}{20\ \text{cm}^2}$$
$$= 30\ \text{N/cm}^2$$

▲ The pressure is bigger if your weight is concentrated over a smaller area, such as your hand.

▲ The studs increase the grip on the ground.

▲ Snowshoes increase the area of your feet so the pressure is less.

Studs increase the pressure. At other times it is useful to make the pressure smaller, as with the earthmover.

If you need to walk over a soft surface such as snow, you need to increase the area of your feet in contact with the ground so that you do not sink.

## Finding the force

Which of these is the correct equation for working out the force?

A force = pressure/area
B force = pressure × area
C force = area/pressure

## Summary Questions

1  Copy the sentences below, choosing the correct bold words.

Pressure is a measure of how much **force/pressure** there is on a certain **area/volume**. If you exert a **big/small** force on a **big/small** area the pressure will be large. Pressure is measured in **N/m²/Nm**.

*(5 marks)*

2  A gymnast has a weight of 600 N. The area of each hand is 150 cm². Calculate the pressure on the floor when he is doing a handstand.

*(3 marks)*

3  The point of a nail has an area of 0.25 cm², and an average person has a weight of 700 N. Explain in detail why it is possible to lie on a bed of 4000 nails, but not on a single nail.

*(6 marks)*

## Learning objectives

After this topic you will be able to:

- describe what is meant by a moment
- calculate the moment of a force.

▲ Tightrope walking over Niagara Falls.

▲ You need to apply a turning force to open a door.

### Key Words

pivot, moment, newton metres, law of moments, centre of gravity, centre of mass

**A tightrope walker uses a long pole to help him to balance.**

### A force that turns

Whenever you open a door you are using a turning force. A turning force acts a certain distance from a **pivot**.

The turning effect of a force is called a **moment**. The moment depends on the force being applied and how far it is from the pivot.

moment (Nm) = force (N) × perpendicular distance from the pivot (m)

You measure force in newtons (N) and distance in metres (m). You calculate a moment in **newton metres** (Nm).

**A** State the unit of a 'moment'.

### The law of moments

You sit on the left of a see-saw with your friend at the other end. It balances.

The moment of your weight acts anticlockwise. The moment of your friend's weight acts clockwise.

When an object is in equilibrium the sum of the clockwise moments is equal to the sum of the anticlockwise moments. This is the **law of moments**.

▲ These apples are in equilibrium because the clockwise moment equals the anticlockwise moment.

**B** State the law of moments.

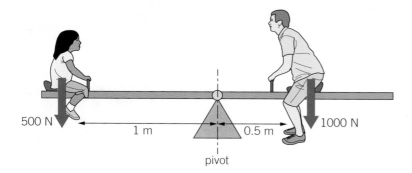

500 N    1 m    0.5 m    1000 N

pivot

▲ The see-saw doesn't turn if it is in equilibrium.

You can work out if a see-saw is going to be balanced by calculating the clockwise and the anticlockwise moments.

clockwise moment = force × distance on the right
= 1000 N × 0.5 m
= 500 Nm

anticlockwise moment = force × distance on the left
= 500 N × 1 m
= 500 Nm

The moments are the same. The see-saw balances.

## Falling over

When you lean back and tip your chair slightly, there is a turning force that brings your chair back. That turning force is your weight acting about the point where the legs touch the floor. If you lean back far enough you will topple over.

All the weight of an object seems to act through a point called the **centre of gravity** (or **centre of mass**). If the centre of gravity is above the pivot there is no turning force. If the centre of gravity is to the left or right of the pivot there will be a turning force.

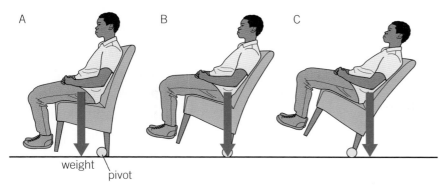

A    B    C

weight    pivot

▲ There is a turning force in A and C, but not in B.

C  Describe what is meant by centre of gravity.

## Fantastic Fact

The world's largest see-saw is in New York. It is just over 24 metres long. It lifts you higher than a house.

### Sitting on a see-saw

A mother and daughter are on a see-saw 2 m long. The mother has a weight of 600 N and the child has a weight of 150 N.

Calculate where the mother must sit to balance the child who is sitting at the other end.

## Summary Questions

1  🧪 Copy and complete the sentences below.

The _____ effect of a force is called a moment. You can calculate the moment of a force by multiplying the _____ by the _____. If the anticlockwise moments equal the clockwise moments the object will be in _____. This is the _____ of moments. The _____ of an object acts through a point called the centre of _____.

*(7 marks)*

2  🧪🧪 A girl applies a force of 5 N to close a door. The handle is 0.75 m from the hinge. Calculate the moment of the force.

*(2 marks)*

3  🧪🧪🧪 Design a balancing game that children can play. Explain in terms of the law of moments and centre of gravity how to play it.

*(6 marks)*

## Key Points

- Speed = distance/time, measured in metres per second (m/s). Average speed is the total distance travelled/total time taken.
- You can show what is happening to the position of an object on a distance–time graph. The slope of the distance–time graph is the speed.
- Gas pressure is due to the collisions of gas molecules with the sides of the container or object. If the gas is hotter, or compressed into a smaller volume, or if there are more gas molecules in the same space, there will be more collisions and the pressure will be greater.
- Atmospheric pressure is due to the collisions of air molecules with objects. Atmospheric pressure decreases with height because there are fewer air molecules higher up.
- Liquids are incompressible. The pressure at a particular depth in a liquid depends on the weight of water above it. Pressure increases with depth.
- Pressure = force/area, measured in $N/m^2$ or $N/cm^2$. The pressure tells you how the force is spread out over an area.
- The turning effect of a force is called a moment. You calculate a moment by multiplying the force by the distance from a pivot.
- If the clockwise moments acting on an object equal the anticlockwise moments the object will be in equilibrium. This is how see-saws balance.
- The centre of gravity is the point at which all the weight of the object appears to act.
- The weight of an object acting through the centre of mass can produce a turning force.

## Case study

### Alien landing

When NASA sent a probe to Cassini, one of the moons of Saturn, they did not know what would happen. They called it 'crash or splash'.

Imagine landing a spacecraft on an unknown planet.

### Task

Tell the story of the journey of your spacecraft as it approaches and lands.

### Tips

- Include the type of atmosphere on the planet, and how it changes close to the surface.
- Decide whether there are oceans, and what they are made of.
- Say whether your spacecraft would float or sink on any ocean.

## Key Words

speed, metres per second, instantaneous speed, average speed, relative motion, distance–time graph, acceleration, gas pressure, compressed, atmospheric pressure, density, liquid pressure, incompressible, pressure, newtons per metre squared, pivot, moment, newton metres, law of moments, centre of gravity, centre of mass

# End-of-chapter questions

1 ⚗ Choose units of speed from the list below.

m/s   m   s   h   mph   km/s   km

*(3 marks)*

2 ⚗ You can make a hole in a piece of wood if you bang in a nail with a hammer. If you hit the wood with the hammer it does not make a hole. Choose the best explanation for this from the statements below:

**A** The area of the nail is much smaller so the pressure is smaller.

**B** The area of the nail is much smaller so the pressure is bigger.

**C** The area of the hammer is bigger so the pressure is bigger.

*(1 mark)*

3 ⚗ Here is a graph of a person riding his bike.

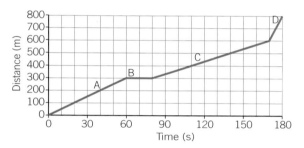

State the letter of the section where the student was:

**a** stationary *(1 mark)*

**b** moving fastest *(1 mark)*

**c** moving slowest. *(1 mark)*

*(3 marks)*

4 ⚗⚗

**a** Explain why it can hurt your hands when you carry heavy shopping in carrier bags. *(2 marks)*

**b** Explain why road bikes have narrow tyres but off-road bikes have wide tyres. *(2 marks)*

*(4 marks)*

5 ⚗⚗ A car is travelling at 70 mph and a lorry is travelling at 50 mph.

**a** Calculate the speed of the car relative to the lorry. *(2 marks)*

The car slows down to 50 mph.

**b** State the new speed of the car relative to the lorry. *(1 mark)*

*(3 marks)*

6 ⚗⚗ Here is a distance–time graph for three snails Cyril, Gertie, and Harold.

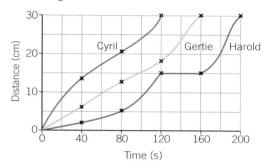

Compare the journeys of the three snails, and describe what happened to their speed during the journeys.

*(6 marks)*

7 ⚗⚗⚗ Look at the diagram of an arm holding a phone. The phone has a weight of 1.5 N.

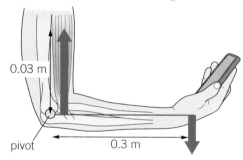

**a** Calculate the moment of the force exerted by the phone. *(2 marks)*

**b** Calculate the force that the muscle exerts to keep the phone in equilibrium. *(2 marks)*

**c** Explain why the force exerted by the muscle is much greater than the weight of the phone. *(2 marks)*

*(6 marks)*

8 You buy a bag of crisps in an airport. After take-off you take the crisps out of your rucksack. Explain in detail why the bag has expanded.

*(6 marks)*

# Glossary

**acceleration**   The amount by which speed increases in one second.

**acid rain**   Rain that has a non-metal dissolved in it.

**adaptation**   Characteristic that helps an organism to survive in its environment.

**addiction**   A need to keep taking a drug in order to feel normal.

**aerobic respiration**   Chemical reaction where glucose reacts with oxygen to release energy, carbon dioxide, and water.

**alcoholic**   A person who is addicted to alcohol.

**algae**   Green unicellular or multicellular organisms that perform photosynthesis and live underwater.

**ammeter**   A device for measuring electric current in a circuit.

**amps**   Units of measurement of electric current, symbol A.

**anaerobic respiration**   Chemical reaction that takes place without oxygen. Glucose is converted into lactic acid and energy is released.

**anus**   Muscular ring through which feces pass out of the body.

**atmosphere**   The mixture of gases surrounding the Earth.

**atmospheric pressure**   Pressure caused by the collisions of air molecules that produce a force on an area.

**atom**   A neutral particle; everything is made of atoms.

**attract**   Be pulled together, for example, opposite poles of a magnet attract and positive and negative charges attract.

**average speed**   The total distance travelled in the total time taken for a complete journey.

**balanced diet**   Eating food containing the right nutrients in the correct amounts.

**battery**   Two or more electrical cells joined together.

**bile**   Substance that breaks fat into small droplets.

**bioaccumulation**   The build up of toxic chemicals inside organisms in a food chain.

**biodiversity**   The range of organisms living in an area.

**biological weathering**   The breaking up or wearing down of rocks by the action of living things.

**carbohydrase**   Enzyme that breaks down carbohydrates into sugar molecules.

**carbohydrate**   Nutrient that provides energy.

**carbon cycle**   The carbon cycle shows stores of carbon, and summarises how carbon and its compounds enter and leave these stores.

**carbon fibre**   A material made of thin tubes of carbon.

**carbon store**   A place where carbon and its compounds may remain for a long time. Carbon stores include the atmosphere, oceans, sedimentary rocks, fossil fuels, the soil, and living organisms.

**catalyst**   Substance that speeds up a reaction without being used up.

**cell**   A chemical store of energy, which provides the push that moves charge around a circuit.

**cementation**   The 'gluing together' of sediments by different chemicals to make sedimentary rocks.

**centre of gravity**   The point in an object where the force of gravity seems to act.

**centre of mass**   The point in an object where the mass of an object seems to act.

**ceramic** A compound such as a metal silicate or oxide that is hard, strong, and has a high melting point.

**chemical property** How a substance behaves in its chemical reactions.

**chemical store** Energy stored in food and fuels.

**chemical weathering** The breaking up or wearing down of rocks by the action of chemicals such as those in rainwater.

**chemosynthesis** Reaction performed by bacteria, using energy transferred from chemical reactions to produce glucose.

**chlorophyll** Green pigment that absorbs light for use in photosynthesis.

**chromatogram** An image obtained from chromatography.

**chromatography** A technique to separate mixtures of liquids that are soluble in the same solvent.

**chromosome** Long strand of DNA, which contains many genes.

**climate change** A long-term change in weather patterns.

**co-exist** Plants and animals living in the same habitat at the same time.

**combustion** A burning reaction, in which a substance reacts quickly with oxygen, and gives out light and heats the surroundings.

**community** The collection of the different types of organism present in an ecosystem.

**compaction** The process of squashing sediments together to make new rocks by the weight of layers above.

**competition** Competing with other organisms for resources.

**composite** A mixture of materials with properties that are a combination of those of the materials in it.

**compressed** Squashed into a smaller space.

**conduction** The way in which energy is transferred through solids, and to a much lesser extent in liquids and gases.

**conductor** A material that conducts charge or energy well, such as a metal or graphite.

**consumer** Organisms that eat other organisms as food.

**continuous variation** Characteristic that can take any value within a range of values.

**convection** The transfer of energy by the movement of gases or liquids.

**convection current** The movement of heated liquids or gasses.

**core** A rod of a magnetic material placed inside a coil to make the magnetic field of an electromagnet stronger.

**crust** The rocky outer layer of the Earth.

**current** The flow of electrical charge (electrons) around a complete circuit per second.

**deficiency** A lack of minerals, that causes poor growth.

**deforestation** The cutting down or burning of trees in forests.

**density** The mass of a material in a certain volume.

**deposition** The settling of sediments that have moved away from their original rock.

**depressant** A drug that slows down the body's reactions by slowing down the nervous system.

**digestion** Process where large molecules are broken down into small molecules.

**digestive system** Group of organs that work together to break down food.

**discontinuous variation** Characteristic that can only be a certain value.

**displace** A more reactive metal displaces – or pushes out – a less reactive metal from its compound.

**displacement reaction**   In a displacement reaction, a more reactive metal displaces – or pushes out – a less reactive metal from its compound.

**dissipated**   Energy that has become spread out or 'wasted' by heating the environment.

**dissolve**   The mixing of a substance (the solute) with a liquid (the solvent) to make a solution.

**distance–time graph**   A graph that shows how far an object moves each second.

**distillation**   A technique that uses evaporation and condensation to obtain a solvent from a solution.

**DNA**   Chemical that contains all the information needed to make an organism.

**drug**   Chemical substance that affects the way your body works.

**durable**   A property of a material meaning that it is difficult to damage.

**ecosystem**   The name given to the interaction between plants, animals, and their habitat in a particular location.

**elastic store**   Energy stored when objects change shape.

**electric charge**   A property of a material or particle that can be positive or negative.

**electric field**   A region where a charged material or particle experiences a force.

**electromagnet**   A temporary magnet produced using an electric current.

**electron**   A negatively charged particle found in atoms. Electrons flow through a wire when a current flows.

**endangered**   Species of plants and animals that have only a small population in the world.

**energy**   Associated with changes in temperature or with work.

**energy resources**   Materials or mechanisms for heating or generating electricity.

**energy store**   Something such as a food or hot object that enables you to account for the energy at the start and end of a transfer.

**enzyme**   Special protein that can break large molecules into small molecules.

**equilibrium**   Objects are at thermal eqilibrium when they are at the same temperature.

**erosion**   The breaking of a rock into sediments, and their movement away from the original rock.

**ethanol**   The drug found in alcoholic drinks.

**evolution**   Development of a species over time.

**extinct**   When no more individuals of a species are left anywhere in the world.

**feces**   Undigested food that leaves the body as waste.

**fermentation**   Chemical reaction used by microorganisms to convert glucose into ethanol, carbon dioxide, and energy.

**fertiliser**   Chemical containing minerals, normally applied to soil.

**fibre**   Provides bulk to food to keep it moving through the digestive system.

**filtering**   A way of separating pieces of solid that are mixed with a liquid or solution by pouring through filter paper.

**filtrate**   The liquid or solution that collects in the container after the mixture has passed through the filter paper.

**filtration**   A way of separating pieces of solid that are mixed with a liquid or solution by pouring through filter paper.

**food chain**   A diagram that shows the transfer of energy between organisms.

**food test** Chemical test to detect the presence of particular nutrients in a food.

**food web** A diagram showing a set of linked food chains.

**fossil** The remains of plants and animals that have turned to stone.

**fossil fuel** Coal, oil, and gas made from the remains of trees and sea creatures over millions of years.

**freeze–thaw** Weathering of rocks that happens as a result of water repeatedly freezing and thawing.

**gas pressure** The force exerted by air particles when they collide with a surface.

**gear** A rotating lever that reduces the force required to do work.

**gene** Section of DNA that contains the information for a characteristic.

**gene bank** A store of genetic samples, used for research and to try to prevent extinction.

**global warming** The gradual increase in the Earth's mean air temperature.

**gravitational potential store** Energy due to the position of an object in a gravitational field.

**greenhouse effect** The absorbing of energy by gases in the atmosphere, such as carbon dioxide, which keeps the Earth warmer than it would otherwise be.

**greenhouse gas** A gas that contributes to climate change, such as carbon dioxide.

**group** A vertical column of the Periodic Table. The elements in a group have similar properties.

**Group 0** Group 0 is on the right of the Periodic Table. Group 0 elements include helium, neon, argon, and krypton.

**Group 1** The elements in the left column of the Periodic Table, including lithium, sodium, and potassium.

**Group 7** Group 7, is second from the right of the Periodic Table. Group 7 elements include fluorine, chlorine, bromine, and iodine.

**gullet** Tube that food travels down into the stomach.

**habitat** The area in which an organism lives.

**haemoglobin** The substance in blood that carries oxygen around the body.

**halogen** Another name for the Group 7 elements.

**hypothesis** An idea that is a way of explaining scientists' observations.

**igneous (rock)** Rock made when liquid rock (magma or lava) cools and freezes.

**impure** A subsatnce is impure if it has different substances mixed with it.

**incompressible** Cannot be compressed (squashed).

**infrared radiation** Radiation given off by the Sun and other objects that brings about energy transfer.

**inner core** The solid iron and nickel at the centre of the Earth.

**insoluble** A substance that cannot dissolve in a certain solvent is insoluble in that solvent.

**instantaneous speed** The speed at a particular moment.

**insulator** A material that does not conduct electricity or transfer energy well.

**interdependence** The way in which living organisms depend on each other to survive, grow, and reproduce.

**joules** The unit of energy, symbol J.

**kilojoules** 1 kilojoule = 1000 J, symbol kJ.

**kilowatt hours** The unit of energy used by electricity companies, symbol kWh.

**kilowatts** 1 kilowatt = 1000 W, symbol kW.

**kinetic store**   Energy of moving objects.

**large intestine**   Organ where water passes back into the body, leaving a solid waste of undigested food called feces.

**lava**   Liquid rock that is above the Earth's surface.

**law of conservation of energy**   Energy cannot be created or destroyed, only transferred.

**law of moments**   An object is in equilibrium if the clockwise moments equal the anticlockwise moments.

**lever**   A simple machine that multiplies the force.

**lightning**   A current through the air that produces light and sound.

**lipase**   Enzyme that breaks down lipids into fatty acids and glycerol.

**lipids**   Nutrients that provide a store of energy and insulate the body.

**liquid pressure**   The pressure produced by collisions of particles in a liquid.

**magma**   Liquid rock that is below the Earth's surface.

**magnesium**   A mineral needed by plants for making chlorophyll.

**magnetic field**   A region where there is a force on a magnet or magnetic material.

**magnetic field lines**   Imaginary lines that show the direction of the force on magnetic material.

**magnetic material**   A material that is attracted to a magnet, such as iron, steel, nickel, or cobalt.

**magnetise**   Make into a magnet.

**malnourishment**   Eating the wrong amount or the wrong types of food.

**mantle**   The layer of Earth that is below the crust. It is solid but can flow very slowly.

**medicinal drug**   Drug that has a medical benefit to your health.

**metal**   Elements on the left of the stepped line of the Periodic Table. Most elements are metals. They are good conductors of energy and electricity.

**metalloid**   Elements near the stepped line of the Periodic Table are metalloids.

**metamorphic (rock)**   Rock fomed by the action of heating and/or pressure on sedimentary or igneous rock.

**metres per second**   A unit of speed.

**mineral**   Essential nutrient needed in small amounts to keep you healthy.

**mixture**   A mixture is made up of substances that are not chemically joined together.

**moment**   A measure of the ability of a force to rotate an object about a pivot.

**motor**   A component or machine that spins when a current flows through it.

**natural polymer**   Polymers made by plants and animals, including wool, cotton, and rubber.

**natural selection**   Process by which the organisms with the characteristics that are most suited to the environment survive and reproduce, passing on their genes.

**negative**   The charge on an electron, or on an object that has had electrons transferred to it.

**neutral**   Describes an object or particle that has no charge, or in which positive and negative charges cancel out, giving no charge overall.

**neutron**   A neutral particle found in atoms.

**newton metre**   The unit of moment.

**newtons per metre squared**   A unit of pressure.

**niche**   A particular place or role that an organism has in an ecosystem.

**nitrates**   Minerals containing nitrogen for healthy growth.

**noble gas**   Another name for the Group 0 elements.

**non-metal**   Elements on the right of the stepped line of the Periodic Table. They are poor conductors of energy and electricity.

**non-renewable**   Energy resources that have a limited supply.

**north pole**   The pole of a magnet that points towards the north.

**nutrient**   Essential substance that your body needs to survive, provided by food.

**obese**   Extremely overweight.

**ohms**   The units of resistance, symbol $\Omega$.

**ore**   A rock that you can extract a metal from.

**outer core**   The liquid iron and nickel between the Earth's mantle and inner core.

**oxygen debt**   Extra oxygen required after anaerobic respiration to break down lactic acid.

**parallel**   A circuit in which there are two or more paths or branches for the current.

**passive smoking**   Breathing in other people's smoke.

**period**   A horizontal row of the Periodic Table. There are trends in the properties of the elements across a period.

**phosphate**   Mineral containing phosporus for healthy roots.

**photosynthesis**   The process plants use to make their own food, glucose. In photosynthesis, carbon dioxide and water react together to make glucose and oxygen.

**physical property**   A property of a material that you can observe or measure.

**physical weathering**   The breaking up or wearing down of rocks by the effects of changing temperature.

**pivot**   The point about which a lever or see-saw balances.

**plasma**   The liquid part of blood, which carries carbon dioxide to the lungs where it is exhaled.

**polymer**   A substance made up of very long molecules.

**population**   The number of plants or animals of the same type that live in the same area.

**porous**   A porous material has small gaps that may contain substances in their liquid or gas states. Water can soak into a porous material.

**positive**   The charge on a proton, or on an object that has had electrons transferred from it.

**potassium**   A mineral needed by plants for healthy leaves and flowers.

**potential difference**   A measure of the push of a cell or battery, or the energy that the cell or battery can supply.

**power rating**   The number in watts or kilowatts that tells you the rate at which an appliance transfers energy.

**predator**   An animal that eats other animals.

**pressure**   The force exerted on a certain area.

**prey**   An animal that is eaten by another animal.

**producer**   Organism that make its own food using photosynthesis.

**protease**   Enzyme that breaks down proteins into amino acids.

**protein**   Nutrient used for growth and repair.

**proton**   A positively charged particle found in atoms.

**pure**   A substance is pure if it has no other substances mixed with it.

**radiation**   The transfer of energy as a wave.

**rating**   The value of potential difference at which a cell or bulb operates.

**reactive**   A substance is reactive if it reacts vigorously with substances such as dilute acids and water.

**reactivity series**   A list of metals in order of how vigorously they react.

**recreational drug**   Drug that is taken for enjoyment.

**rectum**   Feces are stored here, before being passed out of the body.

**recycling**   Collecting and processing materials that have been used, to make new objects.

**reinforced concrete**   A composite material consisting of steel bars surrounded by concrete.

**relative motion**   The difference between the speeds of two moving objects, or of a moving and a stationary object.

**relay**   Electrical device that uses current flowing through it in one circuit to switch on and off a current in a second circuit.

**renewable**   Energy resources whose supply will not run out.

**repel**   Be pushed away from each other, for example, like magnetic poles repel or like electric charges repel.

**residue**   The solid that collects in the filter paper.

**resistance**   How difficult it is for current to flow through a component in a circuit.

**respiration**   The process that transfers energy from plants and animals. In respiration, glucose reacts with oxygen to make carbon dioxide and water.

**rock cycle**   The rock cycle explains how rocks change and are recycled into new rocks over millions of years.

**saturated solution**   A solution in which no more solute can dissolve.

**sediment**   Pieces of rock that have broken away from their original rock.

**sedimentary (rock)**   Rock made from sediments.

**series**   A circuit in which components are joined in a single loop.

**simple machine**   Lever or gear that reduces the force required to do something, but increases the distance.

**small intestine**   Organ where small digested molecules are absorbed into the bloodstream.

**solubility**   The solubility of a substance is the mass that dissolves in 100 g of water.

**solute**   The solid or gas that dissolves in a liquid.

**solution**   A mixture of a liquid with a solid or a gas. All parts of the mixture are the same.

**solvent**   The liquid in which a solid or gas dissolves.

**south pole**   The pole of a magnet that points towards the south.

**species**   Organisms that have lots of characteristics in common, and can mate to produce fertile offspring.

**speed**   A measure of how far something travels in a given time.

**starvation**   Extreme case of not eating enough food.

**state symbol**   A state symbol gives the state of a substance in a chemical equation. (s) means solid, (l) means liquid, (g) means gas, and (aq) means dissolved in water.

**stimulant**   A drug that speeds up the body's reactions by speeding up the nervous system.

**stomach**   Organ where food is churned with digestive juices and acids.

**stomata**   Holes found on the bottom of the leaf that allow gases to diffuse in and out of the leaf.

**switch**   A component that controls the current by making or breaking the circuit.

**synthetic polymer**   A substance made up of very long molecules that does not occur naturally.

**temperature**   A measure of how hot or cold something is, measured in degrees Celsius.

**thermal imaging camera**   A camera that absorbs infrared and produces a (false-colour) image.

**thermal power station**   A power station that uses fossil fuels to generate electricity.

**thermal store**   Energy in objects as a result of the motion of their particles.

**thermite reaction**   Reaction of aluminium with iron oxide to make aluminium oxide and iron.

**thermometer**   Instrument used to measure temperature.

**transport**   Movement of sediments far from their original rock.

**troposphere**   The part of the atmosphere nearest the Earth.

**unit of alcohol**   10 ml of pure alcohol.

**unreactive**   Elements that take part in few chemical reactions are unreactive.

**uplift**   Uplift happens when huge forces from inside the Earth push rocks upwards.

**variation**   Differences in characteristics within a species.

**villi**   Tiny projections in the small intestine wall that increase the area for absorption.

**vitamin**   Essential nutrients needed in small amounts to keep you healthy.

**voltage**   A measure of the strength of a cell or battery used to send a current around a circuit.

**voltmeter**   A device for measuring voltage.

**volt**   Unit of measurement of voltage, symbol V.

**watt**   The unit of power, symbol W.

**weathering**   Weathering breaks up all types of rock into smaller pieces, called sediments.

**withdrawal symptom**   Unpleasant symptom a person with a drug addiction suffers from when they stop taking the drug.

**work**   A way of transferring energy that does not involve heating.

# Index

# The Periodic Table

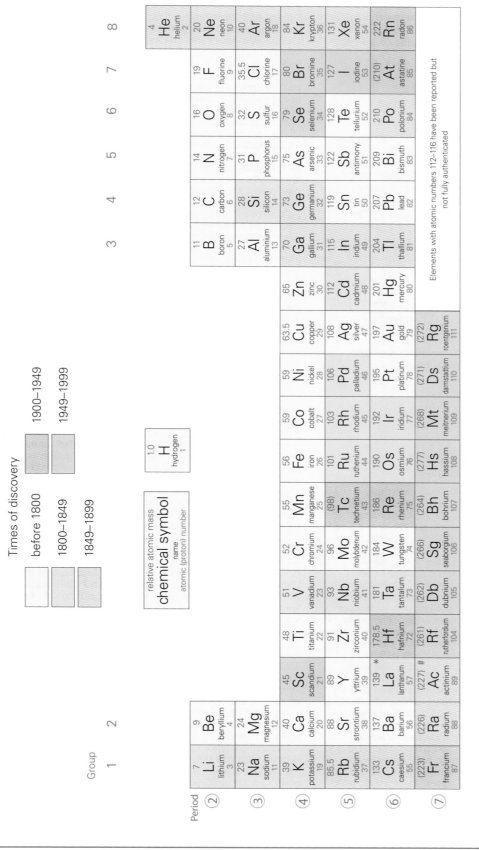

Times of discovery

- before 1800
- 1800–1849
- 1849–1899
- 1900–1949
- 1949–1999

Key: relative atomic mass / **chemical symbol** / name / atomic (proton) number

1.0 H hydrogen 1

| Period | Group 1 | 2 | | | | | | | | | | | 3 | 4 | 5 | 6 | 7 | 8 |
|---|---|---|---|---|---|---|---|---|---|---|---|---|---|---|---|---|---|---|
| | | | | | | | | | | | | | | | | | | 4 He helium 2 |
| 2 | 7 Li lithium 3 | 9 Be beryllium 4 | | | | | | | | | | | 11 B boron 5 | 12 C carbon 6 | 14 N nitrogen 7 | 16 O oxygen 8 | 19 F fluorine 9 | 20 Ne neon 10 |
| 3 | 23 Na sodium 11 | 24 Mg magnesium 12 | | | | | | | | | | | 27 Al aluminium 13 | 28 Si silicon 14 | 31 P phosphorus 15 | 32 S sulfur 16 | 35.5 Cl chlorine 17 | 40 Ar argon 18 |
| 4 | 39 K potassium 19 | 40 Ca calcium 20 | 45 Sc scandium 21 | 48 Ti titanium 22 | 51 V vanadium 23 | 52 Cr chromium 24 | 55 Mn manganese 25 | 56 Fe iron 26 | 59 Co cobalt 27 | 59 Ni nickel 28 | 63.5 Cu copper 29 | 65 Zn zinc 30 | 70 Ga gallium 31 | 73 Ge germanium 32 | 75 As arsenic 33 | 79 Se selenium 34 | 80 Br bromine 35 | 84 Kr krypton 36 |
| 5 | 85.5 Rb rubidium 37 | 88 Sr strontium 38 | 89 Y yttrium 39 | 91 Zr zirconium 40 | 93 Nb niobium 41 | 96 Mo molybdenum 42 | (98) Tc technetium 43 | 101 Ru ruthenium 44 | 103 Rh rhodium 45 | 106 Pd palladium 46 | 108 Ag silver 47 | 112 Cd cadmium 48 | 115 In indium 49 | 119 Sn tin 50 | 122 Sb antimony 51 | 128 Te tellurium 52 | 127 I iodine 53 | 131 Xe xenon 54 |
| 6 | 133 Cs caesium 55 | 137 Ba barium 56 | 139 * La lanthanum 57 | 178.5 Hf hafnium 72 | 181 Ta tantalum 73 | 184 W tungsten 74 | 186 Re rhenium 75 | 190 Os osmium 76 | 192 Ir iridium 77 | 195 Pt platinum 78 | 197 Au gold 79 | 201 Hg mercury 80 | 204 Tl thallium 81 | 207 Pb lead 82 | 209 Bi bismuth 83 | 210 Po polonium 84 | (210) At astatine 85 | 222 Rn radon 86 |
| 7 | (223) Fr francium 87 | (226) Ra radium 88 | (227) # Ac actinium 89 | (261) Rf rutherfordium 104 | (262) Db dubnium 105 | (266) Sg seaborgium 106 | (264) Bh bohrium 107 | (277) Hs hassium 108 | (268) Mt meitnerium 109 | (271) Ds darmstadtium 110 | (272) Rg roentgenium 111 | Elements with atomic numbers 112–116 have been reported but not fully authenticated | | | | | | |

| | | | | | | | | | | | | | | |
|---|---|---|---|---|---|---|---|---|---|---|---|---|---|---|
| *58–71 Lanthanides | 140 Ce cerium 58 | 141 Pr praseodymium 59 | 144 Nd neodymium 60 | (145) Pm promethium 61 | 150 Sm samarium 62 | 152 Eu europium 63 | 157 Gd gadolinium 64 | 159 Tb terbium 65 | 163 Dy dysprosium 66 | 165 Ho holmium 67 | 167 Er erbium 68 | 169 Tm thulium 69 | 173 Yb ytterbium 70 | 175 Lu lutetium 71 |
| #90–103 Actinides | 232 Th thorium 90 | 231 Pa protactinium 91 | 238 U uranium 92 | 237 Np neptunium 93 | 239 Pu plutonium 94 | 243 Am americium 95 | 247 Cm curium 96 | 247 Bk berkelium 97 | 252 Cf californium 98 | (252) Es einsteinium 99 | (257) Fm fermium 100 | (258) Md mendelevium 101 | (259) No nobelium 102 | (260) Lr lawrencium 103 |

# OXFORD
## UNIVERSITY PRESS

Great Clarendon Street, Oxford, OX2 6DP, United Kingdom

Oxford University Press is a department of the University of Oxford. It furthers the University's objective of excellence in research, scholarship, and education by publishing worldwide. Oxford is a registered trade mark of Oxford University Press in the UK and in certain other countries

© Oxford University Press 2014

The moral rights of the authors have been asserted

First published in 2014

All rights reserved. No part of this publication may be reproduced, stored in a retrieval system, or transmitted, in any form or by any means, without the prior permission in writing of Oxford University Press, or as expressly permitted by law, by licence or under terms agreed with the appropriate reprographics rights organization. Enquiries concerning reproduction outside the scope of the above should be sent to the Rights Department, Oxford University Press, at the address above.

You must not circulate this work in any other form and you must impose this same condition on any acquirer

British Library Cataloguing in Publication Data
Data available

978-0-19-839257-6

20 19 18 17

**MIX**
Paper from responsible sources
FSC
www.fsc.org  FSC® C007785

Paper used in the production of this book is a natural, recyclable product made from wood grown in sustainable forests. The manufacturing process conforms to the environmental regulations of the country of origin.

Printed in Great Britain by Bell and Bain Ltd, Glasgow

## Acknowledgements

The publisher and the authors would like to thank the following for permissions to use their photographs:

**Cover image**: Anekoho/Shutterstock; **p3**: Kotist/Dreamstime; **p3**: Pasieka/Science Photo Library; **p3**: Frans Lanting/Mint Images/ Science Photo Library; **p3**: Ninell Art/iStock; **p3**: Raj Creationzs/ Shutterstock; **p3**: Dudarev Mikhail/Shutterstock; **p3**: Power and Syred/ Science Photo Library; **p4**: Surakit Harntongkul/iStock; **p4**: Martyn F Chillmaid/Science Photo Library; **p5**: Martyn F Chillmaid/Science Photo Library; **p5**: Cordelia Molloy/Science Photo Library; p6: Andrew Lambery Photography/Science Photo Library; **p7**: Andrew Lambert Photography/Science Photo Library; **p7**: Andew Lambert Photography/ Science Photo Library; **p8**: Elena Schweitzer/Shutterstock; **p9**: Biophoto Associates/ Science Photo Library; **p11**: Steve Gschmeissner/Science Photo Library; **p12**: Cordielia Molloy/Science Photo Library; **p14**: Gustoimages/Science Photo Library; **p15**: BCFC/iStock; **p15**: Mr Wilke/iStock; **p17**: Arthur Glauberman/Science Photo library; **p18**: Mac99/iStock; **p19**: Matt Meadows, Peter Arnold Inc./Science Photo Library; **p22**: NNehring/ iStock; **p22**: Alan Phillips/iStock; **p24**: Nikada/iStock; **p25**: Vvoe/ Shutterstock; **p25**: Dr Jeremy Burgess/Science Photo Library; **p25**: Dr Jeremy Burgess/Science Photo Library; **p26**: Nigel Cattlin/Science Photo Library; **p27**: Nigel Cattlin/Science Photo Library; **p27**: Northlight Images/iStock; **p28**: Dr Jeremy Burgess/Science Photo Library; **p29**: Woods hole Oceanographic Institution/Visuals Unlimited/ Science Photo Library; **p30**: Via Films/iStock; **p31**: CNRI/Science Photo Library; **p31**: Black Jack 3D/iStock; **p32**: Maridav/iStock; **p33**: Power and Syred/ Science Photo Library; **p33**: Hemeroskopion/iStock; **p34**: Rusak/iStock; **p38**: AMR Image/iStock; **p42**: Cathleen A Clapper/Shutterstock; **p43**: GP232/iStock; **p43**: Skyak/iStock; **p44**: Mouse-Ear/iStock; **p44**: Photos MartYmage/iStock; **p44**: Jane FF/iStock; **p46**: GlobalP/iStock; **p47**: Gehringj/iStock; **p51**: Science Photo Library; **p52**: Impalastock/iStock; **p53**: Michael W. Tweedie/Science Photo Library; **p53**: Michael W Tweedie/iStock; **p54**: Grauy/iStock; **p54**: Denisk0/iStock;

**p55**: Pjmalsbury/iStock; **p55**: James King-Holmes/Science Photo Library; **p57**: John Pitcher/iStock; **p59**: Ventin/Shutterstock; **p59**: Andrew Burgess/Shutterstock; **p59**: Fpm/iStock; **p59**: WC Chow/ Shutterstock; **p59**: Justin Reznick/iStock; **p59**: Frans Lanting/Mint Images/Science Photo Library; **p60**: Science Photo Library; **p60**: Urguplu/iStock; **p60**: Westphalia/iStock; **p61**: Science Photo Library; **p62**: Dien/Shutterstock; **p64**: Hadrian/Shutterstock; **p64**: Simazoran/iStock; **p64**: Lyle Gregg/iStock; **p64**: Martyn F Chillmaid/Science Photo Library; **p65**: Andrew Lambert Photography/ Science Photo Library; **p65**: Martyn F Chillmaid/Science Photo Library; **p66**: Andrew Lambert Photography/Science Photo Library; **p67**: Andrew Lambert Photography/Science Photo Library; **p67**: Andrew Lambert Photography/Science Photo Library; **p68**: Djburrill/Dreamstime; **p68**: UltraONEs/iStock; **p68**: Slobo/iStock; **p68**: iStock; **p69**: Baranozdemir/iStock; **p69**: Graffizone/iStock; **p69**: iStock; **p69**: Stock Solutions/iStock; **p72**: Charles D Winters/Science Photo Library; **p72**: Martyn F Chillmaid/Science Photo Library; **p74**: Martyn F Chillmaid/Science Photo Library; **p75**: Martyn F Chillmaid; **p75**: Urban Cow/iStock; **p77**: Martyn F Chillmaid/Science Photo Library; **p78**: Andrew Lambert Photography/Science Photo Library; **p78**: Lucato/ iStock; **p78**: iphotographer/iStock; **p79**: **p79**: **p80**: Tobiasjo/iStock; **p80**: Julie V Mac/iStock; **p80**: Photo Euphoria/iStock; **p80**: Fernando Podolski/iStock; **p82**: Pgiam/iStock; **p83**: Monica-Photo/iStock; **p83**: Mikeledray/Shutterstock; **p86**: Charles D Winters/Science Photo Library; **p87**: Martyn F Chillmaid/Science Photo Library; **p88**: Andrew lambert Photography/Science Photo Library; **p88**: Martyn F Chillmaid/ Science Photo Library; **p89**: Leks_Laputin/iStock; **p90**: Martyn F Chillmaid/Science Photo Library; **p90**: Martyn F Chillmaid/Science Photo Library; **p90**: nsj images/iStock; **p93**: Jamesdvdsn/iStock; **p94**: Dan_Prat/iStock; **p94**: Dinn/iStock; **p94**: tr3gi/iStock; **p96**: Turner Visual/iStock; **p96**: Turner Visual/iStock; **p96**: Mary Looo/iStock; **p97**: Tatty Welshie/iStock; **p97**: Dszc/iStock; **p97**: Angelika/iStock; **p98**: Alexandrumagurean/iStock; **p98**: Sunara/iStock; **p98**: Pete Pattavina/iStock; **p98**: Tom Wang/Shutterstock; **p98**: Merlion/iStock; **p98**: Solidago/iStock; **p99**: Vladmir Melnik/Shutterstock; **p100**: Small Frog/iStock; **p101**: Bim/iStock; **p101**: carbonmods.co.uk; **p104**: Larsgustav/iStock; **p106**: Alan Phillips/iStock; **p106**: Suzifoo/ iStock; **p106**: Hadel Productions/iStock; **p106**: Trevor Clifford Photography/Science photo Library; **p106**: Fikretozk/iStock; **p106**: Eric Foltz/iStock; **p107**: f9photos/iStock; **p107**: ChrisAt/iStock; **p108**: Mount Lynx/iStock; **p108**: Nick pit/iStock; **p108**: Inger Al Haosului/Wikipedia; **p108**: Yuttasak Jannarong/Shutterstock; **p108**: Mikeuk/iStock; **p109**: Dirkr/iStock; **p109**: Slim Sepp/ Dreamstime; **p109**: Tyler Boyes/Shutterstock; **p109**: Sisoje/iStock; **p109**: Terry J/iStock; **p111**: TibetTravel; **p112**: Grafikeray/iStock; **p112**: Kamisoka/iStock; **p113**: walesdirectory.co.uk; **p114**: Thomas and Pat Leeson/Science Photo Library; **p114**: Ric Aguiar/iStock; **p114**: Scott Nodine/iStock; **p116**: Kali9/iStock; **p116**: Anthony Berenyi/ Shutterstock; **p116**: Ria Novosti/Science Photo Library; **p117**: Catherine Gardom/iStock; **p121**: Martyn F Chillmaid/Science Photo Library; **p121**: Marcel Clemens/Shutterstock; **p121**: Triff/Shutterstock; **p121**: Science Source/Science photo Library; **p122**: Charles D Winters/ Science Photo library; **p123**: Erik Simonsen/Getty Images; **p123**: Ted Kinsman/Science Photo Library; **p124**: Peter Ryan/Science Photo Library; **p124**: Matthew Oldfield/Science Photo Library; **p126**: Michael Donne/Science photo Library; **p126**: Martyn F Chillmaid/Science Photo Library; **p126**: Tek Image/Science Photo Library; **p128**: Romakoma/ Shutterstock; **p130**: Pincasso/Shutterstock; **p131**: Andrew Lambert/ Science Photo Library; **p132**: Oliver Hoffman/Shutterstock; **p132**: JJ Studio/Shutterstock; **p133**: Mark Garlick/Science Photo Library; **p135**: Clive Streeter/Dorling Kindersley/Getty Images; **p136**: Martin Bond/ Science Photo Library; **p140**: Graf Vision/Shutterstock; **p140**: Anglian Art/Shutterstock; **p140**: Danymages/Shutterstock; **p140**: Volosina/ Shutterstock; **p141**: Ajan Alen/Shutterstock; **p141**: Michael Jung/ Shutterstock; **p141**: CLS Design/Shutterstock; **p141**: Levent Konuk; **p142**: Art Allianz/Shutterstock; **p142**: Liane M/Shutterstock; **p143**: Peter Gudella/Shutterstock; **p143**: Edward Kinsman/Science Photo Library; **p144**: Alberto Pellaschiar/Associated Press; **p144**: Lebazele/Getty Images; **p144**: Mehau Kulyk and Victor De Schwanberg/Science Photo Library; **p144**: Bikerriderlondon/ Shutterstock; **p144**: Andrew Lambert photography/Science Photo Library; **p146**: Nrel/US Department of Energy/Science Photo Library; **p146**: Qin Xianan/Color China Photo/Associated Press; **p147**: Blue Ring Media/Shutterstock; **p147**: Jeff Schmaltz, Lance/Eosdis Modis Rapid Response Team/NASA/Science Photo Library; **p148**: GIP Photosstock/ Science Photo Library; **p148**: Noao/Science Photo Library; **p148**: Edward Kinsman/Science Photo Library; **p149**: Dario Sabljak/ Shutterstock; **p149**: Jason Hetherington/Getty Images; **p150**: Tim

Burrett/Shutterstock; **p151**: Irina Belousa/iStock; **p151**: Kshishtof/
iStock; **p151**: Skynavin/Shutterstock; **p151**: Tides Stream;
**p151**: Martin Bond/Science Photo library; **p151**: iStock;
**p151**: gprentice/iStock; **p152**: Tony McConnell/Science Photo Library;
**p153**: Cecile Degremont/Look at Sciences; **p153**: Sheila Terry/Science
Photo Library; **p154**: Antonov Roman/Shutterstock; **p155**: Science
Source/Science Photo library; **p155**: Kkgas/iStock; **p158**: Frans Lanting/
Mint Images/Science Photo Library; **p158**: Joe Gough/Shutterstock;
**p159**: Ostill/Shutterstock; **p160**: Christian Mueller/Shutterstock;
**p162**: Ted Kinsman/Science Photo Library; **p163**: Charles D Winters/
Science Photo Library; **p163**: Charles D Winters/Science Photo Library;
**p164**: Dr Ken MacDonald/Science Photo Library; **p164**: David Parker/
Science Photo Library; **p166**: NASA/Science Photo Library;
**p166**: Jeremy Bishop/Science Photo Library; **p167**: Warren Goldswain/
Shutterstock; **p167**: Racheal Grazias; **p167**: Bigchen/Shutterstock;
**p168**: Frank Gunn/The Canadian Press/Associated Press;
**p168**: Benedektibor/Shutterstock

Artwork by Phoenix Photosetting and Q2A Media

Although we have made every effort to trace and contact all
copyright holders before publication this has not been possible in all
cases. If notified, the publisher will rectify any errors or omissions at
the earliest opportunity.

Links to the third-party websites are provided by Oxford in good faith
and for information only. Oxford disclaims any responsibility for
materials contained in any third-party website referenced in
this work.